The Origin of Ancient American Cultures

Paul Shao

IOWA STATE UNIVERSITY PRESS, AMES, 1983

Contents

Acknowledgments

I am grateful to Dr. Daniel Zaffarano and Mr. Daniel Griffen without whose generous support this book would not have been possible. I thank my friends, Hsiao-mei Ku, Heide Exner, Najin Hooman, Somchai Arunsiripate, Der-An Jan, Elizabeth Rooney and Wesley Shank for their help in preparing the manuscript. I am especially indebted to M. J. Kitzman for his constant encouragement and advice.

I would like to take this opportunity to thank Kao Hua-Cheng, Academia Sinica, and Chu Wan-Li, Institute of History and Philology, Academia Sinica, Taiwan, for their kind support and cooperation. I am indebted to Mrs. Katherina Edsall, Peabody Museum, Harvard University, for her encouragement and patient assistance. I am deeply grateful to Harvard University for the use of their magnificent Peabody Archive and the Archive of the Carnegie Institute of Washington.

I am indebted to Xia Nai, An Zhimin of the Institute of Archaeology, Chinese Academy of Social Sciences and to Tsou Heng of Peking University for their enlightenment. To Pei Wenzhong, Jia Lanpo, Gai Pei, Wei Qi, Li Zhaorong, You Yushu, Sun Jianzhong, Wang Yuzhue, Jiang Peng of the Institute of Vertebrate Paleontology and other institutions, I am grateful for their dedicated teaching from which some of the illustrations in Chapter II and III are based.

To the following institutions I would like to express my indebtedness for granting me access to the artifacts in their collections or else supplying me with photographs of their art works: The National Institute of Anthropology and History and the National Museum of Anthropology, Mexico City; the Regional Museum of Mayan Archaeology, Copan; the Museum of Palenque; the Frissell Museum, Mitla; the National Museum of Anthropology, Guatemala City; the Regional Museum of Villahermosa; the University of Veracruz Museum, Jalapa; the American Museum of Natural History, the Museum of the American Indian.

Finally, I convey my deep appreciation to the Iowa State University Research Foundation and the Graduate School for their generous support.

fact that in most primitive cultures the custom of interior mass worship simply was not practiced. The temple, as constructed in Mesoamerica, was to accommodate not the common people but a specific social group: priest-king, shaman, etc. Thus, the entire temple complex was conceived as a symbol of worship or monument of authority rather than an interior space for assembly.

Corroboratively, it is noteworthy that all major traditional Chinese architecture featured the corbel system in the form "dou-gun" (corbel brackets). Furthermore, all significant temple complexes erected prior to the 15th century A.D. in Java, Cambodia, Thailand, Vietnam, and a number of other southeast Asian cultures were constructed exclusively with the corbel arch—including such noted religious centers as Barabudur, Chandi Sari, Chandi Kalasan, Chandi Mendut, Chandi Sewu, Prambanan, the Ankor Thom, Ankor Wat. Clearly in spite of the close contact with advanced cultural centers in the Old World and the resulting knowledge of the true arch, these southeast Asian peoples had chosen to employ the corbel arch in preference to the true arch for environmental and ideological reasons apparently similar to those of their ancient American counterparts. This was, presumably, because they were located in earthquake and volcanic zones and because they regarded temples as monuments rather than interiors for congregational assembly. Consistent with the architectural dictum, "form follows function," there simply was no demand for substantially large interior spaces and no need to discard a proven efficient method of building, such as the false arch. It would appear that the absence of the true arch in the New World argues for cultural contact between Asia and the Precolumbian Americas rather than for indigenous origin within the Americas.

The second often used argument of the independent inventionists centers on the absence of the wheel in the American cultures. This absence can be explained by reasons of environmental and economic necessity just as in the case of the corbel versus the true arch. Productive application of the wheel is directly related to the presence of draft animals, metals, good roads, bridges, and voluminous trade requirements. Without metals and draft animals, the durability and practicality of the wheeled vehicle is seriously limited. The rugged terrain of the highlands and the heavy rainfall of the tropic lowlands render the construction and maintenance of roads suitable for vehicular travel economically prohibitive, in terms of small scale trade.

It is inconceivable that tiny groups of traders could maintain a far-reaching road system which, soon after construction, would be devoured by tropical vegetation and rainfall. Under conditions typical in much of Mexico and Guatemala for example, the flexibility of human legs and bodies capable of transporting substantial volumes of materials was far more efficient and economical. With bad roads, rugged terrain, lack of vehicular bridges and the absence of a suitable pulling force such as horses or oxen, the wheeled vehicle would be, more often than not, a liability. That the wheeled vehicle can be a liability, or certainly not an asset, is borne out by modern travelers attempting to reach remote ruins in Central America: There are hundreds of ancient sites and contemporary villages where even powerful four-wheel drive vehicles are helpless, while two strong feet and a machete penetrate with relative ease. In these remote areas of Central America and Mexico, as well as in east Asia, humans rather than wheeled vehicles remain the primary mode of cargo transportation.

As we proceed to examine the third argument against diffusion, we shall digress for a moment to study the following news quoted from the *Asian Student* (a fortnightly published by the Asia Foundation in San Francisco), dated December 17, 1977:

A boat carrying 75 Vietnamese refugees arrived in Darwin on December 1, adding to the flood of Vietnamese who have reached Australia since Thailand began to enforce its policy of turning them away. The number of Vietnamese refugees to enter Australia since mid-November has now reached almost 600.

On another page of the same paper, a photograph of a small boat crowded with people was shown. Under the photograph is a description which reads as follows:

This 30-foot fishing boat loaded with 50 Vietnamese refugees sits in Kampuchean waters after being towed to that area of the sea by Thai police, who refused them entry. Vietnamese refugees are increasingly being turned away from most Asian countries.

Let us now consider the third argument: absence of "bona fide stratigraphically excavated Old World artifacts" in Precolumbian America. Had one been in the boat among those above-mentioned southeast Asian refugees, perhaps the absence of Old World artifacts in America would not have been difficult to understand. People who flee their homeland under duress are not likely to carry with them an abundance of articles, since each article carried would displace valuable space which could otherwise have been available for additional people in the boat. Moreover, any excess baggage would have made the voyage more hazardous. This is not only true of sea journeys, but also true of travel by land; not only true of fleeing but also true of migration in search of better habitats. One cannot travel far or fast on foot if one carries even a minimum amount of metal or stone objects. Thus it can be assumed most of the items carried by the early immigrants to the New World were of a relatively light, small, and perishable character. Due to their scarcity and irreplaceable nature, the limited number of permanent objects these early travellers managed to bring to the Americas, would not likely have been buried with the dead. This, together with the vast span of space separating the two cultures under study and the relatively small number of immigrants, renders the likelihood of discovering "bona fide" Old World artifacts in well-stratified deposits in America extremely remote. It must also be kept in mind that most of the Precolumbian immigrants to America were probably nomads on the periphery of the Chinese heartland, possessing only a semblance of culture. Under these circumstances even burials containing genuine Old World artifacts might not be easily identified as such because of their hybrid and morphotic character.

Another factor that accounts for the absence of Old Word artifacts in the Precolumbian New World was the plundering and indiscriminate, wholesale destruction of the early American cultural relics by the Hispanic conquerors of the New World. In *Asiatic Influences in Pre-Columbian American Art* (Shao 1976: 10–11), I cited a number of historical records describing such lamentable events. It will suffice to repeat only two here:

These people also made use of certain characters of letters, with which they wrote in their books their ancient matters and their sciences, and by these and by drawings, they understood their affairs and made others understand them and taught them. We found a large number of books in these characters and, as they contained nothing in which there were not to be seen superstition and lies of the devil, we burned them all, which they regretted to an amazing degree, and which caused them much affliction (Landa ca. A.D. 1566: 169):

Introduction

Recent archaeological breakthroughs have radically altered the outline of China's history and prehistory. They have also provided new impetus and data for unlocking the mystery concerning the origin of ancient American cultures. Because of their freshness, however, little of these discoveries have been applied to the problem of circum- or transpacific cultural contacts. It is hoped that this book will help to fill the existing vacuum of knowledge on the subject.

With new data increasingly coming to light, the consensus of scholars in recent decades has been that: 1) ancient America was peopled by east Asians of a primarily Mongoloid stock possessing a semblance of culture and 2) lithic industries from east Asia were diffused to the New World from the inception of the Paleolithic Period down to the later millennia. As pointed out by Gordon Willey, one of the foremost authorities in American archaeology, these contacts "provided the bifacial-flaked blade technology which eventually gave rise to the early American Clovis [projectile point] and related industries". They "formed the bases for arctic and subarctic techniculture prior to the appearance of the more typical Eskimo complexes."[1]

In spite of this, the present trend in American archaeology is against diffusionist theories in favor of those that postulate indigenous invention of ancient American cultures.[2] At the end of the last Ice Age, approximately 10,000 years ago, melting glaciers gradually submerged the Bering land bridge. Accordingly, these scholars hypothesized, the American continent had since been isolated from the Old World. Cultures evolved in the Americas independently without external influences until Columbus "discovered" America. I believe new evidence and correlations presented in this book shall modify this trend and stimulate cross-disciplinary cooperation among Asian and American archaeologists, anthropologists, historians and art specialists in search of America's beginning.

In Chapter I, a holistic continuum proposition is advanced as a theoretical framework for cultural evolution. Since I actively embarked on this project nine years ago, I have visited most of the principal cultural centers around the world including major Olmec, Mayan, Chavin, and Chinese archaeological sites. With the passage of time during these studies, the classic Chinese knowledge which I had learned by rote when I was a child in Guangzhou, China, gradually resurfaced from a hidden and blocked corner of my mind. It did not make much sense as a child; but as an adult investigator it suddenly became profoundly revealing and inspiring. It now appears to me that a common thread runs through all major cultures. This chapter expands from *I Jing* (The Book of Changes), one of the oldest Chinese classics, written more than two thousand years ago.

Chapters II and III trace the roots of the ancient Americans and their techno-lithic cultures, establishing a genetic context for the emergence of civilization in the Americas.

In Chapter IV, multiple correlated evidence is presented, which documents the oneness of Old and New World cultures. As the culmination of nine years of vigorous investigation, this chapter is the pivotal component of this volume. Since the Mesoamerican Olmec has been accepted by most leading Americanists as the "Mother Culture" of the New World, a substantial portion of this chapter is devoted to synchronic and diachronic comparison of the Olmec culture with that of ancient China—the oldest, most continuous and influential civilization in east Asia. A gestalt correlational system is employed. A multitude of verifiable cultural traits and trait-complexes are seriated, analyzed and correlated in spatial and temporal context. It is found that the Olmec and the Shang-Zhou Chinese cultural trait-complexes are homogeneous not only in expressive forms, but also in ideological contents.

Chapter V identifies the forces, mechanisms and processes responsible for the genesis and growth of civilization in the ancient Americas. It ramifies the findings presented in this volume and delineates new frontier needed to further the knowledge of cultural evolution in general and the cultural origin of the New World in particular.

Since I have reviewed various speculations and theories concerning interhemispheric cultural contacts in an earlier publication: *Asiastic Influences in Pre-Columbian American Art* (1976), I shall not restate these issues in this volume. Instead I shall introduce the theme of this study by addressing a number of lingering contentions against circum- and transpacific cultural diffusion.

Few single subjects in archaeology have stirred keener controversies and more opposing passions than that of interhemispheric cultural diffusion.

The three arguments most frequently cited by scholars who believe the origins of ancient American culture to be indigenous are: 1) non-existence of the true arch; 2) absence of the wheel; 3) absence of "bona fide" stratigraphically excavated Old World artifacts in Precolumbian America.

Scholars holding the notion of indigenous origins of New World culture discount theories of cultural contact by asking, "If there were contacts, why was the true arch never employed in the ancient Americas?" It is surprising that no one has previously enumerated the two logical reasons for the non-use of the true arch. First, most ancient American cultural centers were located on or near seismic faults: an arch with radial-joint construction is inferior to corbelled construction in its ability to withstand ground vibration. The true arch constructed with the principle of the lateral thrust of the key stone, is more vulnerable to side pressures resulting from seismic activities. The falling of only one arched stone would result in failure of the arch.

In contrast, the vaulting system, with stacked horizontal layers (false or corbel arch), exerts only vertical pressure on the walls, this force being applied in such a way that each component is in a state of constant static equilibrium. The rending of one or more corbelled layers has only limited effect on the general stability of the whole. Thus, the vaulting system with stacked horizontal joints was not only better adapted to the environment of the early Americans but also more productive and economical. The corbel arch does not require precise dressing of the stone, nor rigid adherence to specifications and formulas, as required in the true arch.

It should be noted, however, that not all so-called corbel arches in the Americas were indeed true corbel systems. In the strict sense, some are a false version of the corbel arch, since there was not enough vertical purchase between layers to attain the level of equilibrium necessary to bear the load from above (and withstand earth vibration). To compensate for this, the Mayan builders made extensive use of mortar between layers, mortar cores, and heavy stuccoing of the inner face of the vault. This is, however, irrelevant to the isolationists' argument since their proposition deals with the absence of the true arch.

The second reason for the non-use of the true arch and vaulting system may be recognized by examining the socialization pattern of early American people. Indigenous origin scholars hold that the absence of the true arch and, therefore, large interior spaces in the ancient American architecture is synonymous with the absence of cultural contact between the Old and New Worlds. This tenuous position is, no doubt, based on our experience in congregational worship within interior spaces, whereby we automatically assume large interior space to be more desirable as in the case of temples. This ignores the

From some notes of D. Pablo Moreno and from a letter of a Yucateca Jesuit, D. Domingo Rodriquez to Illmo. Sr. Estevez, dated Bologna, March 20, 1805, we are able without other authority to offer to our readers the following annotation of the objects some of which were destroyed and others burned:

5000 idols of different form and dimension
13 great stones which served as altars
22 small stones of various forms
27 rolls of signs and heiroglyphics on deer skin
197 vases of all sizes and shapes
(Cogolludo 1867: 603–604)

In a manner resembling the practice of today—that we treasure and preserve in museums the cultural relics of the 16th and 17th century immigrants to America—whatever permanent artifacts early immigrants from Asia brought with them were probably collectively kept as heirlooms by the ancient Americans and, as such, were subsequently vulnerable to collective destruction by the conquistadores.

The following working hypothesis is postulated in this book for the birth of America's first civilization during the late second millenium B.C.: the alternating hegemony in east Asia of the Chinese with the surrounding nomadic peoples activated a chain of events leading to the dislocation and subsequent emigration of people from east Asia. These exoduses resulted in sporadic, involuntary arrivals in the Americas. As immigrants in the Americas, these east Asians could have provided the initial cultural stimuli and the succeeding cultural recharges necessary for the emergence and development of civilization in the New World. This hypothesis seems to be a more reasonable explanation than the indigenous evolution theory for the sudden emergence of the highly developed Olmec-Chavin cultures and the subsequent blossoming of the Mayan civilization. The theoretical foundation upon which this hypothesis is constructed shall be discussed in Chapter One.

Notes

1. Gordon R. Willey and Jereme Sabloff, *A History of American Archaeology,* London: Thames and Hudson, 1974, p. 172.
2. Ibid., p. 174.

CHAPTER I
The Tao of Cultural Changes:
A Theoretical Framework

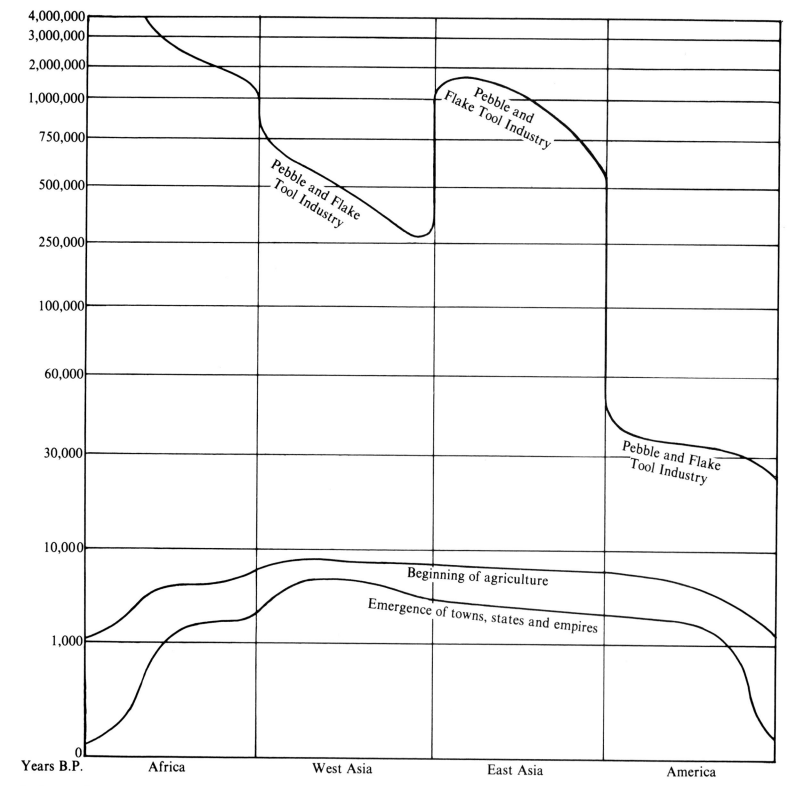

1. Comparative chronologies, indicating the oneness of Old and New World cultures.

2. The Taiji image expressing the unity and differentiation of human cultures.

Culture, not unlike its creator, is the product as well as the process of a single, all-embracing evolutionary continuum. When one's vision is focused upon the total configuration of human culture in a spatial and temporal context, rather than upon the particular localized and transitory appearance of individual culture, the global organic oneness of the cultural evolutionary process becomes quite evident. The universe comes into being from one accidental "Big Bang." The human descends from one primordial line of species. Culture evolves from the same organic origin via a symbiotic process. Cultural diffusion, like many forms of biological behavior, is programmed into the "cultural genes" as a reproductive strategy for the advancement and perpetuation of cultural species. It is the Tao (The Way) of cultural information generation, storage, retrieval and transmission.

Culture, is organic by nature, and is thus characterized by determinated, transitory and differentiated changes. *I Jing* (The Book of Changes, written during the Zhou Dynasty 1122–221 B.C.) offers fascinating revelation in this regard. According to *I Jing* there are three kinds of change: nonchange, cyclical change, and sequential change. The nonchange is *a priori*, determinate and genetic. It is the ultimate metaphysical matrix against which phenomenal, materialistic changes occur.

Cyclical change is transitory: a continual flux of being "to be"—a recurring phenomenon like the full and waning moon, the rotation of the seasons and the rise and fall of cultures.

Sequential change is differentiated: differentiated, that is, in such a way that transformation and permutation can be externally expressed in terms of the high and low, the "creative" (Yang) and the "receptive" (Yin) or the developed and the underdeveloped. These differentiations are organically necessary as they create dynamic potential for change.

A model of cultural origin and development can be constructed under a similar though somewhat modified light.

At the inception there is a postulated "Wuji" (the infinity, the black void) from which emerges the cultural "Taiji" (the primal beginning of culture). "Taiji" is the embodiment of forces. Cultures originate and develop out of an integrated and predetermined system of interplay and transformation of these forces. Cultural changes are transitory, sequential and interrelated. High culture flows to low culture as naturally as high atmospheric pressure moves into the low until its force diminishes and is changed into other forms of energy. Cultures are as differentiated as brothers and sisters of the same parents. They possess *a priori* genetic attributes as well as *a posteriori*, adaptive, individual personalities. The high cultures of the New World, the Olmec, Chavin and Mayan, owed their origins to the Old World culture. Through interaction with environment and creative adoption, they developed their own cultural characters permeated with vitality and splendor.

Great indeed is the Creative beginning to which all beings owe their origins. . . . The Creative Law works through change and transformation so that all beings obtain their determinate nature and acquire their individual character in accordance with the Eternal Law of Harmony.

I Jing, Part I, Jien (The Creative)

The concept of cultural change derived from *I Jing* can be visually symbolized by a circle, the "Wuji." The circle is divided into two parts: the light (Yang) and the dark (Yin); forming a continuous reverse curve. This symbol represents the oneness of world culture as well as the differentiation of cultural character.

The Yang (the cultural generator, stimulator, seed-sower) complements the Yin (the cultural bearer, adopter, regenerator) and vice versa. One is not inferior to the other, since they share a common origin and common bonds as signified by the small black and white circle on either side. Both possess equal potential for interactive change, growth and eventual cross-fertilization.

In the following chapters the bio-cultural roots of the ancient American cultures shall be traced and the organic oneness of the Old and New World civilization documented.

CHAPTER II
The Origin of the Ancient Americans

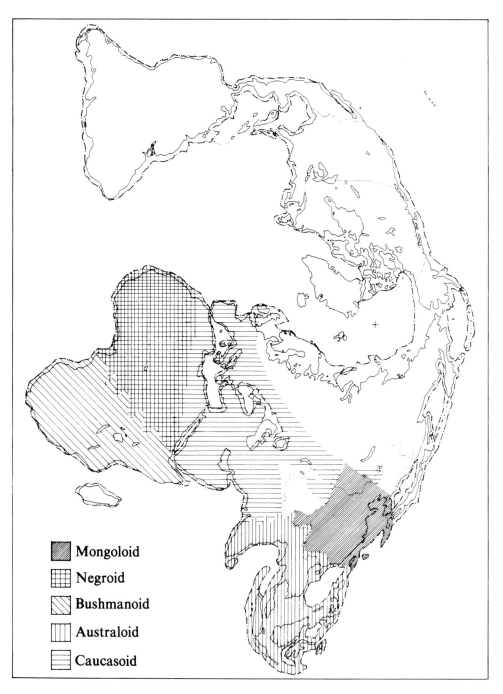

3. Distribution of major racial groups, ca. 60,000 years ago.

Mongoloid

Negroid

Bushmanoid

Australoid

Caucasoid

4. Mongoloid migration, ca. 30,000 years ago.

Mongoloid

Negroid

Bushmanoid

Australoid

Caucasoid

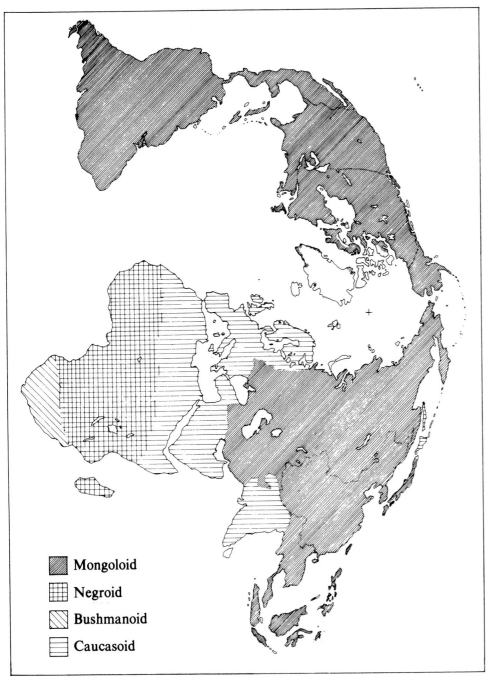

5. Maximum expansion of Mongoloid ca A.D. 1240.

Mongoloid

Negroid

Bushmanoid

Caucasoid

6. Late Pleistocene (ca 40,000–12,000 B.P.) distribution of Mammuthus Primigenius and Coelodonta Antiquitatis.

Mammuthus Primigenius

Coelodonta Antiquitatis

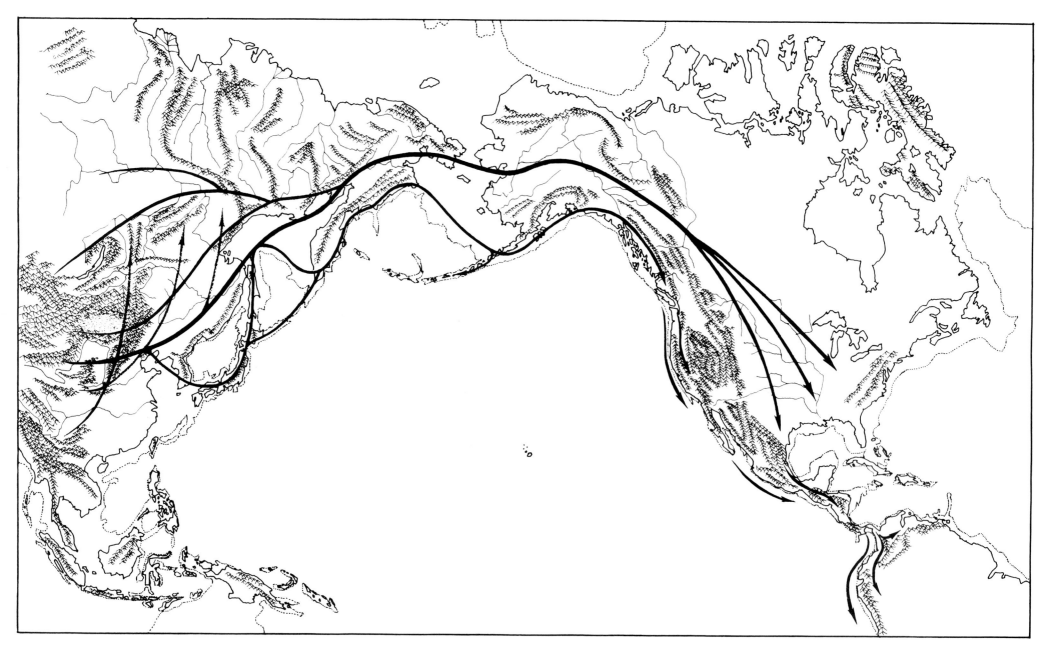

7. Major circumpacific migration routes during the Late Pleistocene period.

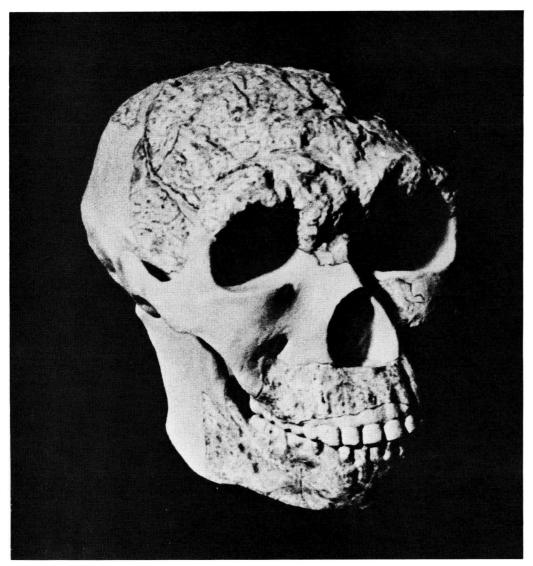

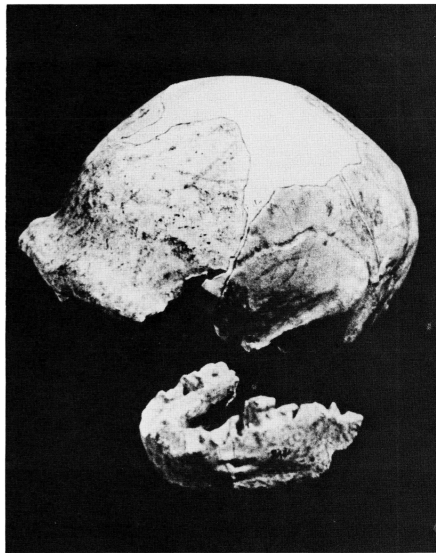

8. The Lantien Man (Sinanthropus Lantienensis) skull (restored), ca. 1 million years B.P. (Before Present).

9. The Peking Man (Sinanthropus Pekinensis) skullcap and mandible, ca. 500,000 B.P.

10. Lantien Man (ca. 1 million years B.P.), reconstruction drawing by the author.

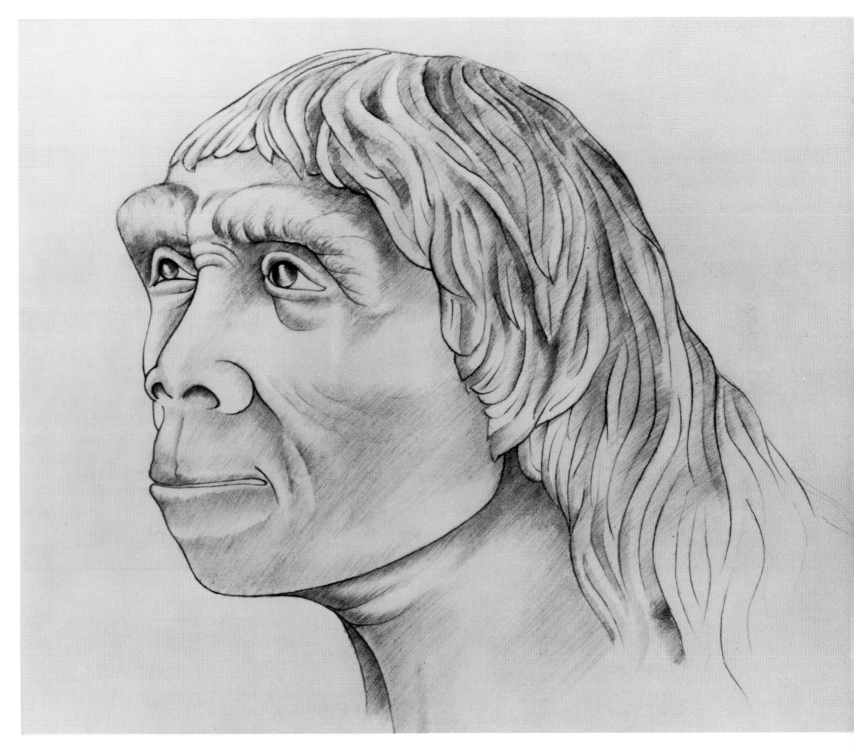

11. Peking Man (ca. 500,000 B.P.), reconstruction drawing by the author.

12. Upper Cave Man (ca. 18,000 B.P.), reconstruction drawing by the author.

13. Northern Chinese, Shanxi Province, 1981.

14. Chippewa native American, 20th Century (Courtesy of the American Museum of Natural History).

> *There is no reasonable doubt as to the ultimate origin of the human population that finally covered the hemisphere. There is consensus among scholars that the first American was of Asian stock. Research in biology, language, and archeology demonstrates this; no space need be wasted here in presenting the varied evidence pointing to the one conclusion. It is the timing of the entry that has not yet been determined.*
>
> *Jesse Jennings.[1]*

Recent research findings buttress Jennings' conclusion and provide new information on the timing of the entry into the Americas.

Outstanding among these research efforts is the latest joint U.S.-Soviet project conducted by Christy G. Turner II,[2] who succeeded in tracing the origin of the early Americans to North China. Assisted by a National Geographic Society grant, Turner studied the teeth of more than 6,000 early American skeletons. He was subsequently invited in 1980 by the Institute of Ethnography, Academy of Science, USSR, to conduct a large-scale study of North Asian dental traits and distribution. A multitude of data was sifted and correlated with the aid of a computer system. It was found that the northeast Asian and the early inhabitants of both North and South America shared the following dental trait-complex: 1) one-root upper first premolars, 2) three-root lower first molars, 3) shovel-shaped incisers.

Turner named this trait-complex Sinodonty after the archetype from Anyang, a major royal capital of the Shang Dynasty (1766–1122 B.C.) in the Central Plains of China.

Together with his Russian colleagues, he further concluded that man migrated from North Asia to America in three waves—the first, about 20,000 but not earlier than 40,000 years B.P. (Before Present); the second, between 14,000 to 12,000; and the third, ca. 8,700 B.P. "The roots of the first Americans lead ultimately to Mongolia, Manchuria and Northern China."[3]

Other scholars, with Richard MacNeish as their exponent, have argued that the first Americans arrived in the New World at a much earlier time. Based on these views, Jason and Rachel Smith stated in an article entitled, "New Light on Early Sociocultural Evolution in the Americas", the following:

Indeed, we suspect that the Siberian evidence speaks rather eloquently of a sparse occupation of the Subarctic of northeast Asia until around 18,000 years B.P. Prior to that, only limited occupation occured. What little chronometric evidence we do have indicates that the earlier period of maximum occupation was from 40,000 to 33,000 B.P., and that the technology of the earlier horizons is rather clearly of a type which could have been derived from the Chinese Lower Paleolithic.

The significance of all of this seems to us to be that people traveled north, probably along the Pacific coast and its immediate inland environs, by at least 50,000 years ago (if not earlier), and crossed the Bering Land Bridge or, using boats, hopped from island to island. Some of these people found their way into the New World and gradually worked their way eastward and southward so that by 20,000+ years ago they were on the Atlantic coast of North America and at least as far south as Ayacucho, Peru.[4]

A brief review of the recent Chinese Paleo-archaeological breakthrough is in order at this juncture.

The earliest hominid presence in China was discovered in 1965 in Yuanmou,[5] southwest China. Two shovel-shaped incisors were found in a Lower Pleistocene deposit dated 1.7 million years B.P.

Another early site, Xihoudu in the Yellow River Valley, which Jia Lanpo considered to be "the earliest population center of North China" and "Contemporaneous with the Yuanmou Man"[6] yielded evidence of fire-use and stone and bone tools.

In 1964 a skullcap of early Middle Pleistocene age (ca. one million years B.P.) had been discovered at Gongwangling, Lantien, Shannsi Province. The skullcap features flat forehead, thick skull wall, prominent brow ridge and small cranial capacity. It was determined to be more "primitive" than the Java Man and the Peking Man.[7]

Since Pei Wenzhong discovered the first Peking Man skullcap in 1929, the well-known Middle Pleistocene site, Zhoukoudian (50 kilometers from Peking now known as Beijing) has been extensively investigated (work still in progress). To this date, 6 skullcaps, 8 skull fragments, 6 facial bones, 15 mandibles, 153 teeth and 13 other miscellaneous bones have been unearthed. These fossils have been determined to belong to forty individuals. In addition, over 100,000 stone artifacts and numerous antler and bone implements have been recovered.[8]

Of the recently discovered Middle Pleistocene sites, Xujiayao is possibly most significant because of its fossils' intermediate links to the Homo sapiens neanderthalensis. Furthermore, the lithic assemblages from this site are regarded by leading Chinese scholars as the progenitor of the microlithic tradition of China and by extension, northeast Asia and northwest America. This point shall be further elaborated in Chapter III. Other Middle Pleistocene human fossils have been found as far south as Guangdong Province (The Maba Man) and Hubei Province (The Changyang Man).

The early Upper Pleistocene Fenhe site (Dingcun), bears the first Neanderthal fossils found in China. Significantly, MacNeish referred to the Fenhe cultural tradition both in his 1971[9] and 1976[10] articles as the predecessor of the early Paleoindian's lithic traditions.

The late Upper Pleistocene period (40,000–10,000 B.P.) witnessed the emergence and spread of Homo sapiens in China as well as in all other parts of the Old World. In China they are represented by the Liujiang Man, Guangxi Province in southwest China and the Upper Cave Man from Zhoukoudian near Beijing. Most scholars believed that the first Asians arrived in the New World during this period when the fall of the sea level at least twice exposed the Bering land bridge.

In summary, the following model can be constructed:

1. Throughout the Pleistocene era, east Asia in general, and North China in particular, experienced relatively favorable natural conditions in contrast to northwestern Eurasia, which suffered "catastrophic changes of climate".[11]
2. Favorable natural conditions nourished the evolution and expansion of an east Asiatic population with its original center in North China.
3. Following the retreating glaciers and animals, parts of the east Asiatic population migrated northward and northeastward, eventually crossing the Bering land bridge in pursuit of new habitats available for hunters and gatherers.

This is a highly simplified and generalized description. Much of it may be modified by subsequent findings, such as the latest discovery of "the best preserved and the most complete Homo erectus skull found in China."[12] Although details of this find have not been published, it was reported that the age of the skull fossil approximated that of the Peking Man. The fossil was unearthed in He Xien, Anhui Province, southeast China.

Notes

1. Jesse Jennings, Editor, *Ancient Native Americans,* San Francisco: W. H. Freeman, 1978, p. 1.
2. Franklin and Mary Folsom, "Sinodonty and Sundadonty", *Early Man,* Vol. 4, No. 2, 1982, pp. 16–21.
3. Ibid, p. 16.
4. Jason W. Smith and Rachel A. Smith, "New Light on Early Sociocultural Evolution in the Americas", *Peopling of the New World,* Edited by Jonathon Ericson et al, Los Altos: Ballena Press, 1982, p. 234.
5. Hu Chengzhi, "Fossil Teeth of Homo Erectus found at Yuanmou, Yunnan", *Acta Geologica Sinica,* No. 1, 1973.
6. Jia Lanpo, *Early Man in China,* Beijing: Foreign Language Press, 1980, p. 10.
7. Wu Rukang, "Paeoanthropology in China (1949–1979)", *Vertebrata PalAsiatica,* Vol. 18, No. 1, 1980, p. 2.
8. Jia, ibid., p. 27.
9. Richard S. MacNeish, "Early Man in the Andes" (1971), *Biology and Culture in Modern Perspective,* San Francisco: W. H. Freeman, 1972, p. 257.
10. Richard S. MacNeish, "Early Man in the New World", *American Scientist,* Vol. 64, No. 3, 1976 p. 317.
11. A. P. Derevianko, "The Problem of the Lower Paleolithic in the South of the Soviet Far East", *Early Paleolithic in South and East Asia,* Edited by Fumiko Ikawa-Smith, Hague: Mouton Publishers, 1978, p. 311.
12. Wang Shihmin, "Chinese Archaeological Research in 1980", *Kaogu,* No. 3, 1981, p. 243.

CHAPTER III
The Origin of the Ancient American Technologies

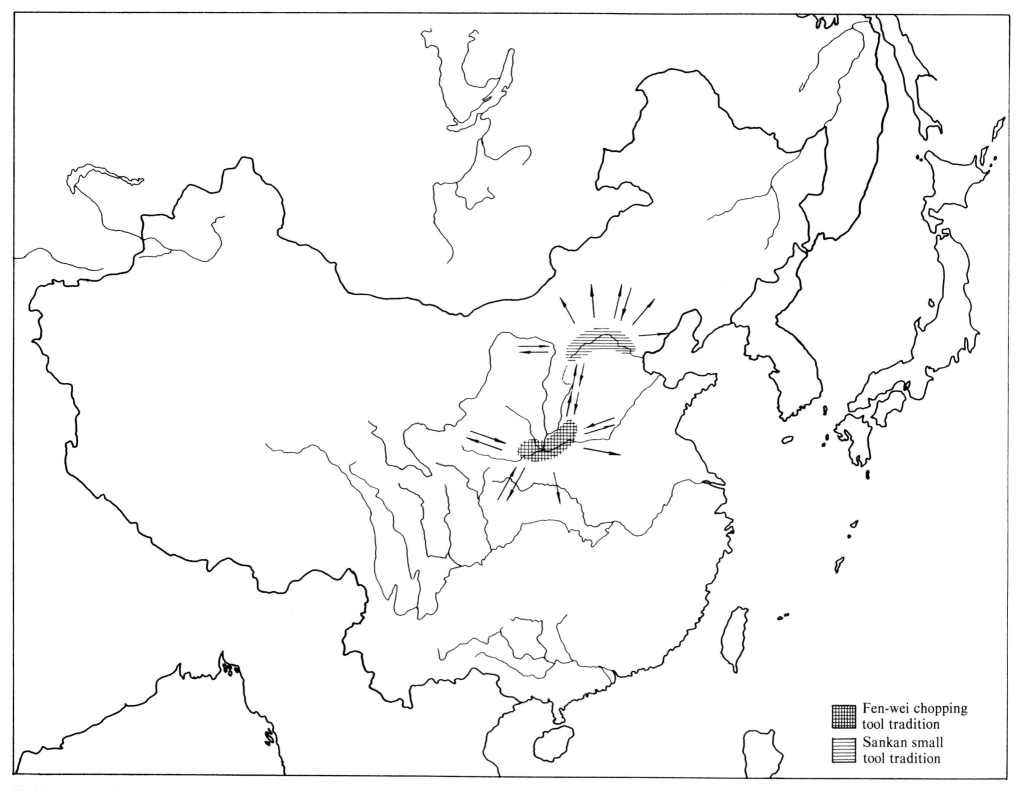

15. Nucleus areas of the two major Chinese Paleolithic traditions.

Fen-wei chopping
tool tradition

Sankan small
tool tradition

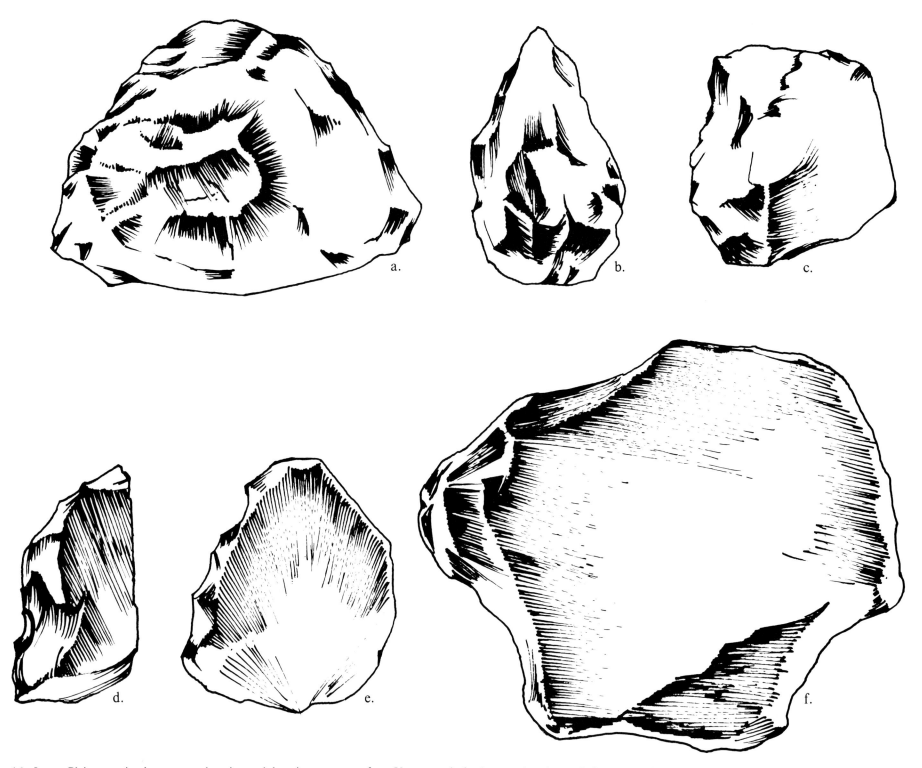

16. Lower Pleistocene implements: a. chopping tool, b. point, c. scraper, from Yuanmou; d.–f., chopper-chopping tools from Xihoudu.

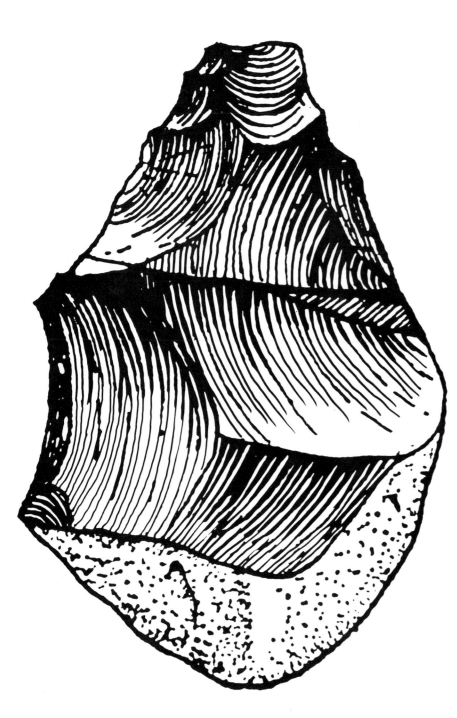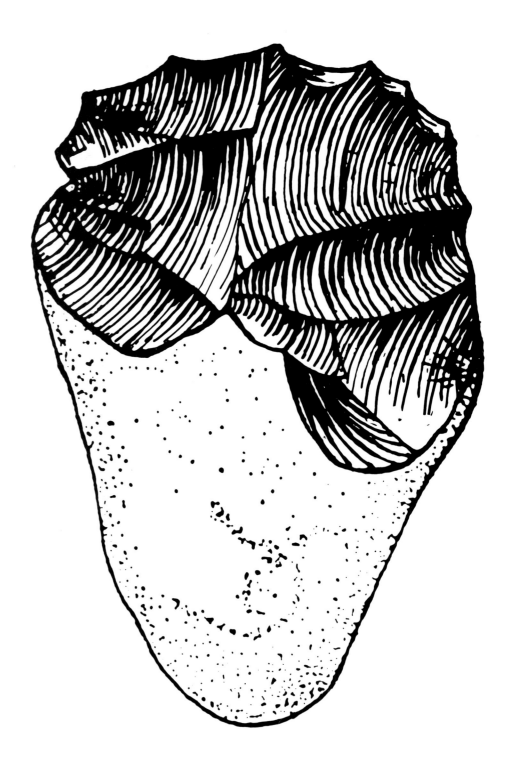

17. Middle Pleistocene chopper-chopping tools from Lantien (actual size).

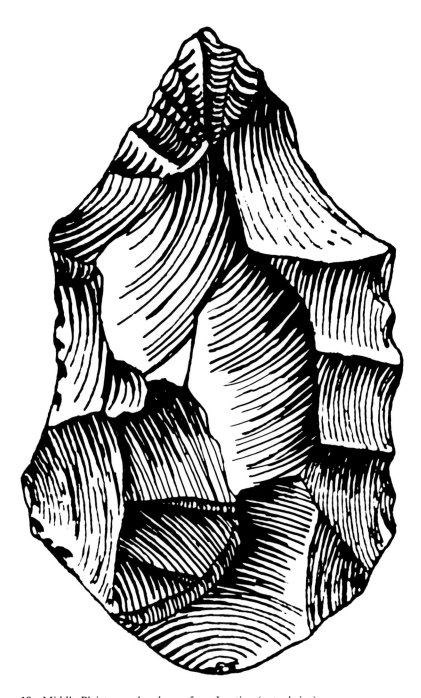 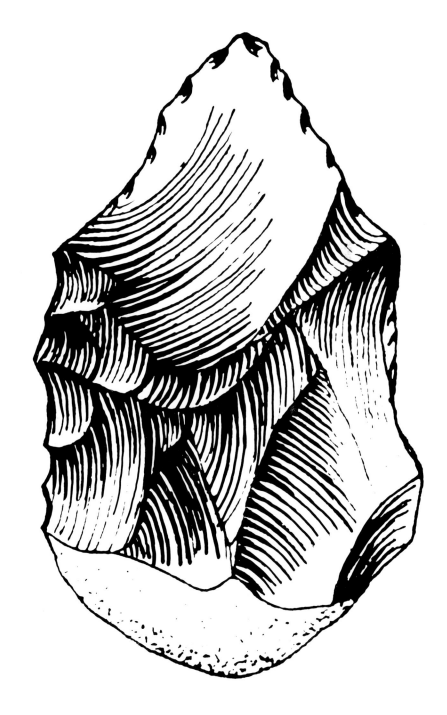

18. Middle Pleistocene hand-axes from Lantien (actual size).

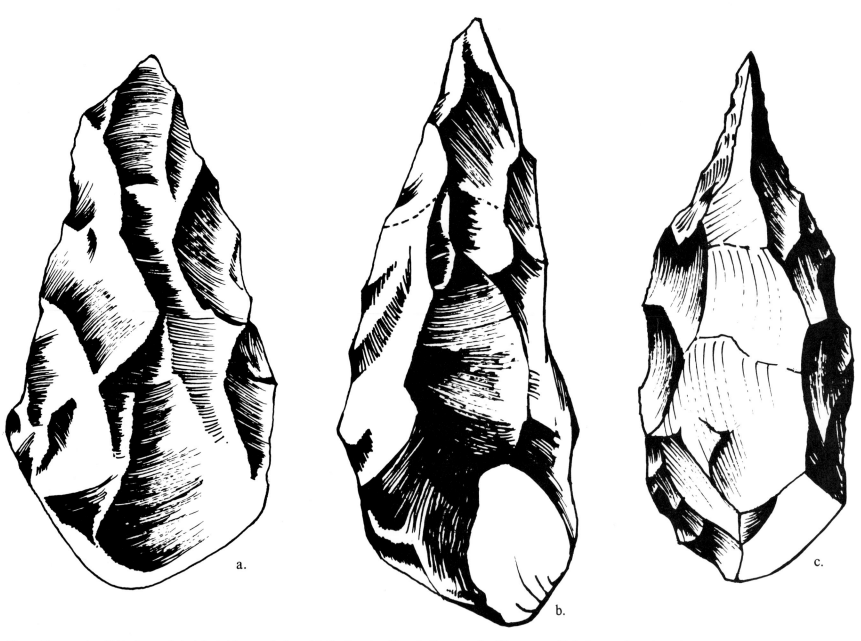

19. a. Heavy point (3/4 of actual size) found in association with the Lantien Man skullcap, ca. 1 million years old; b. heavy triangular point (actual size, upper part restored) from Gehe, ca. 600,000 B.P.; c. heavy triangular point (3/4 actual size) from Dingcun, ca. 80,000 B.P.

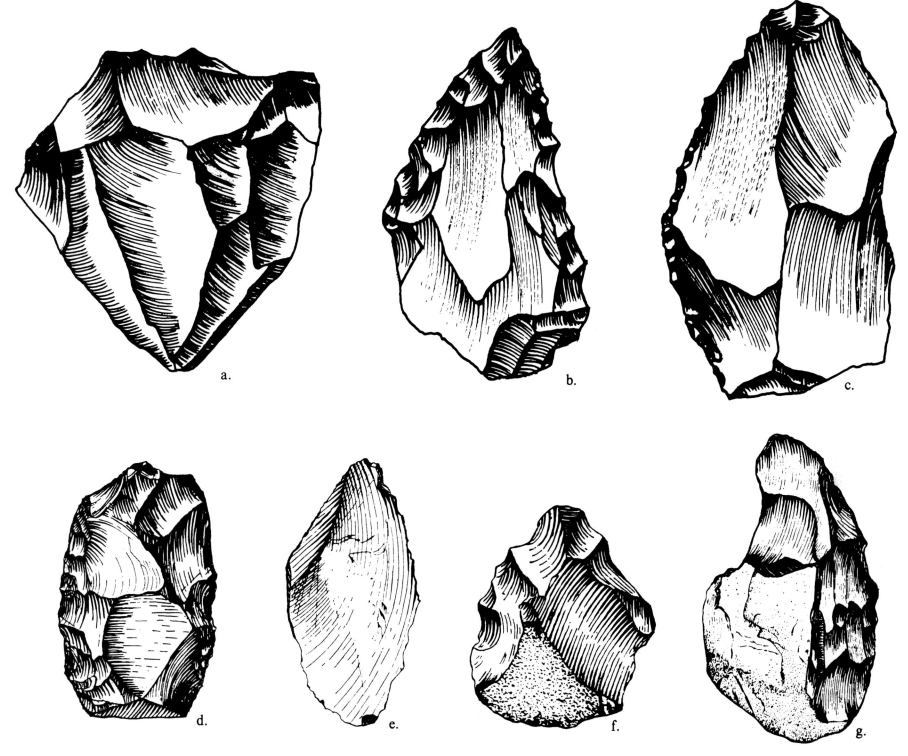

20. Middle Paleolithic implements (not in scale) from Dingcun: a. core; b. flake with secondary chipping; c.–g. various flake and chopping tools, ca. 80,000 B.P.

21. Peking Man's implements from Zhoukoudian Locality 1, ca. 500,000 B.P.

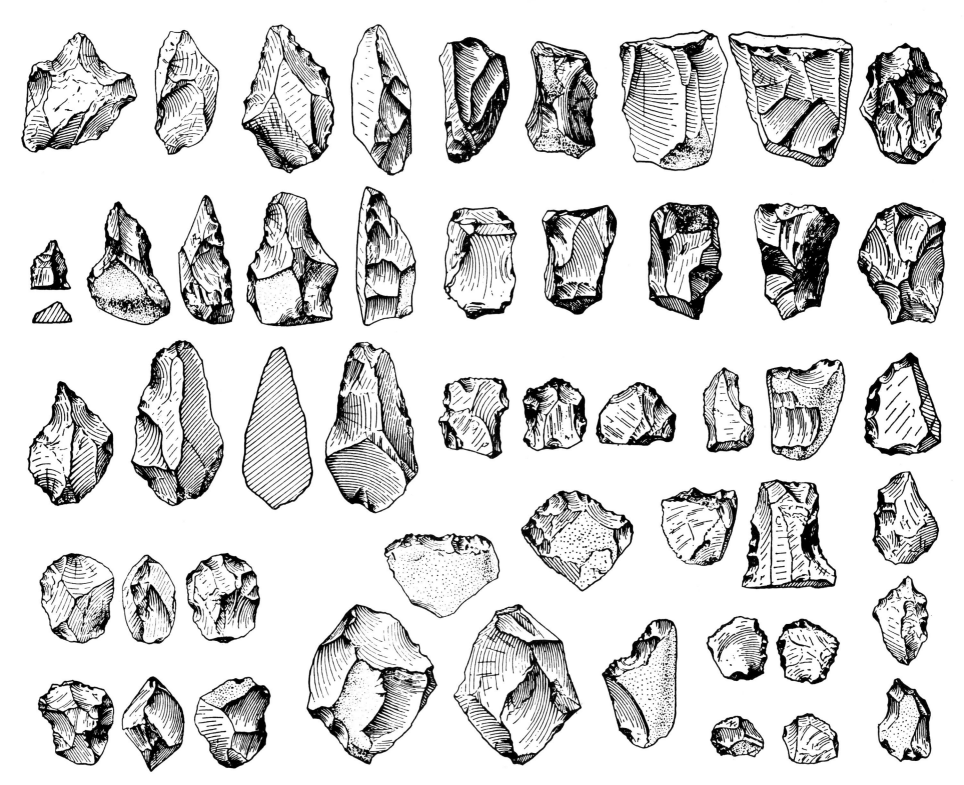

22. Microliths (actual size) from Xujiayao, ca. 100,000 to 60,000 B.P.

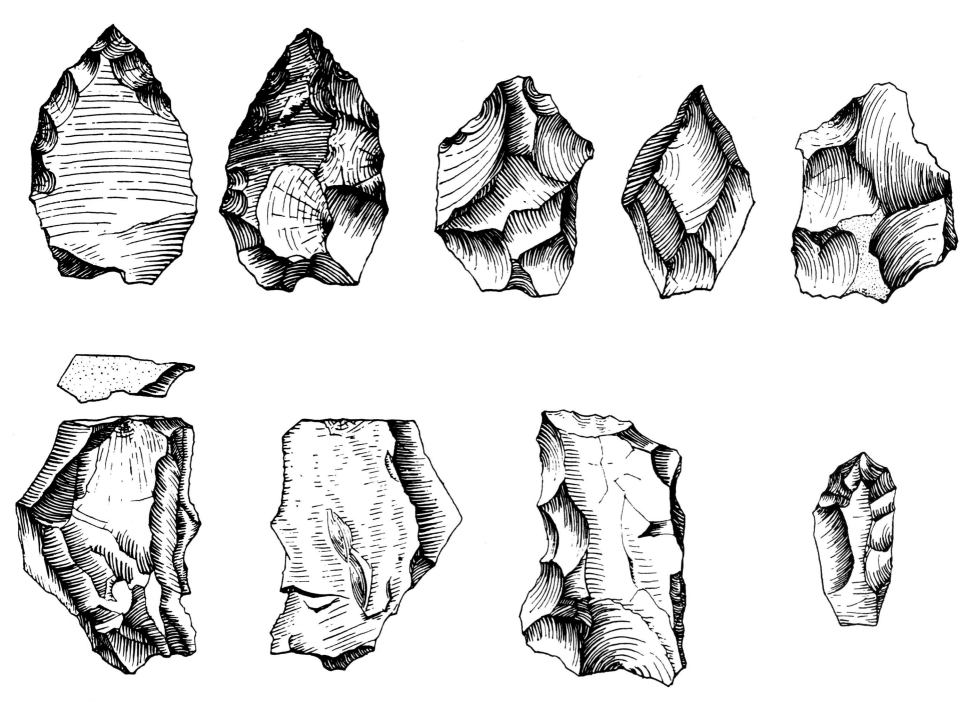

23. Late Middle Paleolithic implements discovered together with mammuthus-coelodonta fauna (see Fig. 6), ca. 70,000–40,000 B.P., at Zhoujia Youfang, Jilin Province, northeast China.

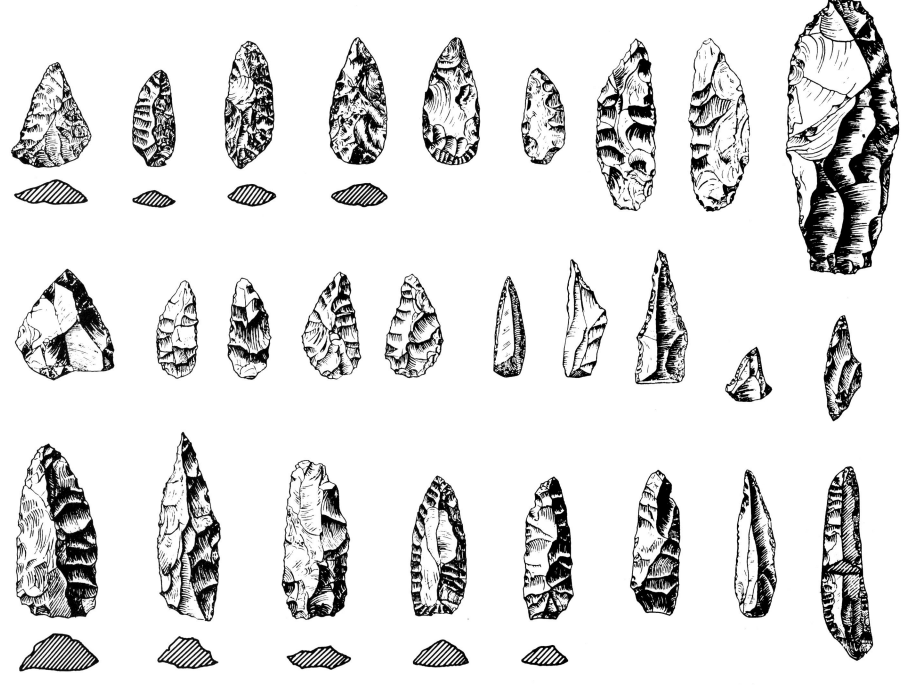

24. Arrowheads, points and other microlithic implements from Xiachuan, ca. 24,000–17,000 B.P.

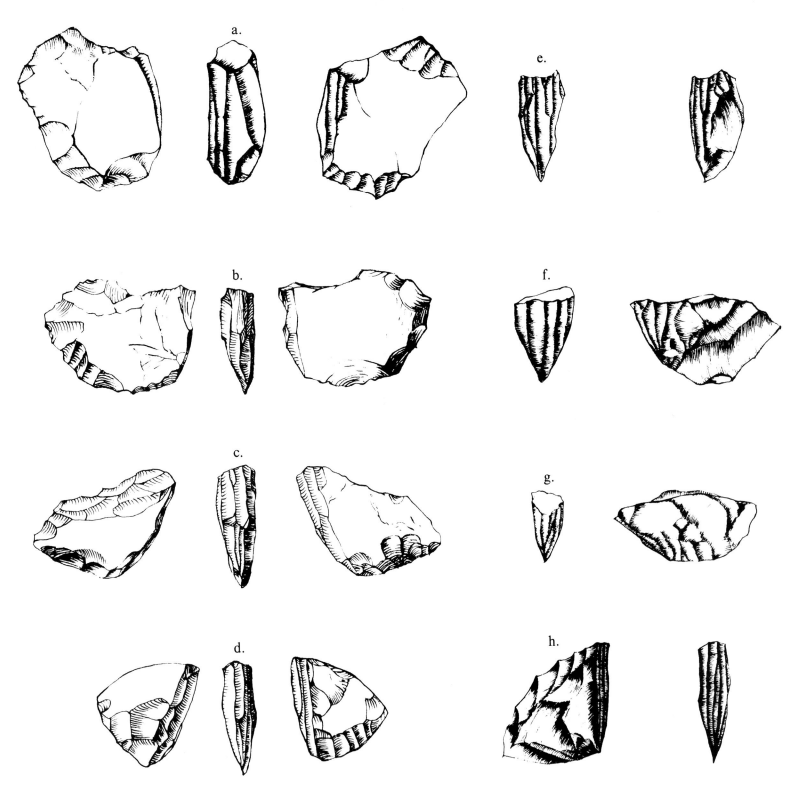

25. North China wedge-shaped microblade cores, carbon 14 dated from 28,900 to 10,000 B.P.: a. Zhiyu, b.–d. Hutouliang, e.–f. Xiachuan, g. Shayuan, h. Zhibajan

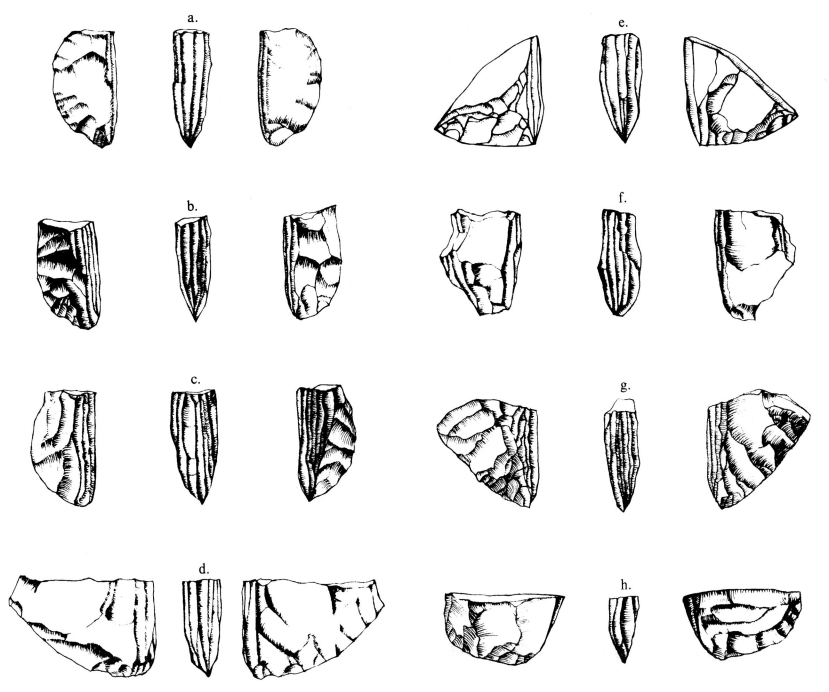

26. Related wedge-shaped microblade cores in northeast Asia and Alaska: a. Hailar (Heilongjiang Province, extreme northeast China); b. Brooks Range, Alaska; c. Mongolia; d. U.A. campus, Alaska; e. Diuktai Cave, Siberia; f. Shishkino, Siberia; g. Okedo-Azum, Japan; h. Tachikawa, Japan.

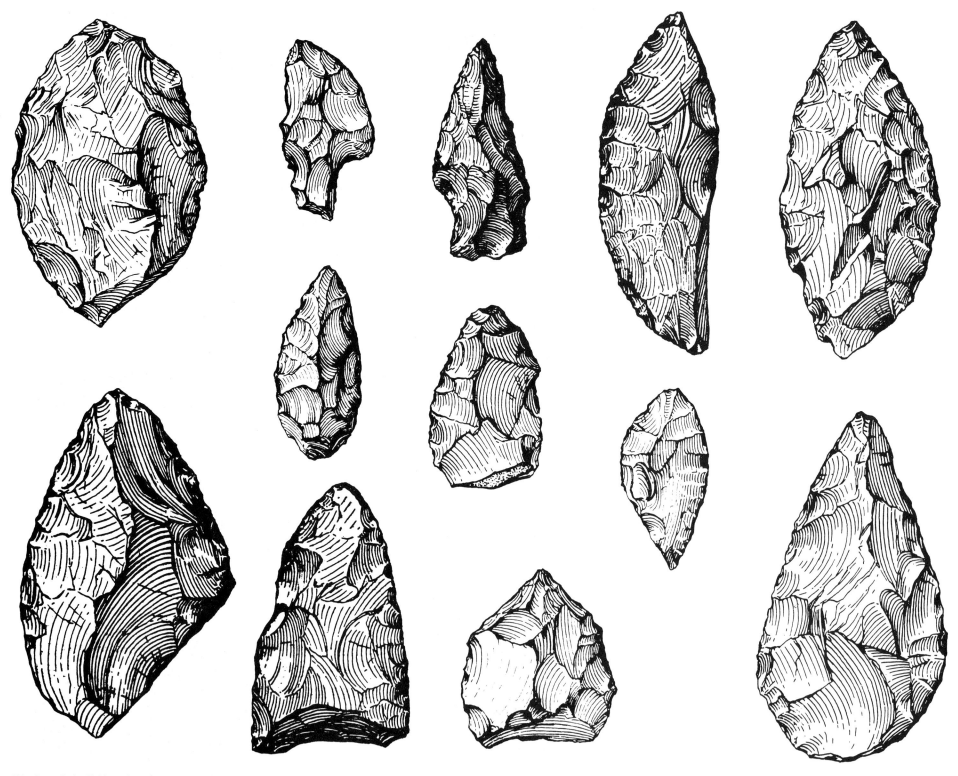

27. Late Paleolithic points from Hutouliang, ca. 10,000 B.P.

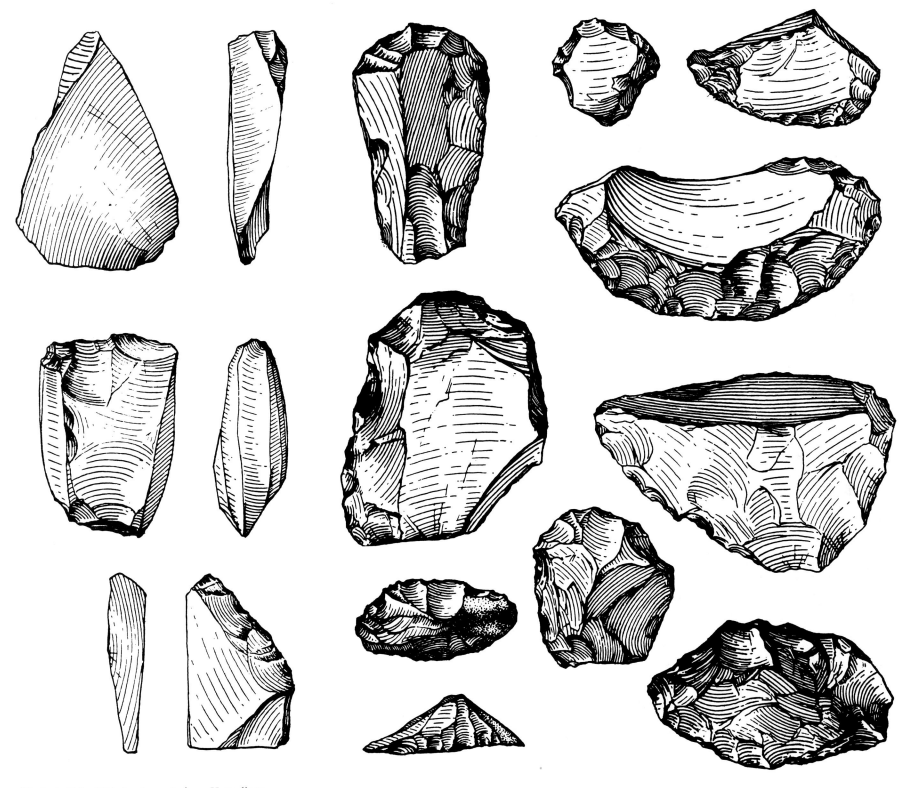

28. Late Paleolithic implements from Hutouliang.

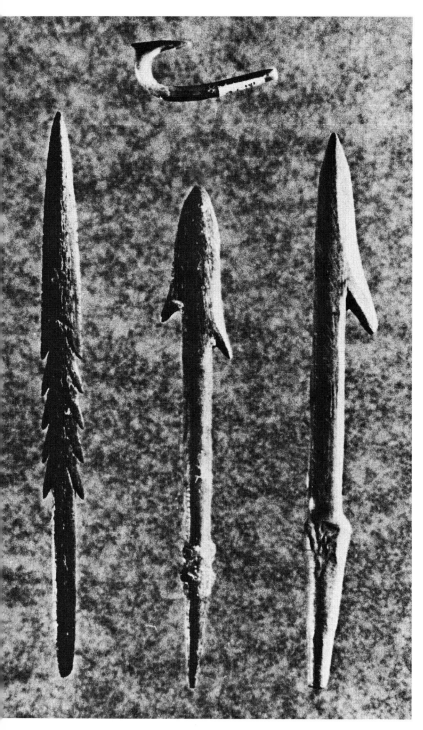

29. Bone fishing implements of Neolithic Period: top, from Heilongjiang; left, from Shanxi; center, from Shaanxi; right, from Jiangsu Province.

30. Neolithic implements from Jaohe, Heilongjiang, Province.

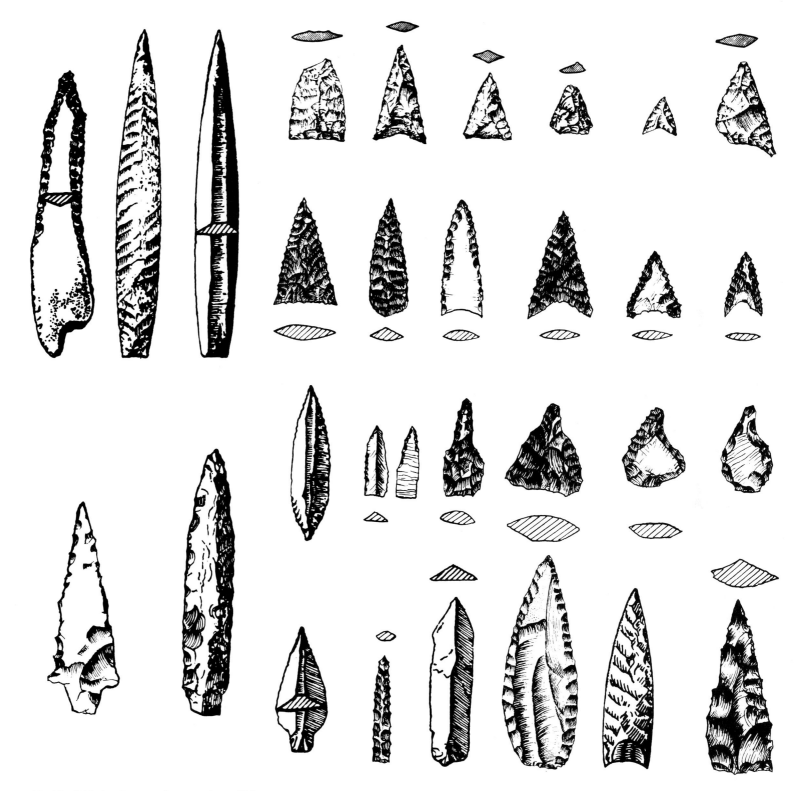

31. Neolithic implements from northeast China.

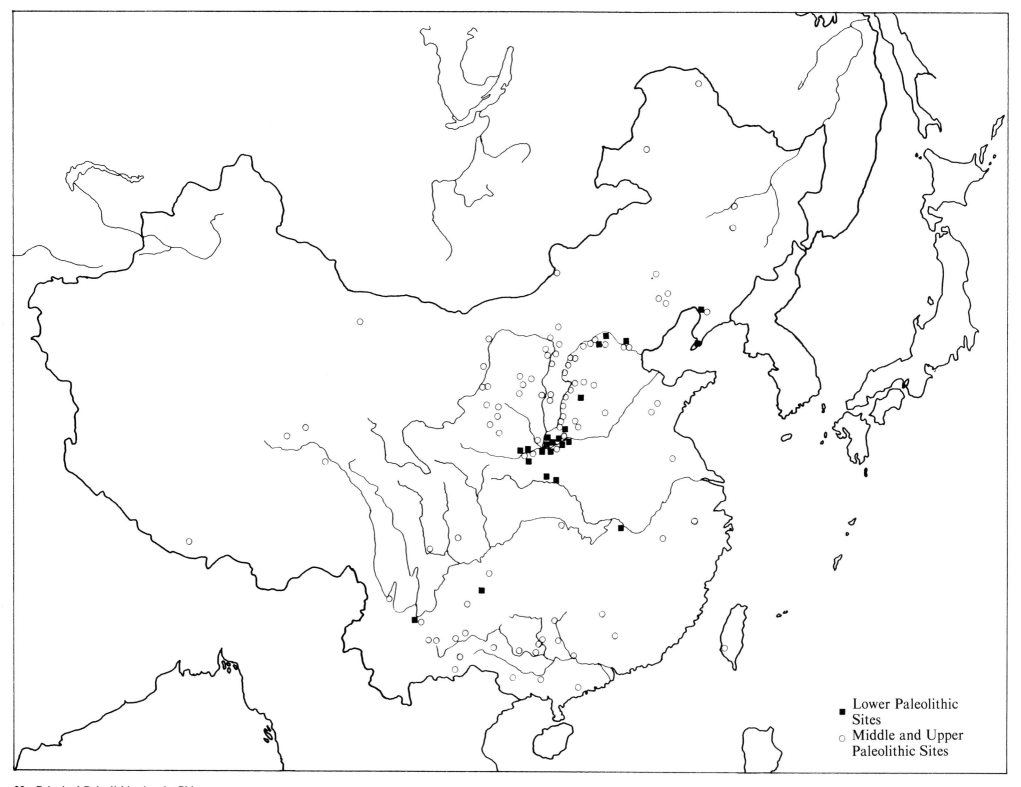

32. Principal Paleolithic sites in China.

Lower Paleolithic Sites

Middle and Upper Paleolithic Sites

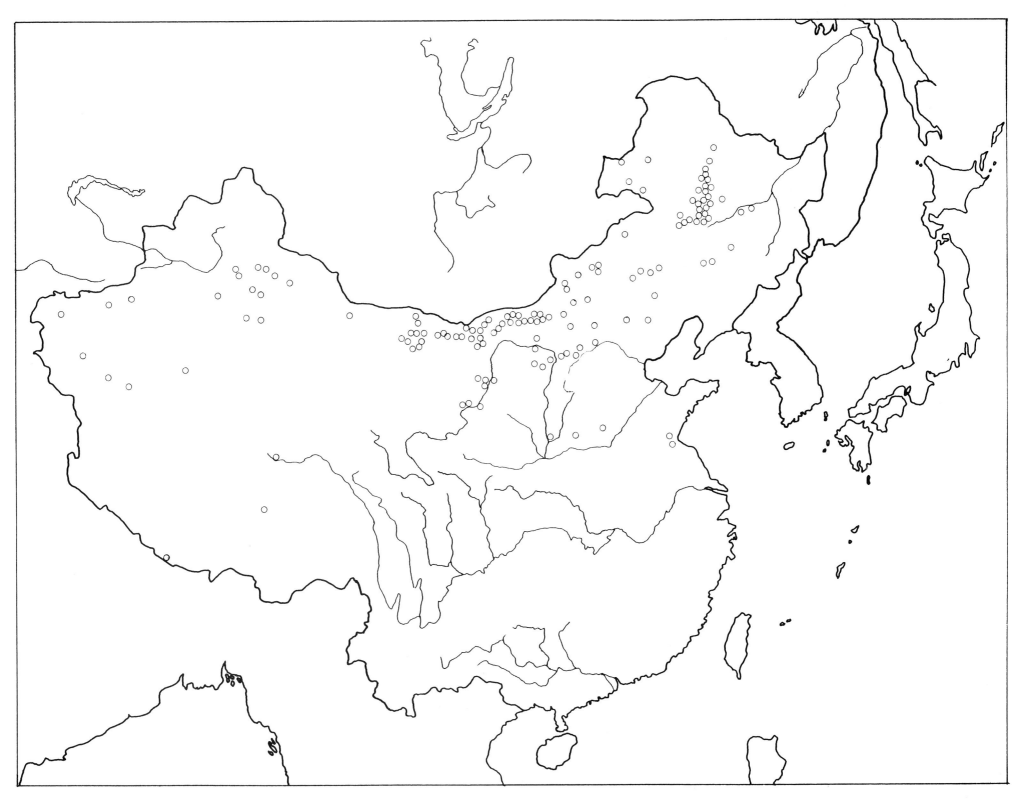

33. Major microlithic sites of Neolithic period in China.

Man crossed the Bering land bridge in search of mammoth and other food sources. As the archaeologist and historian Gordon R. Willey points out: "This means that he came with a cultural heritage." "There can be little question but that the first Paleolithic immigrants to the New World brought from Asia such basic skills as fire-making, flint-chipping, and at least a rude competence in procuring food, shelter, and clothing."[1]

Commenting on the early Americans' lithic traditions, another leading American archaeologist states: "The age of each tradition in North America, in cases where the age of a representative site is known, is substantially greater than it is in South America, suggesting that they stem from earlier Old World roots."[2]

Where then in the Old World did those roots originate? Most scholars including MacNeish point to North China as one of the probable sources. MacNeish compares his earliest stage of Paleoindian development, Stage I, to the "chopper-chopping complexes of the Fen-Ho industry and the Upper Cave culture of Choukoutien in China,"[3] and his Stage II to that of the "Ordos industry of China."[4]

In China, evidence of the earliest tool-making was discovered in 1973 in Yuanmou, Yunnan Province. Three scrapers, one stone core and one point were found in association with the Yuanmou Man deposit which has been paleomagnetic dated 1.7 million years B.P.[5]

Another site of equal antiquity at Xihoudu, Shanxi Province has yielded an assemblage of cores, flakes, choppers, scrapers and heavy triangular points. The latter were to become the prototype for the later Gehe-Dingcun tradition-marker. The cores range from bipolar to funnel-shaped forms. The flakes were produced by the stone-hammer and stone-anvil techniques and the scrapers were fashioned with straight, concave as well as convex contours. Both unifacial and bifacial choppers were present at the site of Xihoudu.[6]

Xihoudu together with a later site, Lantian (of early middle Pleistocene period ca. 1 million years B.P.), presaged one of the two major Paleolithic traditions of North China—the Fen-Wei River (Gehe-Dingcun) tradition. The markers of this tradition are: large flake tools, pebble cores, choppers, and heavy triangular chopping points (picks). Located at the heart of the Central Plains and on the thoroughfare of the much later "silk road," the Gehe-Dingcun people had cultural contact and exchange with their Eurasia neighbors in the west since early time. Like most high cultures in the world, the Chinese culture did not bud in complete isolation. Bifacial hand-axes of the Paleolithic European types have been found in both Gehe and Dingcun sites. Perhaps this is one of the reasons some scholars observed a blending of east Asian pebble-tool with Moustero-Aurignacoid traits in the early American tool kit.[7]

The other major Paleolithic tradition of North China—the Sankan River (Zhoukoudian-Hutouliang) tradition, is characterized by the small size of its tools.

The reason we have traced the microliths of this tradition to Peking Man's culture is that in this assemblage, there are not only large numbers of microliths, but also a great variety of other types of stone implements—bipolar cores, flakes, various forms of small points, scrapers and gravers, which have occurred in the various cultures at Xujiayao, Zhiyu, Xiachuan and Hutouliang, and more or less in all microlithic cultures of the Neolithic Age. Since the sites of earlier dating in this tradition are all in north China, the term "North China microlithic tradition" may be an appropriate designation. Personally, I have become ever more convinced that north China is the place of origin of the microlithic cultures of East Asia, North Asia and North America.[8]

Another characteristic of this tradition is the occurrence of tools in large quantities. At the Zhoukoudian site alone, 100,000 stone artifacts have been collected. The bulk of these are small flake tools. Large pebble choppers are not common. The 1976 excavation of the Xujiayao site (ca. 100,000 B.P.) yielded 13,650 artifacts: 8,302 flakes and blades, 2,532 cores, 1,526 scrapers, 1,095 stone balls, 106 burins, 105 points, 11 borers and only 5 choppers—chopping tools.[9]

The Xujiayao culture is a more documentable progenitor of the North China small tool tradition. The pyramidal and proto-prismatic cores made their early appearance at the site, providing a link between the Zhoukoudian bipolar core and the Zhiyu wedge-shaped core.

In addition to the wedge-shaped cores, the Zhiyu site (carbon 14 dated 28135 ± 1330 B.P.) yielded over 15,000 other stone implements among which are: microblades, thumb-nail scrapers, and projectile points.[10]

The Zhiyu artifacts are directly connected with the Xiachuan middle Upper Paleolithic assemblages (carbon 14 dated 23,900 and 16,400 B.P.). By this time the North China small tool industries were fully developed. Among the 1,800 stone artifacts found at Xiachuan, there are various types of wedge-shaped cores, conical cores and prismatic cores, totaling 300 in number.[11] Microblades are trapezoidal in section and are trimmed at one end or both ends for composite fitting on handles as knives. Projectile points, arrowheads, and scrapers are abundant.

The full blossoming of this tradition is manifested at the late Upper Paleolithic site of Hutouliang,[12] located halfway between Beijing and Zhiyu on the north bank of the Sankan River. An unparalleled total of 236 wedge-shaped cores have been excavated. Gai Pei, the chief investigator of the site, remarked:

At the Hutouliang sites over 200 wedge-shaped cores were unearthed between 1972 and 1974, more than the total found in all the Paleolithic sites in North America. No other site in Asia has contained this many. This suggests the origin and subsequent distribution of the wedge-shaped cores. . . .

. . . the cores unearthed at Hutouliang prove that the techniques used to make them originated in north China. Almost identical cores have also been discovered in Alaska at the Akmak site on the Kobuk River and the Brooks Range site, and also in northern British Columbia in Canada. They are so similar in shape and method of making to those found at Hutouliang that both look as if they had been made by the same craftsman. The pointed implements and scrapers found in north America are also strikingly similar to those at Hutouliang. In prehistorical terms, both north China and north America belonged to the same cultural tradition in the Late Pleistocene. This cultural tradition spread from east Asia (including the Japanese islands), the Mongolian plateau and northeast Asia across the land bridge which is now the Bering Strait to northwest America.[13]

Close cultural ties continued during the Neolithic period between China, northeast Asia and northwest America. Thus, wrote Larichev in an article titled, "Neolithic Remains in the Upper Amur Basin at Ang-Ang-Hsi in Tungpei":

The ancient cultures of northern Asia long felt the powerful influence of one of the most important and advanced centers of man's development—ancient China. This influence penetrated to the neighboring areas of Korea, southern Manchuria, and Inner Mongolia, to the steppes of central Asia and the Siberian taiga as far as Lake Baykal, and reached even further, into Yakutia.

In the literature concerning the Siberian Neolithic, connections have been noted between the Kitoy stage of the Cis-Baykal Neolithic on the one hand, and the culture represented by the finds in the case of Sha-kuo-t'un on the other. . . .

. . . There are adequate grounds for postulating a close relationship between the cultures of Siberia and China also during Paleolithic times.[14]

China-Siberia-Pacific Northwest America connections are best exemplified by the sites at the lower reaches of the Fraser River, British Columbia. The Asia-rooted microblade and core-complex, ground slates projectile points, knives, saws, and most outstanding of all, polished nephrite and jadeite adze blades and narrow-bit chisels, have been found in large quantities. In visiting museums in British Columbia, I have noticed an array of stone figures from this and later periods, bearing striking Asiatic traits. As will be demonstrated in Chapter IV, the Fraser River artifacts provide a crucial link between the ancient Chinese and Mesoamerican culture.

Data accumulating from both the Old and New World make it increasingly evident that a protracted inter-continental cultural exchange was in progress in the millennia before Eskimos occupied Bering Strait. . . .[15]

In addition to the ground slates, which include projectiles, knives, adze blades, and saws, other traits in the Fraser delta assemblages of the first millennium B.C. suggest influences of the Siberian Neolithic. Among these are the previously mentioned neatly sawed and polished adze blades of nephrite. . . .[16]

Moreover, it is becoming increasingly apparent that during the last millennia B.C. the Gulf of Georgia region was a center of intense cultural elaboration where influences from Asia overlapped with those coming up the Pacific slope from the south.[17]

The cultural continuum of Asia, the Gulf of Georgia region of British Columbia, the Pacific slope of Mexico and Guatemala, the Isthmus of Tehuantepec, and the south Veracruz-west Tabasco regions will be documented in the next chapter.

Notes

1. Gordon R. Willey, *An Introduction to American Archaeology: Volume One—North and Middle American,* New Jersey: Prentice-Hall, 1966, p. 19.
2. Richard S. MacNeish, ibid., 1971, p. 256.
3. Richard S. MacNeish, ibid., 1976, p. 317.
4. Ibid., p. 318.
5. Jia Lanpo, *Early Man in China,* Beijing: Foreign Languages Press, 1980, p. 8.
6. Ibid., p. 11.
7. Hansjurgen Muller-Beck, "Paleohunters in America; Origins and Diffusion", *Science,* Vol. 152, No. 3726, 1966, pp. 1190–1210. Also see MacNeish, ibid., 1976, pp. 317 and 318.
8. Jia Lanpo, *Early Man in China,* ibid., 1980, pp. 59–60.
9. Jia Lanpo, Wei Qi and Li Jaorong, "Report on the Excavation of Hsuchiayao Man site in 1976", *Vertebrata PalAsiatica,* Vol. 17, No. 4, 1979, pp. 291–292.
10. Jia Lanpo, Gai Pei and You Yuzhu, "Report on the Excavation of the Late Paleolithic Site at Zhiyu, Shoxien, Shanxi Province", *Kaogu Xuebao,* No. 1, 1972, pp. 39–58.

11. Wang Jien, Wang Xiangjien and Chen Zheying, "Archaeological Reconnaissances at Xiachuan, Qin Qu county, Shanxi province", *Kaogu Xuebao,* No. 3, 1978, p. 264.

12. Gai Pei and Wei Qi, "Discovery of the Late Paleolithic Site at Hutouliang Hebei", *Vertebrata PalAsiatica,* Vol. 15, No. 4, pp. 287–300.

13. Gai Pei, "From China to North America", *China Reconstructs,* May 1978, pp. 46–48.

14. V. Ye. Larichev, "Neolithic Remains in the Upper Amur Basin at Ang-Ang-Hsi in Tungpei", in *The Archaeology and Geomorphology of Northern Asia: Selected Works,* (Henry N. Michael, ed.), Montreal: Arctic Institute of North America, 1964, p. 181.

15. Charles E. Borden, "West Coast Crossties with Alaska", in *Prehistoric Cultural Relationships Between the Arctic and Temperate Zones of North America,* (John M. Campbell, ed.), Montreal: Arctic Institute of America, 1962, p. 17.

16. Ibid., p. 16.

17. Ibid., p. 19.

CHAPTER IV
The Origin of Ancient American Cultures

Ancient American cultures did not, any more than the early Americans and their lithic industries, evolve in complete isolation. The very definition of culture hinges on accumulation, transmission and cross-fertilization of knowledge. It is this unique, evolutionary ability that renders our species superior to all others. A given culture, not unlike an individual, is a living and continuously changing organism capable of independent problem-solving, feeling and action. From a macro-evolutionary point of view, however, the independence of individual cultures is limited. The character and developmental potential of a given culture is molded not only by external ecological and other interactive factors but also by internal bio-cultural genealogy. As Figure 1 indicates, ancient American cultures developed in spatial as well as temporal context with those of the Old World which were ancestral to them.

The purpose of this chapter is to document the organic oneness of the Old and New World cultures in general and of the Chinese and Mesoamerican cultures in particular, by illustrating seventeen samples of juxtaposed Sino-American cultural trait-complexes.[1]

The seventeen interrelated trait-complexes are chosen according to the following criteria:

1. They can be dated to the formative stages of the earliest known New World cultures.
2. They played a primary and fundamental role in the cultures under investigation.
3. They occurred fully evolved and without antecedents in the New World.
4. They are so complex, abstract and unique that their being independently invented as a result of functional causality is not within the realm of probability.
5. The postulated Old World archetypes predate the American "new growths."
6. The Old and New World traits being compared are congruous not only in tangible, expressive forms but also in abstract iconographic contents.
7. These traits are comparable not only as individual complexes but also as interrelated traditions: two differentiated expressions of a genealogical whole.

A brief review of the earliest New World cultures is appropriate at this juncture for better understanding of the correlations to be presented later.

I will begin with the definition of culture. In the previous chapters, the term culture has been employed in a "primitive" context—culture of a pre-civilized nature. Culture of the Mesoamerican Preclassic (ca. 1150 B.C.–A.D. 300) and subsequent periods postulated in this chapter, however, encompasses the following: (1) community centers supported directly or indirectly by settled agriculture, (2) hierarchical social organization with marked division of labor, (3) high-tech achievements such as refined jade-working, elaborate stela-carving, irrigation and monumental public architecture, and (4) hieroglyphic, calendric and allied religious systems.

The appearance of pottery artifacts is generally regarded by archaeologists as signs of man's approaching the threshold of civilization. The first traces of ancient American ceramics were detected along the Pacific Coast in northwest South America and Mesoamerica.

At Valdivia and other related Pacific sites in Ecuador, the earliest ceramic phases (ca. 3000 B.C.) of the New World were discovered by Meggers, Evans, and Estrada. Based on extensive comparisons, they concluded that this tradition had its origin in the Middle Jomon culture of Japan.

Arriving on the Ecuadorian shore, the travelers were met or soon found by the local residents, who presumably were living much the same kind of life as had been left behind on Kyushu. . . . In the process, they introduced the art of pottery making, and very probably new religious practices that are reflected in the stone figurines.[2]

James Ford, in one of the most comprehensive studies of early American cultures, confirmed Meggers, Evans and Estrada's findings of the Jomon-Valdivia cultural connection and went further in linking the Valdivia ceramic repertoire with other early formative cultures of the Americas:

> The Valdivia ceramic complex, which appears suddenly about 3000 B.C. in a limited region on the coast of Ecuador, is by no means primitive. The unusually extensive range of decorations comprises a large part of the techniques (aside from painting) employed in the Americas in the succeeding centuries.

> Within a few years a group of people appears to have proceeded up the Pacific coast of South America and established a colony on the Caribbean coast of present-day Colombia. At the Puerto Hormiga site, a small ring-shaped village was placed on an inlet a short distance from the sea. A limited selection of Valdivia ceramic features was introduced. . . .[3]

> It was also at this early date, about 2300 B.C., that the art of pottery-making arrived in the highlands of central Mexico. . . . Probably the spread of the knowledge of ceramic technology inland from a colony on one of the coasts of Mexico was a diffusion process. . . .[4]

> At about 1800 B.C. ceramics reached the central highlands of Peru. . . .[5]

Even scholars who normally incline towards independent evolution of New World cultures recognize the possibility of cultural diffusion along the Pacific Coast during this gestation period:

> To date the earliest known ceramics in southern Mesoamerica (Swasey and Barra phases) have no Mesoamerican antecedents, although in time antecedents may be found. However, Michael Coe (1960) and Gareth Lowe (1975; Green and Lowe 1967) have detailed a number of co-occurrences of ceramic attributes on ceramics from Ecuador and from Barra and Ocos phase contexts at coastal Chiapas-Guatemala sites. The presence of red-slipped Pox ceramics on the coast of Guerrero and red-slipped bottles and other Ecuadorian-like ceramic traits in early assemblages in Michoacan, Colima, and Jalisco suggest widespread interaction via seaborne contacts along the Pacific Coast during the Early Formative.

> If contacts of this type introduced sophisticated ceramics and a wide variety of decorative attributes to southern and western Mesoamerica during the Early Formative, then less tangible traits were probably introduced as well. Possible introductions into Mesoamerica include such diverse elements as manioc agriculture, cacao, improved corn varieties, pyramid mounds, mound-plaza site arrangements, the rubber ball game, cosmologies and ideologies, etc.[6]

However, the same kind of provincialism that has frustrated Richard MacNeish, in his pioneering investigation of the Tehuacan Valley preceramic-ceramic sequence, also has plagued the search for the ultimate origin of the ancient American cultures:

> At the outset, let me say that it often seems that some archaeologists working in Mesoamerica never change their minds no matter what the new data (Lathrap 1977), or if they do, they never admit it (Lorenzo 1975). Further, there is a great deal of provincialism in respect to both time and space among Mesoamerican archaeologists so that sometimes they may change their minds about one aspect, usually an aspect that concerns their narrow problems, and not change their minds about other conceptions.[7]

There is clearly a need for open-minded interdisciplinary cooperation of a global nature in our effort to deduce why and how New World cultures germinate and grow. Inductive, "particularistic," archaeological approach alone will not be sufficient. "Production-mode" and "production-relationship" analysis in a strict dialectic materialist perspective will not be adequate. Methodologies, which overly emphasize ecological adaptive behavior: subsistence-settlement-demography patterns, oblivious to the humanistic attributes of cultural change, befit zoological studies more than anthropological investigation.

Thus the following insight by a seasoned and astute scholar of American archaeology:

> There is, however, one encouraging aspect of Mesoamerican archaeology. This is its retention of its old, rich humanistic tradition. It is expressed in the way that the subject is embedded in a marvelous ethnographic and ethnohistoric context, and in some of the following chapters it can be seen how this tradition and these contexts have been further enriched and deepened by hieroglyphic and iconographic studies of the very recent years that help us tell the story of the past and, I think, better understand that story in direct, documented human behavioral terms. Is this a moving away from Mesoamerican archaeology's progress as a science? Some of our colleagues might think so, but I would see it as a reinforcement, a betterment as we move forward on a broad front.[8]

It is through this "united front" and the "all world, one nation" spirit that I believe the universal truth of cultural change can be revealed.

> All things under heaven nourish one another, move and change effortlessly . . . the Tao is one.
> *I Jing* (The Book of Changes)

Later in this chapter, I shall focus on the ideational realm of cultural change—the Yang aspect of the Yin materialistic counterpart. I hope, at least to some extent, the form-and-meaning comparisons of the seventeen Sino-American trait-complexes will help to fill the vacuum of knowledge on the subject and stimulate a more integrated and balanced perspective concerning the genesis and development of early American cultures.

In the late second-early first millenium B.C., with a subsistence-surplus derived from settled agriculture and trade (of goods and ideas), two complex cultures emerged abruptly with startling intensity and sophistication—the Olmec culture in Mexico and the Chavin culture in Peru. The Chavin culture produced imposing stone-faced architecture, articulative ceramics and powerful intaglio bas-reliefs but generally lacked the "civil" attributes of the Olmec culture. As a whole, the Chavin belonged to another sub-tradition, although some aspects of its culture are related to those of the early Mesoamerica. For this reason, the emphasis of this volume is placed on the Olmec and Olmec related Mesoamerican cultures.

In recent years, the Olmec culture is widely accepted as the "mother culture," or "the first civilization" of the ancient Americas:

> The first of these great horizon phenomena is the Olmec culture, an apparently autochthonous civilization centered on the Northern Isthmian Plain which had an enormous influence on the rest of Mesoamerica; the Olmecs, who may have invented writing and the Long Count, created the "mother culture" from which are derived all others both here on the Gulf coast and elsewhere.[9]

Is Olmec culture indigenous? Is there a "father culture" involved? I believe the answer to the first question is negative, and to the second question, positive. Following are my reasonings.

The Olmec cultural horizon is defined mainly by its sculptures; however, no evidence indicating the origin and development of these "cultural markers" exists. Coe and Diehl remarked in one of the most elaborate works published on the Olmec:

> On the origins of monumental sculpture at San Lorenzo Tenochtitlan, we have little to say. There are certainly few data to support a slow and inexorable evolution of large-scale quarrying, transportation, and manufacture of these objects, either here or at any other Olmec site.[10]

Unwittingly undermining the indigenous origin hypothesis, Coe and Diehl further concluded that the San Lorenzo sculptures and perhaps also those of the Laguna de los Cerros and La Venta[11], were fashioned in an unknown "workshop site" 60 kilometers away "at the base of the Tuxtlas Range."[12] Significantly, the only known major cultural center near the Tuxtlas Mountains is the much later Tres Zapotes site which is closely associated with the Mayan tradition. Stela C at Tres Zapotes, for example, bears a Long Count date equivalent of 31 B.C. and can be linked to antecedents at the site to Abaj Takalik[13] and others on the Pacific Coast of Guatemala.

Gordon Willey, commenting on the origin of the stela cult and the hieroglyphic system, states:

> For the moment, let me avoid this storm cloud of ultimate origins by saying that to my way of thinking it would not detract anything from the Maya Lowland achievement to see such elements as the stelae cult and the hieroglyphic system having their first development in Pacific or Pacific-Highland Guatemala.[14]

The Olmec-style stela and other monumental sculptures are distributed more extensively on the Pacific Coast of Mesoamerica than on the "heartland" Gulf Coast, spanning over 1100 kilometers from San Miguel Amuco, Guerrero, Mexico to Chalchuapa, El Salvador.

Ceramic sequences at major Olmec sites also point to the Pacific Coast as their immediate source of origin. At San Lorenzo, for instance, the earliest pottery strata, Ojochi, is a direct descendant of the Pacific Coast Barra—Ocos sequence:

> Evidence for the priority of Ojochi with regard to Bajio came from the Monument 20 excavations, in which the Ojochi-bearing Stratum E underlay the Bajio-bearing Stratum D. Thus, Ojochi is the earliest phase at San Lorenzo.

> Ojochi is a country-cousin version of the far more sophisticated Ocos phase of Guatemalan Soconusco (Coe 1961: 48–60) and must be contemporary with it. . . .[15]

> There is considerable similarity to the all-red ceramic types of Soconusco, such as Cotan Grooved Red of the Barra phase (Green and Lowe 1967: Fig. 73); the closest parallels are to be found again in the Ocos phase, in Ocos Specular Red, Ocos Red Burnished, and Ocos Iridescent.[16]

The Barra phase at Altamira on the Pacific Coast of Chiapas is dated between 2000–1500 B.C.[17] and Ocos phase at La Victoria 1500–1150 B.C. Both are related to the Pox ceramics (ca. 2440 B.C.) of Pacific Coast Guerrero[18] and farther south, to the Valdivia ceramics of coastal Ecuador:

> Actually, the entire Isthmian region and contiguous areas contain sites with Ocos-like ceramics (Lowe 1971: 223; 1977: 207–212). The Ojochi phase occupation at San Lorenzo therefore was simply part of a larger, widespread early farming culture influenced by the Pacific Coast.[19]

Another outstanding Olmec cultural "marker", the carved jade effigy objects, were also widely distributed on the Pacific Coast of Middle America: from Guerrero, Mexico, to as far south as Costa Rica (see Figure 241)—a fact which might have prompted Covarrubias's Pacific origin theory:

> One treads on truly dangerous ground when trying to answer the prickly question of who were the creators of the "Olmec" culture. However, the temptation is greater than caution. To judge from the geographic distribution of "Olmec" art—sweeping from the Pacific Coast of Guerrero and Oaxaca northeast into Veracruz and south into Guatemala and Honduras—and taking into consideration the trend of development and elaboration of the culture in those places, it may well have had its origins either on the coast or in the valleys of the Pacific slopes of Oaxaca and Guerrero, where its most archaic forms appear.[20]

Other material evidence strongly against indigenous origin of Olmec culture includes:

1. Negative subsistence-settlement-demography pattern: The Olmec "heartland" is situated in one of the New World's most inhospitable environment: The hot, humid and swampy jungles of Gulf Coast lowland, which was, and still is, sparsely populated. At the height of its grandeur, San Lorenzo had a maximum estimated population of only 1,000. La Venta fared even worse: only 150 people could have been able to subsist on food sources afforded by the environment.[21]
2. Non-evolutionary, sudden appearance of the Olmec dragon culture which engulfed the whole of Mesoamerica with stormy and lightning speed. As will be demonstrated in the following correlations of polycomplexes, almost the entire iconographic embodiment of the Olmec pantheon appears to be a product of interhemispheric Celestial insemination.

The significance of the dragon cult in the Olmec culture has been recognized only recently:

> The iconographic ancestry of God I—the Olmec Dragon—can be traced back to the beginnings of Olmec civilization. Images of the deity have been discovered in early deposits at San Lorenzo in the Olmec heartland and at Las Bocas and Tlapacoya in central Mexico. . . .

> The large number of extant representations of God I indicates that the Dragon was the most important member of the Olmec pantheon.[22]

However, the pivotal position of the dragon deities in the succeeding Maya and Aztec cultures have long been noted by scholars:

> The serpent is more than a common motif in Mayan Art. It is virtually an all-pervading theme which recurs in a great variety of contexts and assumes many different forms. . . . In many cases the identity of the serpent is lost in that of a fantastic monster.[23]

The Itzam were the dragonlike monsters, common in Maya art, with huge saurian heads and bodies at times those of an iguana, but which could take the form of a snake. Frequently they were enriched with features of a deer. . . .[24]

I established, at least to my own satisfaction, that Itzam Na was the supreme god depicted everywhere in the art of the Classic period.[25]

There stood at the head of the Maya Pantheon the Great Itzamna, son of Hunab Ku. . . . He has two name-glyphs . . . which contains as its main element the day-sign Ahau. This day-sign we have already seen, meant "king, emperor, monarch, prince or great lord". . . .[26] [See Figure 381 for Chinese counterpart]

The serpent motive controlled the character of Mayan art and was of first importance in all subsequent arts in Central America and Mexico.[27]

Quetzalcoatl, one of the greatest of gods, provides an example of how different and seemingly unrelated aspects were being synthesized in a single god. . . .
The name Quetzalcoatl means literally "Quetzal-serpent" or "the plumed serpent". . . .

Quetzalcoatl is a very ancient god, among the Mayas and the Quiches he was known as Kukulkan. . . .[28]

Clearly the ancient Mesoamerican iconographic tradition embodied a patterned cosmic structure and its emblematic expression—a coherent system of abstract ideas actualized in the visual images of the supernaturals with well defined messages.

As will be demonstrated by the ensuing 354 juxtaposed illustrations, not only the visual idiom but also the ideological content of the early American cultures are diachronically as well as synchronically consonant with those of China.

The impromptu invention of this highly evolved system of ideo-physical trait-complexes by the Olmec is beyond cognitive probability.

It is recognized that a comprehensive exposition of the interrelationships of ancient American and Chinese cultures will require more space than available in one or two monographs. However, I believe the materials contained in this chapter will provide a stimulative frame of reference for further investigation.

The character of the Mesoamerican iconographic system is roughly sketched below:

1. The Mesoamerican iconographic tradition was marked by a high degree of coherency from the sudden Olmec beginning to the eve of Spanish Conquest, although some secondary elements might have undergone disjointed transformation due to regional-temporal differentiation and permutation.
2. The dragon cult played a dominant and pervasive role in the entire Mesoamerican tradition.
3. The dragon cult is characterized by the following combination of attributes:
   a. Ancestral worship—descent from the dragon, ancestral totem-alter ego.
   b. Royal lineage—dynastic rule sanctified by celestial mandate, deification of clan ancestor.
   c. Dualistic symbiosis—Unification of opposites: sky-dragon vs. earth-dragon; fire dragon vs. water-dragon; life-giving dragon vs. death-inflicting dragon, etc.
   d. Quadruple multiplicity—four dragons associated with four cardinal directions: four colors, four seasons, four differentiated manifestations of a central god and so forth.

e. Polymorphous intensification—selective interface of iconographic human, reptile, feline, avian, and plant elements; sun-eye-paw-wing composite and so on.

f. Temporal and spatial orientation—ordering of ancestors and gods in accordance with time (the day or "sun" on which they were born) and place (the cosmic region or cardinal direction).

These attributes are in complete agreement with those well established in China. An event of special significance regarding the Sino-Mesoamerican dragon cult is reported in a 1983 article in *Kaogu* (Archaeology, No. 1, p. 42):

> The painted dragon pottery basin ca. 4300 B.P. unearthed in a large tomb of the early period, is the earliest sample ever discovered in the Central Plains. It will be of great value to the investigation of the Taosi culture and to the research into the origin of dragon worship.

Importantly, the Taosi sites, located in Xiangfen County, Shanxi Province, is within the heartland of the Xia people, founders of the first historical dynasty of China. Further, it is known from historical records that the clan-name of the Xia was Yi (snake) and that their totem was the dragon.

The significance of the Taosi sites in Xiangfen, however, does not merely consist in its being the cradle of the circumpacific dragon cult. Xiangfen happens also to be the birthplace of the famed Dingcun (Fenho) lithic tradition which Richard MacNeish has linked to the "core-tool tradition" of the early Americans.[29]

The following correlations are intended to serve only as an introduction[30] to the study of the genealogical and diffusional bonds between the ancient American and Chinese cultures. No amount of mortal endeavor will be adequate to fully recapture the vigor and splendor of the early American cultures. The similarities in formal (aesthetic) as well as ideational (iconographic) expressions between the ancient Chinese and Mesoamerican traditions are striking. They are so stylized, so symbolic, so complicated, so numerous and so diachronically and synchronically correlatable, in addition to being unique to these two cultural traditions, as to render the hypothesis of totally independent invention of New World culture, exceedingly improbable.

I have kept my verbal comments to the minimum in the following comparisons so that the reader can experience and visualize individually the aesthetic qualities as well as the correlations being presented.

The myths from the Chinese classics which I have quoted preceding each of the following seventeen parts, all have similar Mesoamerican counterparts.

Notes

1. Other monographs are being prepared to more fully expound on the subject and present the multitude of correlatable data accumulated in the past nine years.
2. Betty J. Meggers, Clifford Evans and Emilio Estrada, *Early Formative Period of Coastal Ecuador: The Valdivia and Machalilla Phases,* Washington, D.C.: Smithsonian Institution, 1965, p. 168.
3. James A. Ford, *A Comparison of Formative Cultures in the Americas,* Washington, D.C.: Smithsonian Institution, 1969, p. 184.
4. Ibid., p. 185.
5. Ibid., p. 186.
6. David Grove, "The Formative Period and the Evolution of Complex Culture," *Supplement to the Handbook of Middle American Indians: Archaeology,* edited by Jeremy Sabloff, Austin: University of Texas Press, 1981, p. 391.
7. Richard MacNeish, "Tehuacan's Accomplishment," *Archaeology,* 1981, ibid., p. 31.

8. Gordon Willey, "Recent Researches and Perspectives in Mesoamerican Archaeology: An Introductory Commentary," *Archaeology,* 1981, ibid., p. 3.

9. Michael Coe, "Archaeological Synthesis of Southern Veracruz and Tabasco," *Handbook of the Middle American Indian,* edited by Gordon Willey, Austin: University of Texas Press, 1965, p. 714.

10. Michael Coe and Richard Diehl, *In the Land of the Olmec,* Austin: University of Texas Press, 1980, Vol. I, p. 295.

11. Michael Coe and Richard Diehl, ibid., p. 295.

12. Michael Coe, "San Lorenzo Tenochtitlan," *Supplement to the Handbook of the Middle American Indians,* ibid., p. 141.

13. John Graham, Maya, "Olmecs and Izapans at Abaj Takalik", *XLII International Congress of Americanists, Acta 8,* 1979, p. 182.

14. Gordon Willey, "A Commentary on Cultural Evolution in the Maya Highlands and Lowlands," ibid., p. 207.

15. Michael Coe and Richard Diehl, ibid., p. 137.

16. Ibid., p. 143.

17. Gareth Lowe, "The Early Preclassic Barra Phase of Altamira, Chiapas", *Papers of the New World Archaeological Foundation,* Provo: New World Archaeological Foundation, No. 38, 1975, p. 1.

18. David Grove, "The Formative Period and the Evolution of Complex Culture", ibid., p. 388.

19. Ibid., p. 376.

20. Miguel Covarrubias, *Indian Art of Mexico and Central America,* New York: Alfred A. Knopf, 1957, p. 76.

21. Warwick Bray, Earl Swanson and Ian Farrington, *The New World,* Oxford: Elseuier, 1975, p. 96.

22. Peter Joralemon, "The Olmec Dragon: A Study in Pre-columbian Iconography," *Origins of Religious Art and Iconography in Preclassic Mesoamerica* edited by H. B. Nicholson, Los Angeles: Latin American Center, 1976, p. 37.

23. Tatiana Proskouriakoff, *A Study of Classic Maya Sculpture,* Washington, D.C.: Carnegie Institution, 1950, p. 39.

24. Eric Thompson, "Maya Rulers of the Classic Period and the Divine Right of Kings," *The Iconography of Middle American Sculpture,* ibid., p. 59.

25. Ibid., p. 58.

26. Sylvanus Morley, *The Ancient Maya,* Palo Alto: Stanford University Press, 1947, p. 222.

27. Herbert Spinden, *Maya Art and Civilization,* Indian Hills: Falcon's Wing Press, 1957, p. 298.

28. Alfonso Caso, *The Aztecs: People of the Sun,* Norman: University of Oklahoma Press, 1958, pp. 23–25.

29. Richard MacNeish, "Early Man in the Andes," *Pre-Columbian Archaeology,* edited by Gordon Willey, San Francisco: W. H. Freeman, 1980, p. 169; see also Notes 9 and 10 in Chapter II and Notes 2, 3, 4 in Chapter III.

30. Three related manuscripts are in advanced state of preparation, *Olmec Art: Form and Meaning, Dragon: A Study of Chinese and American Myth, Art of China and Chavin.*

PART 1
The Dragon Ancestral Cult

The mother of Yao [legendary ruler, ca 2356–2255 B.C.] was called Qingdo. . . . She was constantly covered by yellow clouds and accompanied by dragons. . . . Then darkness and winds converged from all four directions, the red dragon impregnated her. After fourteen months, she gave birth to Yao. . . .

Zhu Shu Ji Nian
(Bamboo Annals)
ca. 300 B.C. with
later annotations

34. Tribal emblem symbolizing ancestral dragon worship, detail of a zun ceremonial vessel, Shang Dynasty, ca. 1766–1122 B.C., China (Collection of the Freer Gallery of Art, Smithsonian Institution, Washington, D.C.).

35, 36. Monument 19, Preclassic Period, ca. 1150 B.C.–A.D. 300, depicting an Olmec ancestral dragon "God I", La Venta, Tabasco, Mexico (Collection of the National Museum of Anthropology, Mexico City).

37. Deity on a dragon, detail of a painting on silk, Han Dynasty, ca. 180 B.C., Mawangdui, Changsha, Hunan, China.

38. Deity on a dragon, late Classic Period, ca. A.D. 600–900, El Tajin, Veracruz, Mexico (Collection of the Museum of Anthropology, University of Veracruz, Jalapa).

39. Deity on a dragon, detail of a Chu silk painting, late Zhou Dynasty, ca. 475–221 B.C., Changsha, Hunan, China.

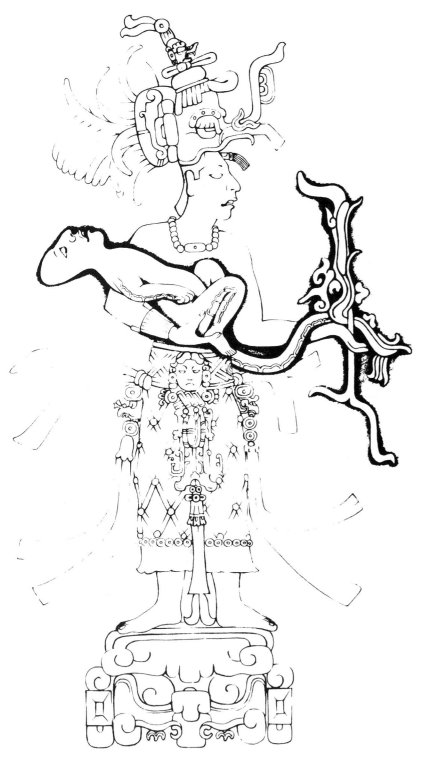

40. Dragon-child, detail of a stucco relief, Classic Period, ca. A.D. 300–900, Temple of Inscription, Palenque, Chiapas, Mexico.

41. Monument 63, Preclassic Period, ca. 1150 B.C.–A.D. 300, La Venta, Tabasco, Mexico (Collection of the La Venta Museum, Villahermosa).

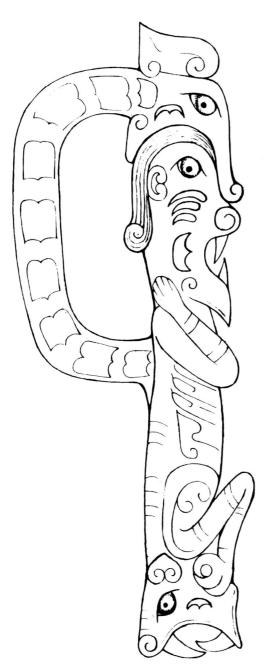

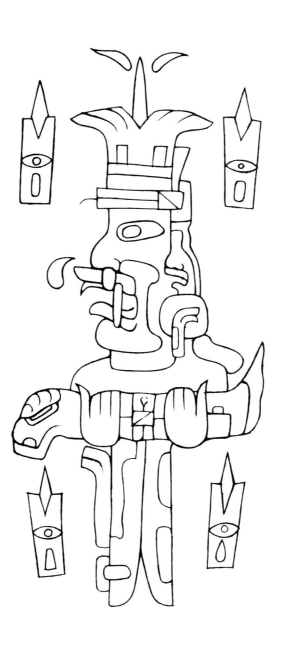

42. Dragon, man and feline, detail of a ceremonial knife, early Zhou Dynasty, ca. 1000 B.C., China (Collection of the Freer Gallery of Art, Smithsonian Institution, Washington, D.C.).

43. Deity holding a dragon, detail of an incised jade celt, Preclassic Period, ca. 1150 B.C.–A.D. 300, Arroya Pesquero, Veracruz, Mexico (Collection of the Museum of Anthropology, University of Veracruz, Jalapa).

44. Deity on a two-headed dragon, late Preclassic Period, ca. A.D. 100–300, Guatemala (Collection of the Museum of American Indian, New York City).

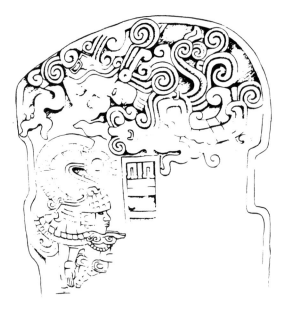

45, 46. Ancestral dragon deity, top portion of Stela 3, late Preclassic Period, ca. A.D. 200, Abaj Takalik, Guatemala.

47. Ancestral dragon deity, top portion of Stela 1, late
Preclassic Period, ca. A.D. 36, El Baul, Guatemala.

48. Monument 63, Preclassic Period, ca. 1150 B.C.–A.D. 300, La Venta, Tabasco, Mexico (Collection of the La Venta Museum, Villahermosa).

49. Ancestral dragon deity, top portion of Stela 1, late Preclassic Period, ca. A.D. 100–300, Abaj Takalik, Guatemala.

50. Ancestral dragon deity, top portion of Stela 11, late Preclassic Period, ca. A.D. 100–300, Kaminaljuyu, Guatemala.

51. Ancestral dragon deity, top portion of Stela 31, Classic Period, ca. A.D. 440, Tikal, Guatemala.

52. Ancestral dragon deity, top portion of Stela 4, early Classic Period, ca. A.D. 300–600, Tikal, Guatemala.

53. Dragon deity, detail of the Bazan incised relief, Monte Alban III Period, ca. A.D. 300–400, Monte Alban, Oaxaca, Mexico (Collection of the Museum of Anthropology, University of Veracruz, Jalapa).

54. Dragon deity, Zhou Dynasty, ca. 1122–256 B.C., China (Collection of the Fogg Art Museum, Cambridge).

55. Guardian dragon above personage, detail of Stela 5, early Classic Period, ca. A.D. 300–600, Cerro de las Mesas, Veracruz, Mexico (Collection of the Museum of Anthropology, University of Veracruz, Jalapa).

56. Guardian dragon above personage, open relief sculpture, late Preclassic Period, ca. A.D. 100–300, Kaminaljuyu, Guatemala.

The people of Xian Yuan [distant ancestors of Xia Yu, founder of the Xia Dynasty, ca. 2205–1766 B.C.], have human faces and snake's bodies. . . .

The name of the Mount Zhong God is "Enlightener". When his eyes are open, it is daytime; when his eyes are closed, it is nighttime. . . . He has a human face and a red snake-body.

Shanhai Jing
(Classics of Mountain
and Sea)
ca. 400–100 B.C.

The God [of Enlightenment] has a human face and a snake's body. . . .

Liu An
Huai Nan Zi
(Book of Prince Huai Nan)
ca. 120 B.C.

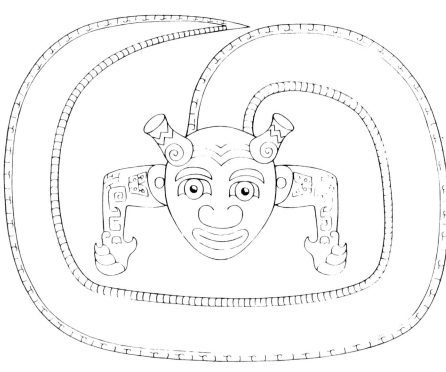

57–59. Anthropomorphic dragon, relief sculpture on a he ceremonial vessel, Shang Dynasty, ca. 1766–1122 B.C., China (Collection of Freer Gallery of Art, Smithsonian Institution, Washington, D.C.).

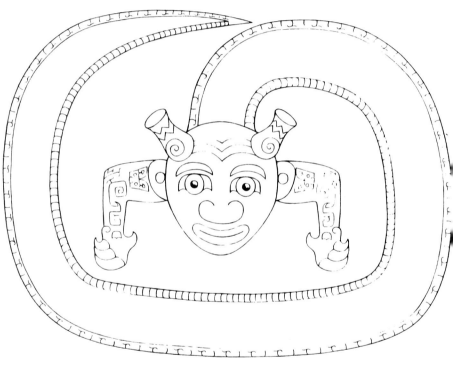

57–59. Anthropomorphic dragon, relief sculpture on a he ceremonial vessel, Shang Dynasty, ca. 1766–1122 B.C., China (Collection of Freer Gallery of Art, Smithsonian Institution, Washington, D.C.).

The people of Xian Yuan [distant ancestors of Xia Yu, founder of the Xia Dynasty, ca. 2205–1766 B.C.], have human faces and snake's bodies. . . .

The name of the Mount Zhong God is "Enlightener". When his eyes are open, it is daytime; when his eyes are closed, it is nighttime. . . . He has a human face and a red snake-body.

Shanhai Jing
(Classics of Mountain
and Sea)
ca. 400–100 B.C.

The God [of Enlightenment] has a human face and a snake's body. . . .

Liu An
Huai Nan Zi
(Book of Prince Huai Nan)
ca. 120 B.C.

60–62. Anthropomorphic feline-dragon, relief carving on bone, Shang Dynasty, ca. 1766–1122 B.C., China (Collection of the Minneapolis Institute of Art, Minneapolis); see Figures 136, 137, 184, 185, 224, 247, and 248.

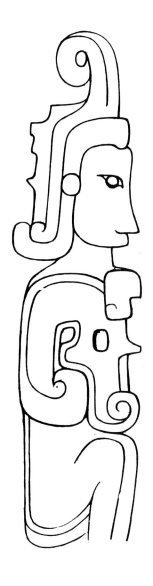

63. Anthropomorphic dragon, relief carving on jade, Zhou Dynasty, ca. 1122–256 B.C., China (Collection of the Field Museum of Natural History, Chicago).

64. Dragon, man and feline, detail of a relief on a ceremonial knife, early Zhou Dynasty, ca. 1000 B.C., China (Collection of Freer Gallery of Art, Smithsonian Institution, Washington, D.C.).

65. Anthropomorphic dragon, detail of a guang ceremonial vessel, early Zhou Dynasty, ca. 1000 B.C., China (Collection of Freer Gallery of Art, Smithsonian Institution, Washington, D.C.).

66. Anthropomorphic dragon, from *Shanhai Jing,* (Classics of Mountain and Sea), ca. 400–100 B.C. This woodblock print is from a later edition.

67. Anthropomorphic dragon, Monument 30, Preclassic Period, ca. 1150 B.C–A.D. 300, San Lorenzo, Veracruz, Mexico; see Figure 387.

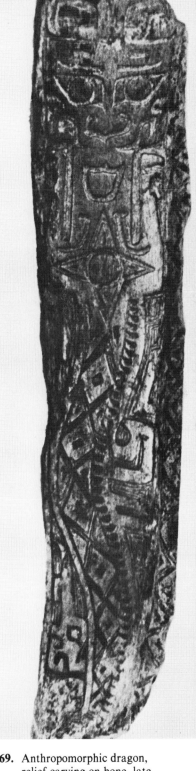

68. Anthropomorphic dragons (Fuxi and Nugua) holding the sun (right) and the moon, Han Dynasty, 206 B.C.–A.D. 220, Sichuan, China.

69. Anthropomorphic dragon, relief carving on bone, late Shang Dynasty, ca. 1400–1100 B.C., Anyang, China.

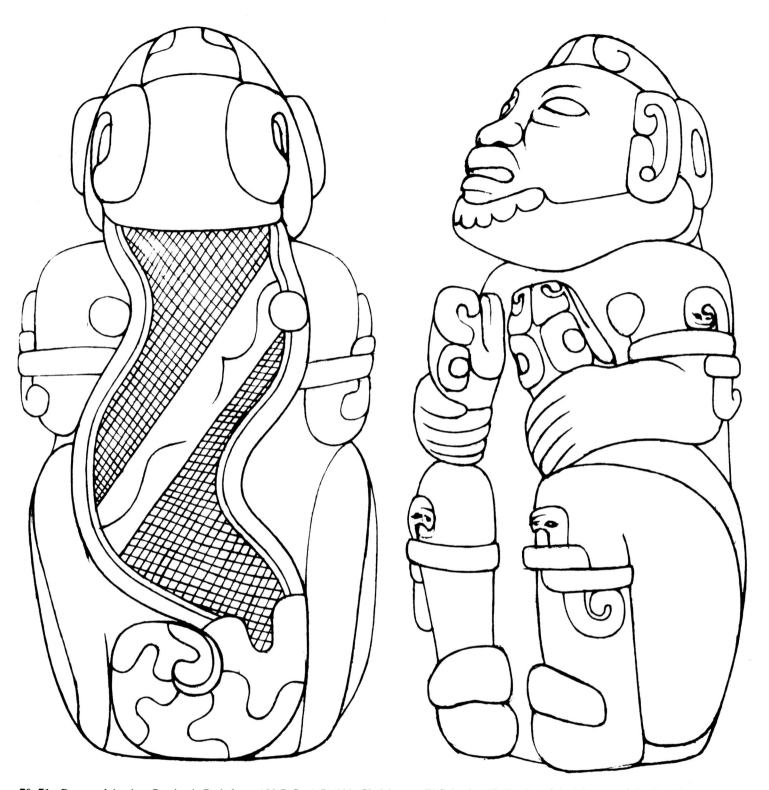

70, 71. Dragon deity, late Preclassic Period, ca. 100 B.C.–A.D. 300, Chalchuapa, El Salvador (Collection of the Museum of the American Indian, New York City); see Figures 57–59, 64, 82–84.

72, 73. Anthropomorphic dragon, Preclassic Period, ca. 1150 B.C.–A.D. 300, Coatepeque, Guatemala (Collection of the National Museum of Anthropology, Guatemala City).

74. Deity emerging from the mouth of a dragon, detail of Lintel 15, Structure 21, late Classic Period, ca. A.D. 725, Yaxchilan, Peten, Guatemala.

75. Deity emerging from the mouth of a dragon, late Zhou Period, ca. 500 B.C., China.

76. Dragon protector, detail of a wall relief, temple of the Jaguars, Postclassic Period, ca. A.D. 1100–1300, Chichen Itza, Yucatan, Mexico.

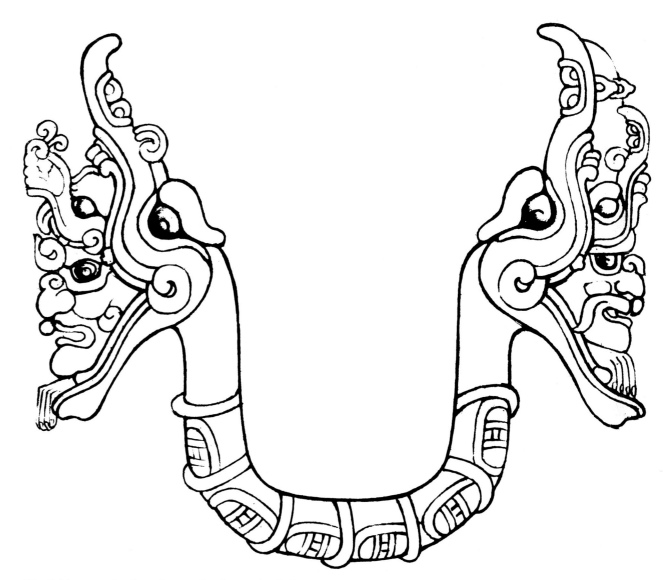

77. Deities emerging from the mouths of a two-headed serpent, detail of Stela P, Classic Period, ca. A.D. 623, Copan, Honduras; see Figures 138–142, 358–361.

PART 3
The Supernatural Power Symbol

The mother of the Huangdi [the legendary Yellow Emperor, ca. 2697–2597 B.C.] was called Fubao. . . . She was pregnant after witnessing a huge lightning which wrapped round the star-Great Bear. . . . After twenty five months she gave birth to the Emperor. . . . When born, he could speak. He possessed the face of a dragon and the virtue of the sage. . . . He could summon a hundred deities to his court and order the feathered dragon to attack Chiyou [rivaling leader of the Miao people, see Figure 225, top] and to fight with the power of tigers, panthers, and bears. . . .

Zhu Shu Ji Nian
(Bamboo Annals)
ca. 300 B.C. with
later annotations.

The Emperor [the legendary Shun, ruled from ca. 2255–2205 B.C.] said: I wish to spread my power in four directions . . . and I wish to see the emblematic images of the ancients on the sacrificial costume—the sun, the moon, the stars, the mountains, the dragons and various creatures.

Shu Jing
(Book of Historical
Documents)
ca. 1122 B.C.–A.D. 320

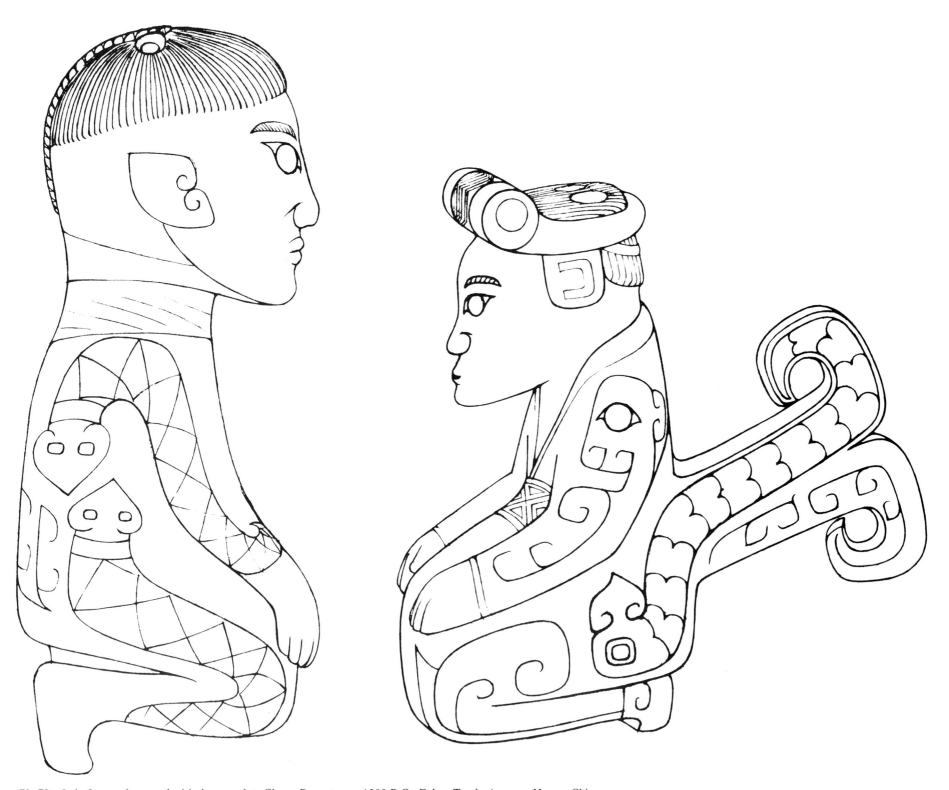

78, 79. Jade figures decorated with dragons, late Shang Dynasty, ca. 1200 B.C., Fuhao Tomb, Anyang, Henan, China.

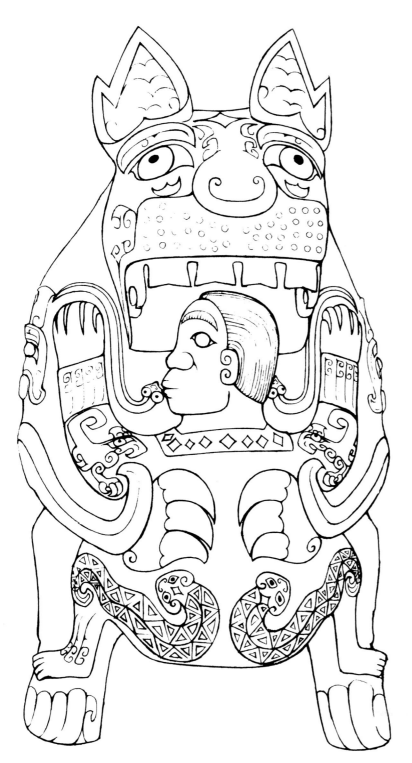

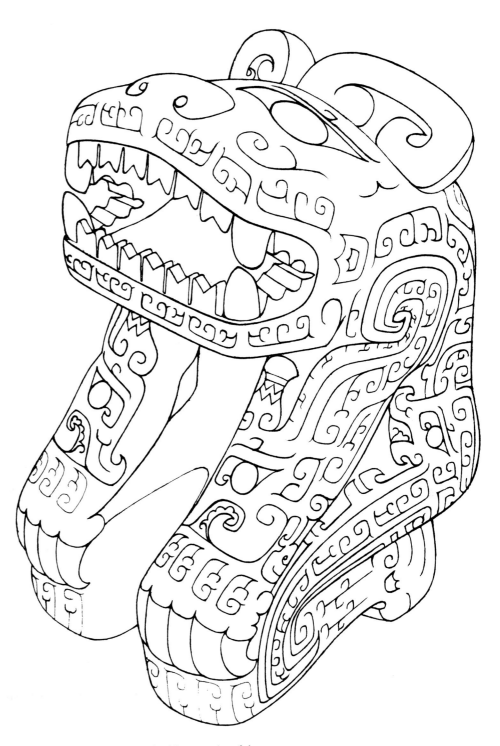

80. Child protected by a feline and flanked by three pairs of dragons, late Shang Dynasty, ca. 1300–1100 B.C., Anhua, Hunan, China (Sumitomo Collection, Kyoto).

81. Seated feline decorated with two pairs of dragons, late Shang Dynasty, ca. 1300–1100 B.C., Tomb 1001, Houjiazhuang, Anyang, Henan, China (Collection of the Academia Sinica, Taipei).

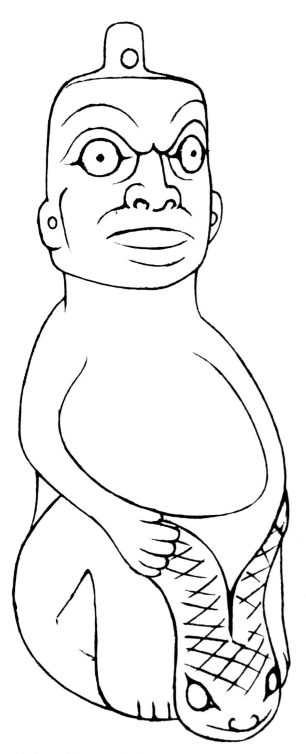

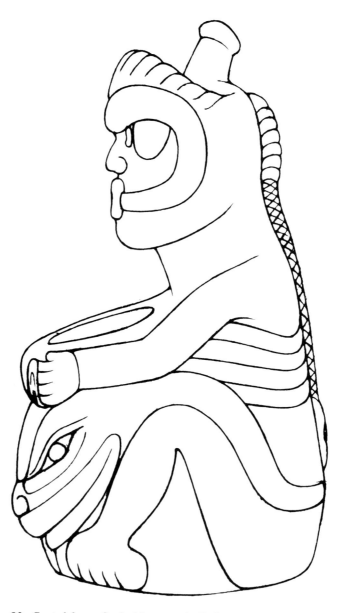

82. Seated figure flanked by a two-bodied reptile, ca. A.D. 500–800, Fraser River near Lillooet, British Columbia (Collection of the Centennial Museum, Vancouver).

83. Seated figure flanked by a two-bodied reptile, ca. A.D. 500–800, Victoria, British Columbia (Collection of R.E.B. Gore-Langton, Victoria).

84. Seated figure flanked by a two-bodied dragon,
Monument 47, Preclassic Period, ca. 1150
B.C.–A.D. 300, San Lorenzo, Veracruz, Mexico.

PART 4

The Transterrestrial Dragon

When the dragon lives in the water he swims with a halo of five colors. Therefore he is divine. If he desires to become small, he changes into a silkworm. If he desires to become big, he dissolves as the universe. If he desires to ascend, he rides on top of the clouds. If he desires to descend, he submerges in an abysmal spring. He whose transformations and movements are not limited by time, is therefore a god.

Guan Zhong
Guan Zi
(Book of Guan)
ca. 300–400 B.C.

A water-snake changes into a fierce four-legged serpent after five hundred years; a fierce jiao serpent changes into a dragon after a thousand years; a dragon changes into a horned dragon after five hundred years; and a horned dragon changes into a feathered dragon after a thousand years.

Ren Fang
Shu Yi Ji
(Record of Strange Things)
ca. A.D. 500–600

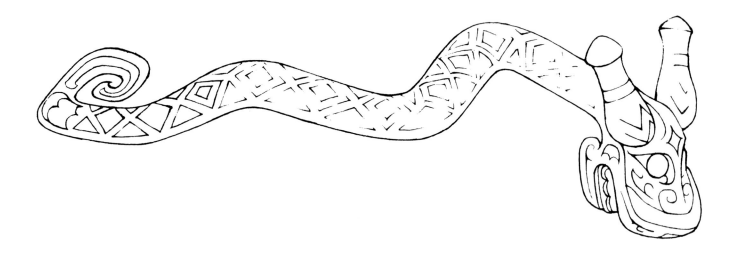

85. Yang (sun, fertility or male) dragons with phallic horns. Top and bottom: bone carving, late Shang Dynasty, ca. 1300–1100 B.C.,
Anyang, Henan; middle: high relief on a zun ceremonial vessel, early Shang Dynasty, ca. 1500 B.C., Funan, Anhui, China.

86. Early American dragons. Top: detail of a relief at the southwest corner of the Castillo, ca. 900–200 B.C., Chavin de Huantar, Peru. Second from top: Monument 19, ca. 1150 B.C.–300 A.D., La Venta, Tabasco, Mexico. Second from bottom: horned dragon design on vessel, Temple Mount II Period, ca. A.D. 1200–1700, lower Mississippi Valley. Bottom: winged sun-dragon design on vessel, ca. A.D. 1500–1700, Arkansas.

87. Bearded dragons, detail of a silk painting, Han Dynasty, ca. 180 B.C., Mawangdui, Changsha, Hunan, China.

88–90. Bearded dragons, Stela D, late Classic Period, ca. A.D. 736, Copan, Honduras.

91. Top: feathered dragon with sun symbols on body, Altar O, late Classic Period, ca. A.D. 700–800, Copan, Honduras. Bottom: feathered or scaled dragon, detail of a fangyi ceremonial vessel, early Zhou Dynasty, ca. 1100 B.C., China (Collection of the Freer Gallery of Art, Smithsonian Institution, Washington, D.C.).

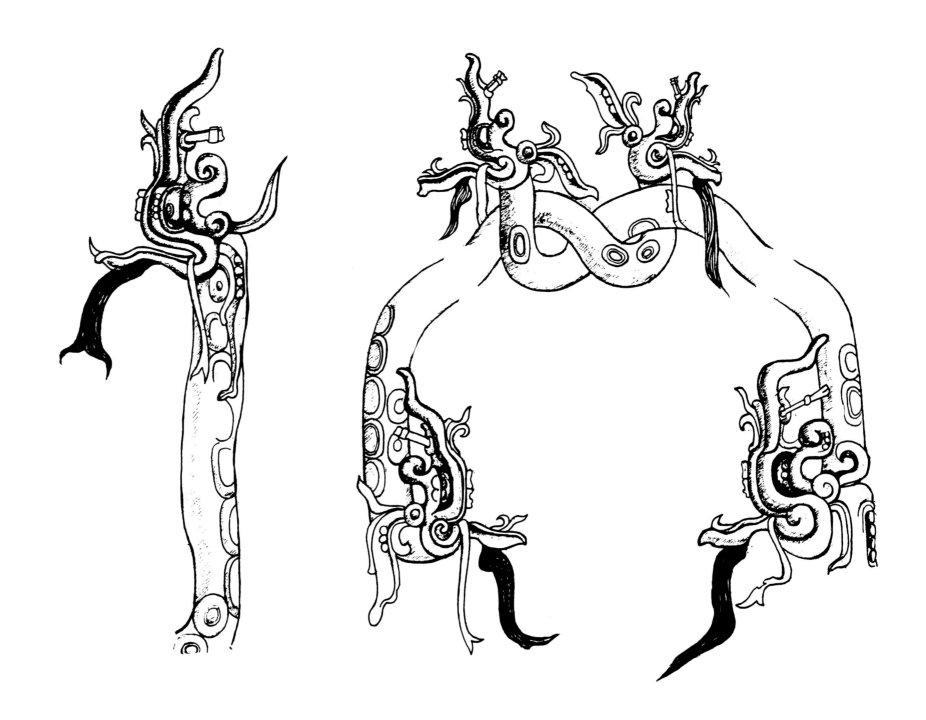

93. Deity of cloud and rain, detail of a lacquered
painting on a se instrument, late Zhou Dynasty, ca.
500–300 B.C., Xinyang, Henan, China.

94. Deity and dragon, drawing of a Stela 3 (restored),
late Preclassic Period, ca. 200 B.C.–A.D. 200,
Izapa, Chiapas, Mexico.

92. Top: dragon with cross in the eye, detail of a fangzun ceremonial vessel, late Shang Dynasty, ca. 1300–1100 B.C., Ningxiang, Hunan (Collection of the National Museum of History, Beijing). Middle: kui dragon with cross on forehead, detail of a gui ceremonial vessel, early Zhou Dynasty, China, ca. 1100–1000 B.C. (Collection of Freer Gallery of Art, Smithsonian Institute, Washington, D.C.). Bottom: dragon with cross inside the phallus-like horn, detail of a fangding, late Shang Dynasty, ca. 1300–1100 B.C., China (Collection of the Indianapolis Museum of Art, Indianapolis).

95. Deities of cloud and rain, detail of a Wuliangzu relief-rubbing, late Han Dynasty, ca. A.D. 150, Jiaxiang, Shandong, China.

96, 97. Deity with dragons, stone relief, ca. 900–200
B.C., Chavin de Huantar, Peru.

98. Fertility deity with dragon, roll-out drawing of Stela 9, late Preclassic Period, ca. 400–200 B.C., Kaminaljuyu, Guatemala (Collection of the National Museum of Anthropology, Guatemala City).

99. Cleft head deity on dragons, detail of a woodblock
print (late edition) from *Shanhai Jing,* ca. 400–100
B.C., ibid.

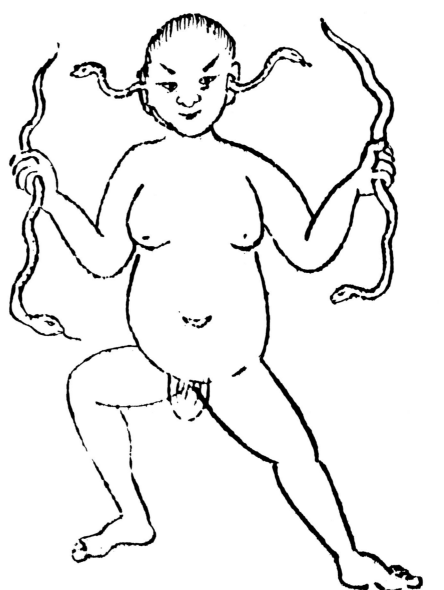

陽谷　之山　圖號　黑茲　兩師　之妾　以蛇

雨師妾

黑身人兩手各操二蛇

左耳有青蛇右耳有赤蛇

100. Goddess of rain holding two snakes, detail of a
woodblock print from *Shanhai Jing,* ibid.

101. Deities with two-headed dragon (symbolizing rainbow), detail of a Wuliangzu relief-rubbing, late Han Dynasty, ca. A.D. 150, Jiaxiang, Shandong, China.

102. Two-headed dragon, detail of a ding ceremonial vessel, late Shang Dynasty, ca. 1300–1100 B.C., China (Collection of the University Museum, Philadelphia).

103. Rain deities, drawing of Stela 1, (restored), late Preclassic Period, ca. 200 B.C.–A.D. 200, Izapa, Chiapas, Mexico.

104. Rain deity and two-headed dragon, drawing of Stela 23, (restored), late Preclassic Period, ca. 200 B.C.–A.D. 200, Chiapas, Mexico.

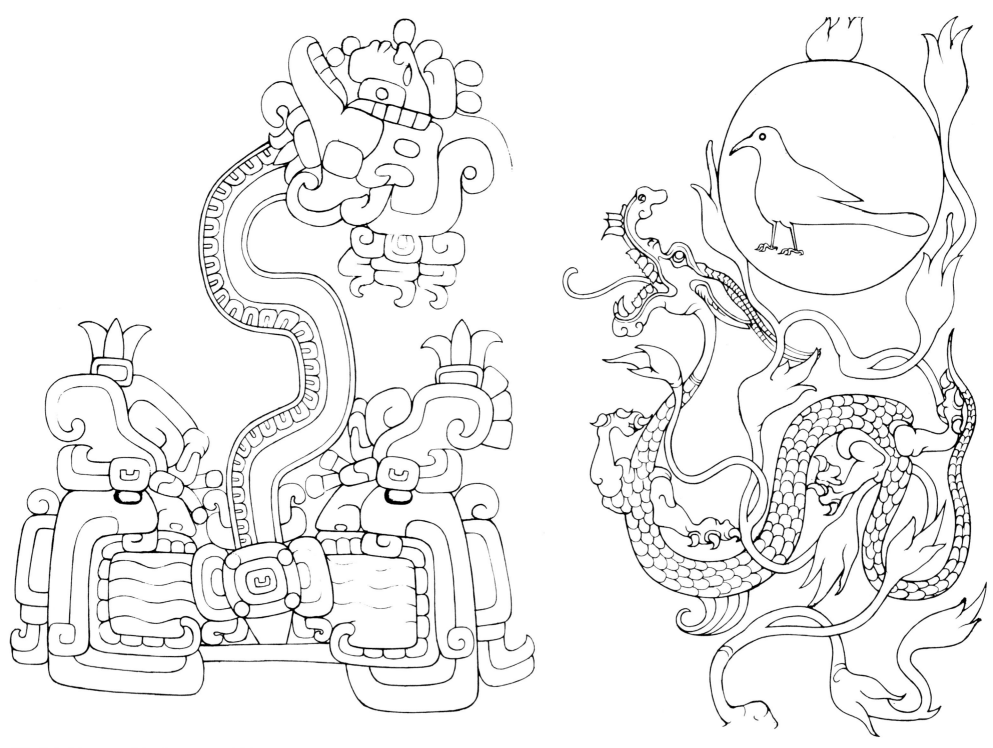

105. Rain deity, terrestrial and transterrestrial dragons, drawing of Stela 4, (restored, other details deleted), late Preclassic Period, ca. 200 B.C.–A.D. 200, Abaj Takalik, Pacific Coast, Guatemala.

106. Sun dragon, detail of a painting on silk, Han Dynasty, ca. 180 B.C., Mawangdui, Changsha, Hunan, China.

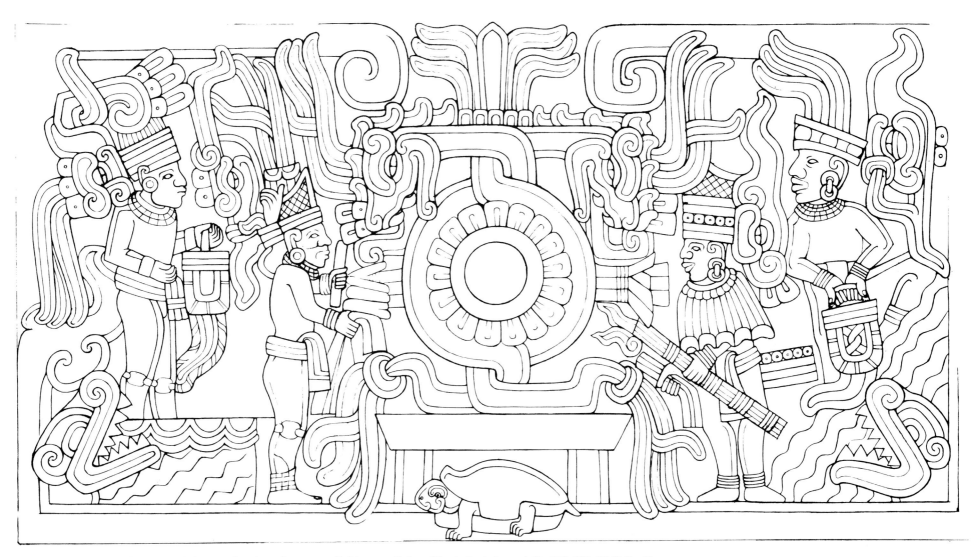

107. Transterrestrial dragons and the sun, drawing of a stone relief (restored), late Classic Period, ca. A.D. 600–900, El Tajin, Veracruz, Mexico (Collection of the Site Museum, El Tajin).

108. Extraterrestrial scene flanked by two dragons, drawing of Stela 5 (restored), late Preclassic Period, ca. 200 B.C.–A.D. 200, Izapa, Chiapas, Mexico.

109. Extraterrestrial scene flanked by two dragons, detail of painting on silk, Han Dynasty, ca. 180 B.C., Mawangdui, Changsha, Hunan, China.

PART 5
The Rain Deity

In time of drought, Tang [the founder of the Shang Dynasty, ruled from ca. 1766–1753 B.C.] made earth-dragon for the "clouds following dragon" ceremony.

Earth-dragon causes rain.

Liu An
Huai Nan Zi
(Book of Prince Huai
Nan)
ca. 120 B.C.

The Mother Goddess of the West traveled on vehicle of purple clouds and drove nine-colored, spotted dragon.

Han Wu Di Nei Zhuan
(The Private Biography
of Emperor Wu of Han Dynasty)
ca. A.D. 250–350

110. Winged deity with snakes emerging from head
and holding two snakes, detail of a rubbing from a
hu ceremonial vessel, late Zhou Dynasty, ca.
600–500 B.C., Hebei, China.

111. Winged deity with snakes emerging from head
and holding composite dragons, roll-out drawing
of the relief on the north portal column, ca.
900–200 B.C., Chavin de Huantar, Peru.

112, 113. Deity holding composite dragons, lower portion of the Raimondi Stone, ca. 900–200 B.C., Chavin de Huantar, Peru (Collection of the National Museum of Anthropology, Lima).

114. Deity with intertwining snakes emerging from head, holding a dragon, drawing of a stone relief in the New Temple, ca. 900–200 B.C., Chavin de Huantar, Peru.

115. Feathered deity holding two composite dragons, detail of a rubbing from the dawu ceremonial dagger-axe, late Zhou Dynasty, ca. 600–300 B.C., Sichuan, China.

116. Deity holding snake and ceremonial object, Preclassic Period, ca. 1150 B.C–A.D. 300, Mexico (Collection of the Metropolitan Museum of Art, New York City).

117. Deity holding similar ceremonial objects, ca. A.D. 300–900, San Agustin, Colombia.

118. Deity holding two composite dragons, restored drawing of a Chavinoid Paracas painting on fabric, ca. 900–200 B.C., Corawa, Peru.

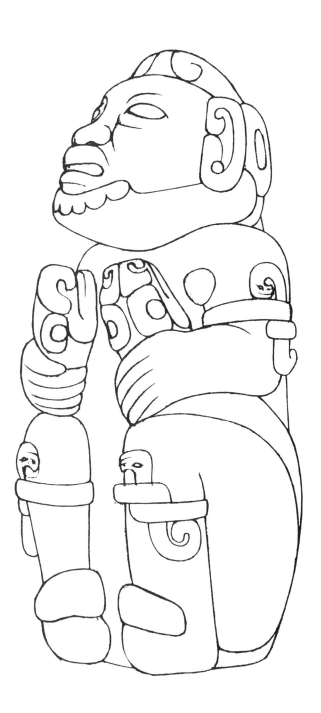

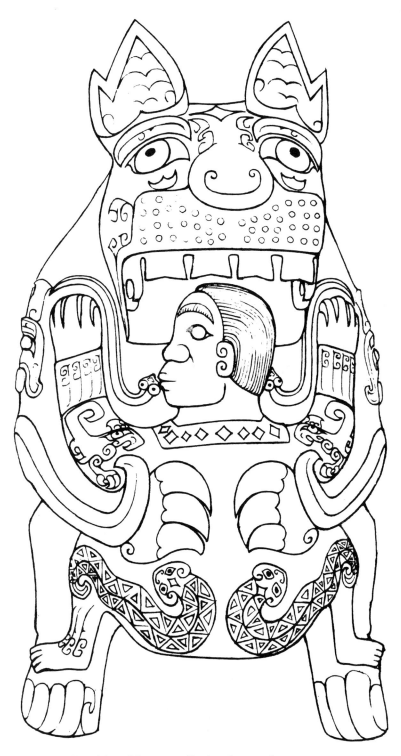

119. Deity holding two dragons, late Preclassic Period, ca. 100 B.C.–A.D. 300, Chalchuapa, El Salvador (Collection of the Museum of the American Indian, Heye Foundation, New York).

120. Guardian deity with arms stylized as dragons (see Figure 179 for another example), late Shang Dynasty, ca., 1300–1100 B.C., Anhua, Hunan, China (Sumitomo Collection, Kyoto).

121. Deity holding two dragons, detail of a lacquered painting on a se instrument, late Zhou Dynasty, ca. 500–300 B.C., Xinyang, Henan, China.

122. Deities holding composite dragons, detail of a Chavinoid painting on fabric, ca. 900–200 B.C. Ica Valley, Peru (Collection of the National Museum of Anthropology, Lima).

123. Left: detail of the Coyotlinahuatl mural, Classic Period, A.D. 300–900, Portico 1, Atetelco, Teotihuacan, Mexico. Right: deity holding two snakes, detail of a Chavinoid painting on fabric, ca. 900–200 B.C., Ica Valley, Peru (Collection of the National Museum of Anthropology, Lima).

124. Deity holding two composite dragons, detail of the Gateway of the Sun, ca. A.D. 600–900, Tiahuanaco, Bolivia.

125. Rain god, Tlaloc, detail of a mural, Classic Period, A.D. 300–900, Tepantitla near Teotihuacan, Mexico.

126. Water goddess, Chalchiutlicue, Classic Period, A.D. 300–900, Teotihuacan, Mexico (Collection of the National Museum of Anthropology, Mexico City).

127. Rain goddess holding two snakes, detail of a woodblock print (late edition) from *Shanhai Jing,* ca. 400–100 B.C., ibid.

PART 6
The Feline-Dragon Alter Ego

The chief of the Taihao Clan [Fuxi, the first
legendary ruler of China, ca. 2852–2737 B.C., see
Figure 68, right], had the dragon as totem,
therefore, was known as the Master of Dragon,
who conferred various dragon titles to his officers.

Zuo Quiming
Zuo Zhuan
(Records of Zuo)
ca. 450–150 B.C.

128. Altar 4, Preclassic Period, ca. 1150 B.C.–A.D. 300, La Venta, Tabasco, Mexico (Collection of the La Venta Museum, Villahermosa).

129. Monument 14, Preclassic Period, ca. 1150 B.C.–A.D. 300, San Lorenzo, Veracruz, Mexico (Collection of the Museum of Anthropology, University of Veracruz, Jalapa).

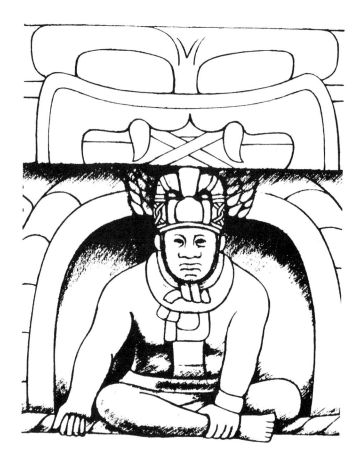

130, 131. Man under the mouth of alter ego, detail of Altar 4, Preclassic Period, ca. 1150 B.C–A.D. 300, La Venta, Tabasco, Mexico (Collection of the La Venta Museum, Villahermosa).

132, 133. Man under the mouth of alter ego, detail of a relief on a ceremonial bronze drum, late Shang Dynasty, ca. 1300–1100 B.C., China (Sumitomo Collection, Kyoto).

134. Child held by alter ego, late Shang Dynasty, ca. 1300–1100 B.C., China (Sumitomo Collection, Kyoto).

135. Child held by alter ego, detail of a Tlingit relief, ca. A.D. 1900, British Columbia (Collection of the University Museum, Philadelphia).

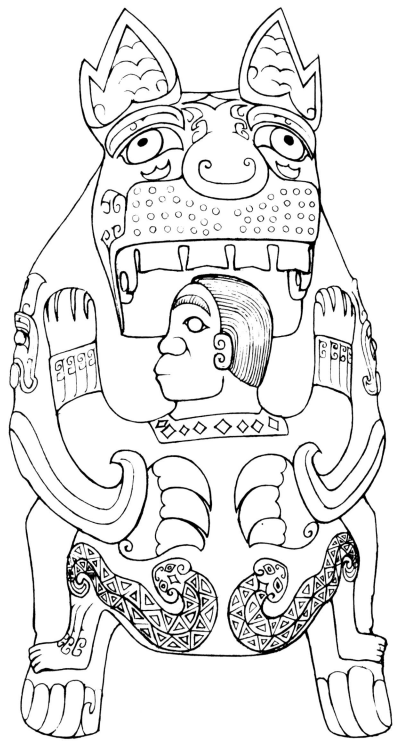

136. Child held by alter ego, drawing of Figure 134.

137. Child held by alter ego, restored drawing of the front panel of a Pacific Coast sculpture, Preclassic Period, ca. 1150 B.C.–A.D. 300, Ojo de Agua, Mazatan, Chiapas, Mexico (Collection of the Regional Museum, Tapachula).

138. Child under the mouth of alter ego, detail of a relief on a zun ceremonial vessel, early Shang Dynasty, ca. 1500 B.C., Funan, Anhui, China (Collection of the National Museum of History, Beijing).

139. Man emerging from the mouth of alter ego, detail of a relief on a fangding ceremonial vessel, late Shang Dynasty, ca. 1300–1100 B.C., Anyang, Henan, China (Collection of the National Museum of History, Beijing).

140. Detail of Figure 138.

141. Man emerging from the mouth of alter ego; see Figure 139.

142. Man emerging from the mouth of alter ego, detail of a ceremonial axe, late Shang Dynasty, ca. 1300–1100 B.C., Anyang, Henan, China (Collection of the National Museum of History, Beijing).

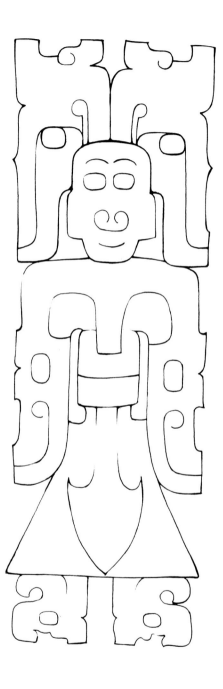

143, 144. Man under the mouth of a stylized alter ego, Stela 1, Preclassic Period, ca. 1150 B.C–A.D. 300, La Venta, Tabasco, Mexico (Collection of the La Venta Museum, Villahermosa).

145. Man under alter ego, drawing of a jade carving, late Zhou Dynasty, ca. 600–300 B.C., China (Collection of the Tianjin Art Museum, Tianjin).

146. Man under the mouth of alter ego, restored drawing of Miscellaneous Monument 2, late Preclassic Period, ca. 200 B.C.–A.D. 300, Izapa, Chiapas, Mexico.

147–149. Men under the mouth of alter ego, Stela D, late Preclassic Period, ca. 300–1 B.C., Tres Zapotes, Veracruz, Mexico (Collection of the Regional Museum of Anthropology, Tres Zapotes).

148.

149.

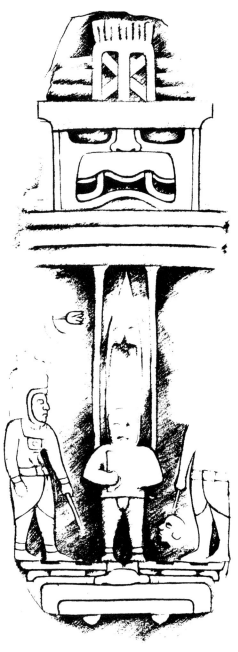

150. Men under the head of alter ego, Stela A, late Preclassic Period, ca. 300–1 B.C., Tres Zapotes, Veracruz, Mexico (Collection of the Regional Museum of Anthropology, Tres Zapotes).

151. Buddha and attendants under the head of feline, detail of a Buddhist stela, Sui Dynasty, ca. A.D. 600, Shanxi, China.

PART 7
The Iconographic Costume

In the last month of the summer, at the sacrificial ceremony for Zhao Kong, the king standing at the eastern steps, was adorned with a dragon-figured costume. . . .

Li Ji
(Record of Rites)
ca. 70 B.C.–A.D. 100

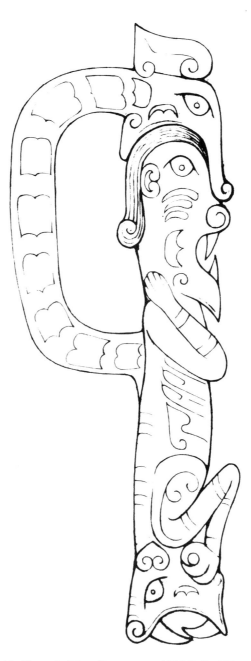

152, 153. Dragon, man and feline, detail of a relief on a ceremonial knife, early Zhou Dynasty, ca. 1000 B.C., China (Collection of the Freer Gallery of Art, Smithsonian Institution, Washington, D.C.).

154, 155. Feline, man and bird, detail of a pole-finale, late Shang-early Zhou Dynasty, ca. 1300–1000 B.C., China (Collection of the British Museum, London).

156–158. Man in iconographic costume, Preclassic
Period, ca. 1150 B.C–A.D. 300, Atlihuayan,
Morelos, Mexico (Collection of the National
Museum of Anthropology, Mexico City).

159. Drawing of Figure 154.

160, 161. Drawings of Figures 156 and 157.

162. Drawing of Figure 155.

163. Detail of Monument 19, Preclassic Period, ca.
1150 B.C–A.D. 300, La Venta; see Figure 36.

164. Detail of a pottery urn, late Preclassic Period, ca.
200 B.C.–A.D. 200, Oaxaca, Mexico (Collection
of the American Museum of Natural History,
New York City).

165. Detail of a stone relief, late Classic Period, ca. A.D. 600–900, Veracruz, Mexico (Collection of the National Museum of Anthropology, Mexico City).

166. Detail of a guang ceremonial vessel, early Zhou Dynasty, ca. 1000 B.C., China (Collection of the Freer Gallery of Art, Smithsonian Institution, Washington, D.C.).

167, 168. Jade relief, Zhou Dynasty, 1122–256 B.C., China (Collection of the Freer Gallery of Art, Smithsonian Institution, Washington, D.C.).

169. Pottery figurine, Preclassic Period, ca. 1000–300 B.C. Uaxactun, Peten Guatemala (Collection of the Peabody Museum, Cambridge).

170. Bronze pole-finale, late Shang Dynasty, ca. 1400–1100 B.C., China (Collection of the Minneapolis Institute of Art, Minneapolis).

171. Bronze pole-finale, late Shang Dynasty, ca. 1400–1100 B.C., China (Collection of the British Museum, London).

172. Lower portion of a stone stela, Nanbei Dynasty, ca. A.D. 500–600, China (Collection of the Metropolitan Museum of Art, New York City).

173. Detail of Altar 4, La Venta; see Figure 128.

175. Detail of a painting on silk, Tang Dynasty, ca.
A.D. 730, China (Collection of the Nelson Gallery
and Atkins Museum, Kansas City).

174. Detail of Stela 1, late Classic Period, ca. A.D. 800, Quirigua, Guatemala.

176. Detail of Stela 6, late Classic Period, ca. A.D. 687, Piedras Negras, Peten, Guatemala.

177. Detail of Stela P, late Classic Period, ca. A.D. 623, Copan, Honduras.

178. Stela H, late Classic Period, ca. A.D. 782, Copan, Honduras.

179. Rubbing of a jade carving, late Zhou Dynasty, ca. 600–300 B.C., China (Collection of the Tianjin Art Museum).

180. Drawing of a jade carving, middle Zhou Dynasty, ca. 800–500 B.C., China (Collection of the Field Museum of Natural History, Chicago).

181. Figure painted on the coffin of Marquis Yi of Zeng State, late Zhou Period, ca. 433 B.C., Suixian, Hubei, China.

All creatures: feathered, scaly, or hairy, owe their origins to the dragon.

Liu An
Huai Nan Zi
(Book of Prince Huai Nan)
ca. 120 B.C.

When Huangdi [the Yellow Emperor] became the emperor, Zhiyu [rivaling tribal leader] had eighty one brothers [allied tribal leaders] who had bodies of animals. . . .

Zhang Shou Jie
Zheng Yi
ca. A.D. 618–906

The Daodi images on the ceremonial vessels of the Zhou people [1122–256 B.C.] were portrayed with heads but without bodies.

Lu Bu Wei
Lu Shi Chun Qiu
(Master Lu's Spring
and Autumn Annals)
ca. 239 B.C.

182, 183. Bronze relief, late Shang Dynasty, ca. 1400–1100 B.C., China (Collection of the Metropolitan Museum, New York City).

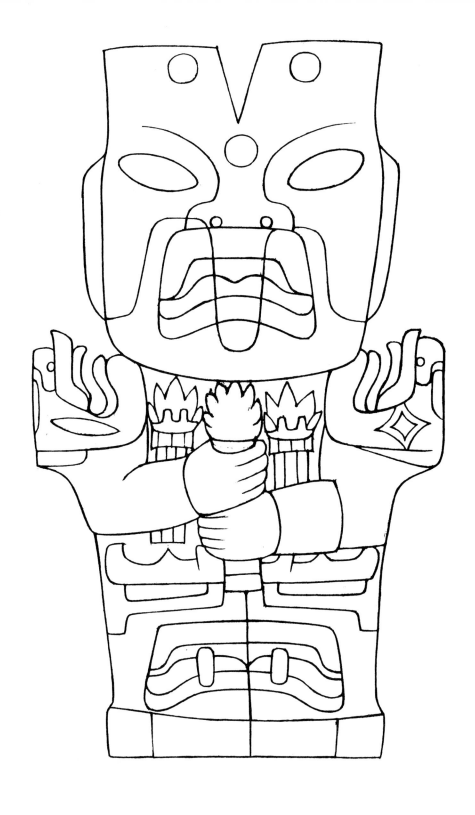 

184, 185. Serpentine celt, Preclassic Period, ca. 1150 B.C.–A.D. 300, Guerrero, Mexico (Collection of the Dallas Museum of Fine Arts).

186, 187. Man on top of an animal head, late Shang Dynasty, ca. 1300–1100 B.C., China (private collection).

188, 189. Man's lower body modeled as an animal head, early Zhou Dynasty, ca. 1100–900 B.C., China (Collection of the Freer Gallery of Art, Smithsonian Institution, Washington, D.C.).

190. Stone celt, Preclassic Period, ca. 1150 B.C.–A.D. 300, Mexico (Collection of the Cleveland Museum of Art).

191, 192. Monument 12, Preclassic Period, ca. 1150 B.C.–A.D. 300, La Venta, Tabasco, Mexico (National Museum of Anthropology, Mexico City).

193. Mural 1, Preclassic Period, ca. 1150 B.C.–A.D. 300, Oxtutitlan, Guerrero, Mexico.

194, 195. Upper and lower portion of Stela C, late Preclassic Period, ca. 31 B.C., Tres Zapotes, Veracruz, Mexico (Collection of the Regional Museum, Tres Zapotes and the National Museum of Anthropology, Mexico City).

195.

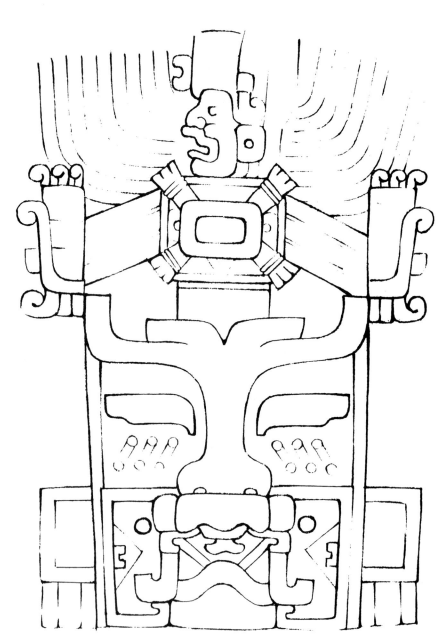

196. Drawing of Stela C (reconstructed), see Figures
194 and 195.

197. Relief on lower portion of Stela F (south side),
late Classic Period, ca. A.D. 761, Quirigua,
Guatemala.

198. Relief-figure on a ceremonial drum with arms and legs deployed forming a frontal animal mask, late Shang Dynasty, ca. 1300–1100 B.C., see Figure 133.

199. Top: bronze relief, early Han Dynasty, ca. 200–100 B.C., Mancheng, Hebei, China (Collection of the National Museum of History, Beijing).
Bottom: relief on a he ceremonial vessel, late Shang-early Zhou Dynasty, ca. 1300–1100 B.C., China (Collection of the Fogg Museum, Cambridge).

200. Dragon, man and feline, early Zhou Dynasty, ca. 1000 B.C., see Figure 42.

201. Stela 11, late Preclassic Period, ca. 200 B.C.–A.D. 200, Izapa, Chiapas, Mexico.

202. Jade carving, late Shang-early Zhou Dynasty, ca.
1300–1000 B.C., China (Collection of the Fogg
Art Museum, Cambridge).

203, 204. El Meson Stela, late Preclassic Period, ca. 200 B.C.–A.D. 300, Veracruz, Mexico (Collection of the Museum of Anthropology, University of Veracruz, Jalapa).

205, 206. Stela 8, late Preclassic Period, ca. 200 B.C.–A.D. 300, Cerro de las Mesas, Veracruz, Mexico (Collection of the Museum of Anthropology, University of Veracruz, Jalapa).

PART 9
The Man-Animal-Plant Interface

. . . dragon is seen in the grain-fields, beneficial omen. . . .

. . . dragon is seen in the sky, beneficial omen. . . .

I Jing
(Book of Changes)
ca. 1120–221 B.C.

. . . His [the dragon's] horns resemble those of a stag, his head that of a camel, his eyes those of a spirit, his neck that of a snake, his belly that of a worm, his scales those of a carp, his claws those of an eagle, his paws those of a tiger, his ears those of a bull. On top of his head he has a triangular protrusion which is called chemu. A dragon without the chemu cannot ascend to the heaven.

Wang Fu
of Han Dynasty
(206 B.C.–A.D. 220)
Quoted in
Er Ya Yi
ca. A.D. 1175

207. Top row: Olmec cleft-head motives, Preclassic Period, ca. 1150 B.C.–A.D. 300, Mexico. Bottom row: Chinese cleft-head motives, Yangshao Period, ca. 4000 B.C., (left three) and late Shang-early Zhou Dynasty, ca. 1300–1000 B.C. (far right).

208. Jade cleft-head, late Shang-early Zhou Dynasty, ca. 1300–1000 B.C., China (Collection of the Fogg Art Museum, Cambridge).

209. Painted cleft-head motives on pottery basins, Yangshao Period, ca. 4000 B.C., Banpo, Shaanxi, China (Collection of the Banpo Museum, Banpo).

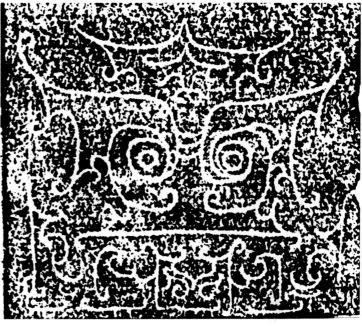

210. Rubbing and drawing of animal masks on a stone adz, late Longshan Period, ca. 2000 B.C., Rizhao, Shandong, China (Collection of the Shandong Museum, Jinan); see Figures 167 and 168.

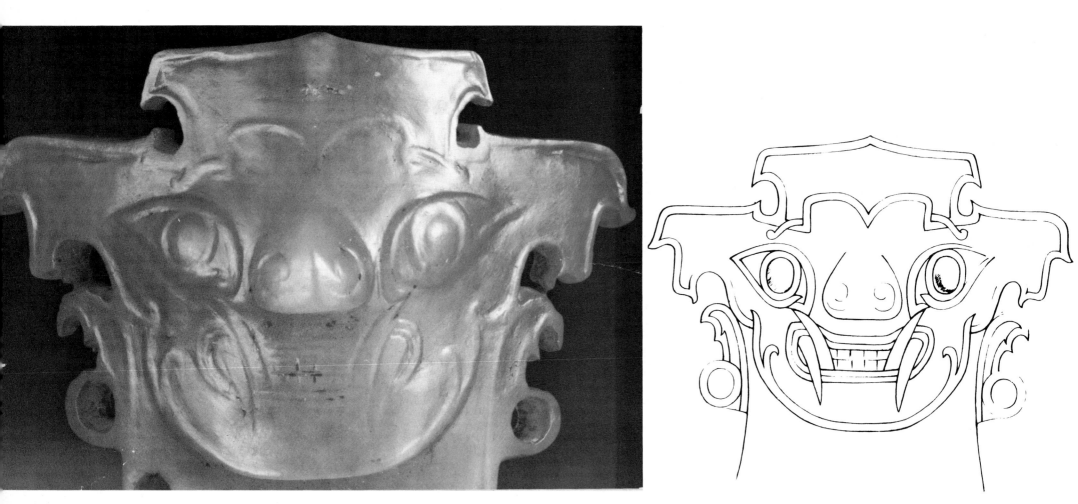

211, 212. Jade cleft-head with protrusion on top, early Zhou Dynasty, ca. 1000–7000 B.C., China (Collection of the Asian Art Museum, San Francisco); see Figures 110, 112, 118, 121, 122.

215. Top: plant-like element on top of animal mask, detail on a ding ceremonial vessel, late Shang Dynasty, ca. 1300–1100 B.C., China (Collection of the Asian Art Museum, San Francisco). Bottom: plant-like element on top of human head, detail of a ceremonial drum, late Shang Dynasty, ca. 1300–1100 B.C.; see Figure 133.

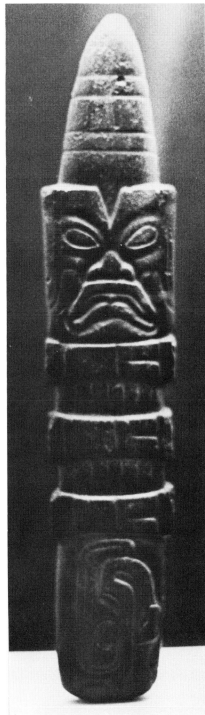

213. Stone cleft-head with protrusion on top, Preclassic Period, ca. 1150 B.C.–A.D. 300, Ejido Ojoshal, Cardenas, Tabasco (Collection of the Tabasco Museum, Villahermosa).

214. Jade ceremonial object, front and back views, early Zhou Style, ca. 1000–700 B.C., China (National Collection of Fine Arts, Smithsonian Institution, Washington, D.C.).

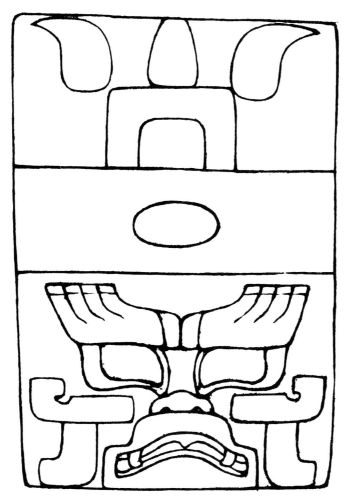

216. Drawing of Monument 15 (restored), Preclassic Period, ca. 1150 B.C.–A.D. 300, La Venta, Tabasco, Mexico.

217. Trifoliate element on top of figure, Preclassic Period, ca. 1150 B.C.–A.D. 300, Arroyo Pesquero, Veracruz, Mexico (Dumbarton Oaks Collections, Washington, D.C.).

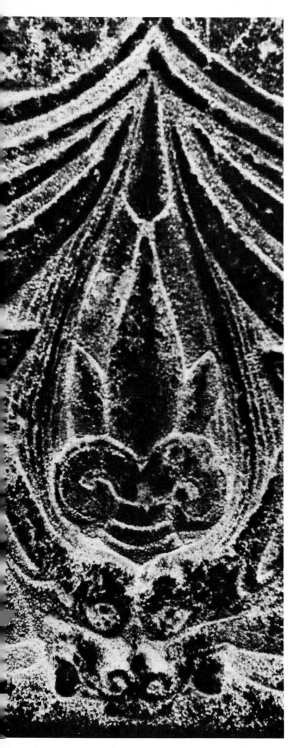

218. Trifoliate element on top of animal mask, detail of a Buddhist stela, Nanbei Dynasty, A.D. 554, China (Collection of the Boston Museum of Fine Arts, Boston).

219. Foliate animal mask, late Zhou Dynasty, ca. 400–200 B.C., China (Collection of the Fogg Art Museum, Cambridge).

220. Cleft animal mask with middle protrusion. Top left: late Zhou Dynasty, ca. 400–200 B.C., China (Collection of the Freer Gallery of Art, Smithsonian Institution, Washington, D.C.). Top right: late Zhou Dynasty, ca. 400–200 B.C., China. Bottom left: Tang Dynasty, ca. A.D. 618–700, China (Collection of the Field Museum of Natural History, Chicago). Bottom right: Han Dynasty, 206 B.C.–A.D. 220, China.

221. Left row: foliate design, ca. 5000–4500 B.C., Hemudu, Zhejiang, China. Middle row: top, foliate design on a celt, ca. 1150 B.C.–A.D. 300, La Venta; bottom, foliate mask, Tang dynasty, ca. A.D. 618–700 China. Right row: top and middle, Han Dynasty, 206 B.C.–A.D. 220; bottom, Nanbei Dynasty, A.D. 554.

222. Left row: top, cleft-head with foliate element, ca. 900–200 B.C., Pachacamac, Peru; bottom, cleft-head with foliate element, ca. 1150 B.C.–A.D. 300, Mexico. Middle row: top, detail of an incense burner, ca. A.D. 800, Tikal Guatemala; bottom, detail of Stela 11, ca. A.D. 100–300, Kaminaljuyu, Guatemala. Right row: all three, ca. 400–200 B.C., China.

Yan Di [legendary emperor, ca. 2737–2697 B.C.], the God of Agriculture, had the clan-name of Qiang. His mother's name was Nudeng. . . . Contacted by a divine dragon, she gave birth to Emperor Yan. . . . He governed by the virtue of fire. Therefore he was called Emperor of Flaming Fire.

Sima Zhen
San Huang Ben Ji
(History of the Three Emperors)
ca. A.D. 618–906

223. Flame-eyebrow mask, Preclassic Period, ca. 1150
B.C.–A.D. 300, Mexico (Collection of the
American Museum of Natural History, New York
City).

224. Stone celt rubbed with red pigment, Preclassic
Period, ca. 1150 B.C.–A.D. 300, La Venta,
Tabasco, Mexico (National Museum of
Anthropology, Mexico City).

225. Top: mask of Chiyou (legendary tribal chief), Shang Dynasty, ca. 1400–1200 B.C., China (Collection of the Dahlem-Berlin Museum, West Berlin). Bottom: flame-eyebrow mask, late Zhou Dynasty, ca. 800–300 B.C., China (Collection of the Rijksmuseum, Amsterdam); see Figures 136, 137, 275–280.

226. Flame-eyebrow "Atlantean Figure", late Zhou Dynasty, ca. 400–300 B.C., Luoyang, Henan, China (Collection of the Museum Guimet, Paris).

227. Flame eyebrow Yamantaka with Sakti, late Ming Dynasty, ca. A.D. 1600, Tibet (Collection of the Museum of Fine Arts, Boston).

228. Flame-eyebrow dragon, late Zhou Dynasty, ca. 600–400 B.C., China (private collection).

229. Left: flame-eyebrow bird-man, Tang Dynasty, A.D. 618–906, China. Right: flame-eyebrow mask, late Zhou Dynasty, ca. 500 B.C., Hebei, China (Collection of the National Museum of History, Beijing).

To the people of Shang, heaven ordered the black
bird to descend, and to give birth.

Shi Jing
(Book of Odes)
ca. 900–500 B.C.

Jiandi, the mother of Qi [ca. 2300–2200 B.C.,
progenitor of the Shang clan] . . . saw a black bird
drop an egg. She swallowed it. As a result she
became pregnant and gave birth to Qi.

Sima Qian
Shi Ji
(Historical Record)
ca. 90 B.C.

Jumang of the East has a bird's body and a human
face. He rides on two dragons.

Shanhai Jing
(Classics of Mountain
and Sea)
ca. 400–100 B.C.
Han Shu
(History of the Han)
ca. A.D. 25–200

230. Jade bird-man, Shang Dynasty, ca. 1400–1200 B.C., China (Collection of the British Museum, London).

231. Jade bird-man, Preclassic Period, ca. 1150 B.C.–A.D. 300, Cerro de las Mesas, Veracruz, Mexico (National Museum of Anthropology, Mexico City).

232. Jade bird-men, Postclassic Period, ca. A.D. 900–1500, Costa Rica (Collection of the American Museum of Natural History, New York City).

233, 234. Jade bird-men, Han Dynasty, 206 B.C.–A.D. 220, China (Collection of the Field Museum of Natural History, Chicago).

235. Jade bird-man, late Shang Dynasty, ca. 1400–1100 B.C., China (Collection of the Freer Gallery of Art, Smithsonian Institution, Washington, D.C.).

236. Stone bird-man, Preclassic Period, ca. 1150 B.C.–A.D. 300, Mexico (Collection of the Peabody Museum, Cambridge).

237, 238. Jade bird-man, two views, middle Zhou Dynasty, ca. 800–500 B.C., China (Collection of the Field Museum of Natural History, Chicago).

239. Jade bird-man, late Preclassic Period, ca. A.D. 162, San Andres Tuxtla, Veracruz, Mexico (National Museum of Anthropology, Mexico City).

240. Bird-man, late Han Dynasty, ca. A.D. 100–200, China (Collection of the Fogg Art Museum, Cambridge).

241. Jade bird-man, Preclassic Period, ca. 1150
B.C.–A.D. 300, Guanacaste, Costa Rica
(Collection of the Brooklyn Museum, Brooklyn).
See Figures 110, 111.

242. Jade bird with round-off square eye-plates, late
Shang Dynasty, ca. 1400–1100 B.C., China
(Collection of the Asian Art Museum, San
Francisco).

With jade and gold in the nine orifices, even a dead body will be everlasting.

Go Hong
Bao Bu Zi
(Book of Master
Bao Bu)
ca. A.D. 320

A dragon has whiskers at the sides of his mouth and a bright pearl under his chin. . . . His breath turns into clouds, then can change into water or fire . . .

Li Shizhen
Ben Cao Gang Mu
(Pharmacopoeia)
ca. A.D. 1596

243. Tenoned stone head with nose plugs, ca. 900–200
B.C., Chavin de Huantar, Peru (Collection of the
National Museum of Anthropology, Lima).

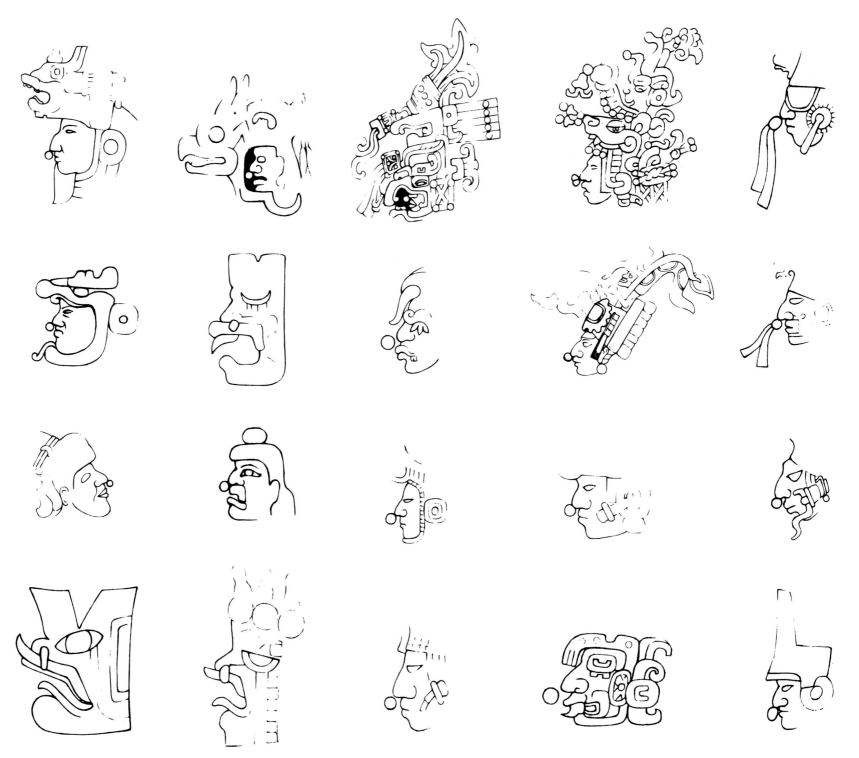

244. Mesoamerican nose beads and plugs: left to right, vertical Row 1 and 2, Preclassic Period, ca. 1150 B.C.–A.D. 300. Row 3: upper two profiles, late Preclassic Period, ca. A.D. 100–300. All others: Classic and Postclassic Period, from ca. A.D. 328 (Row 4, upper most profile) to early Postclassic, ca. A.D. 1100 (Row 5, lower most profile).

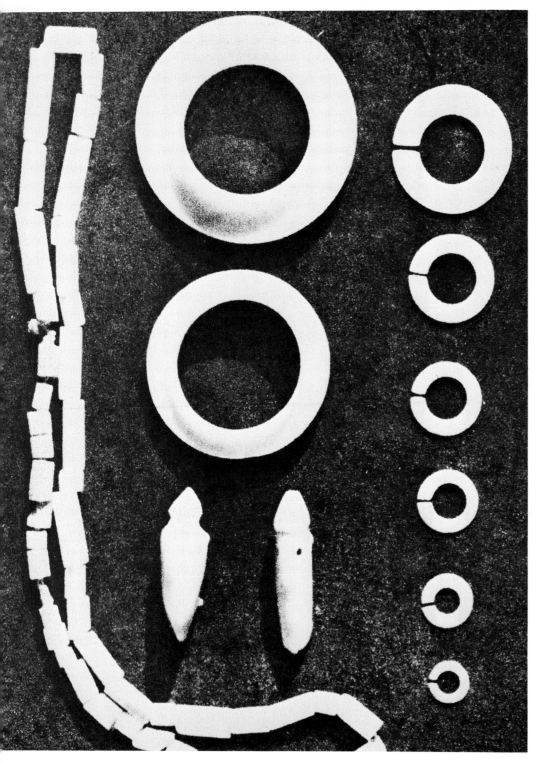

245. Jade nose plugs, earrings, plugs, tubes, flares and assorted ornaments, part of a cache of 329 similar jade pieces unearthed in 1970, late Shang Dynasty, ca. 1400–1100 B.C., Huangcai, Ningxiang, Hunan, China (Collection of the Hunan Museum, Changsha).

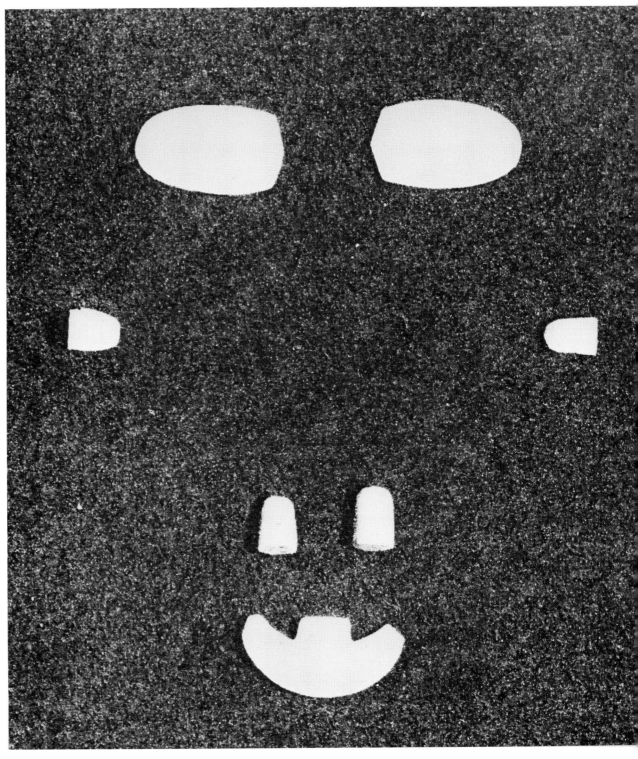

246. Jade nose and ear plugs, eye and mouth covers, early Han Dynasty, ca. 200–100 B.C., Mancheng, Hebei, China (Collection of the National Museum of History, Beijing).

247–248. Monument 52, Preclassic Period, ca. 1150 B.C.–A.D. 300, San Lorenzo, Veracruz, Mexico; see Figures 229, 241, 242, 323.

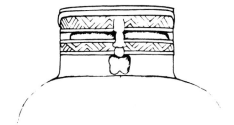

249. Fragment of an effigy vessel, ca. 900 B.C.–A.D. 300, San Lorenzo, Veracruz, Mexico (redrawn after M. Coe and R. Diehl, 1980, p. 185.)

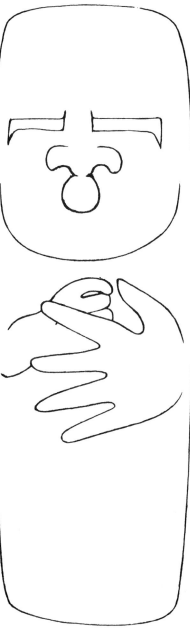

250. Monument 41, Preclassic Period, ca. 1150 B.C.–A.D. 300, San Lorenzo, Veracruz, Mexico.

251. Jade celt, Preclassic Period, ca. 1150 B.C.–A.D. 300, Arroyo Pesquero, Veracruz, Mexico (Collection of the Museum of Anthropology, University of Veracruz, Jalapa)

253. Detail of Monument 19, Preclassic Period, ca. 1150 B.C.–A.D. 300, La Venta, Tabasco, Mexico.

252. Detail of Stela 3, Preclassic Period, ca. 1150 B.C.–A.D. 300, La Venta, Tabasco, Mexico.

254. Detail of Stela 8, late Classic Period, ca. A.D. 850, Seibal, Guatemala.

255. Detail of a stucco mask, late Classic Period, ca. A.D. 600–800, Kohunlich, Rio Bec, Yucatan, Mexico.

256. Chimu gold mask, ca. A.D. 900–1400, Lambayeque, Peru (Collection of the Metropolitan Museum of Art, New York City).

257. Tenoned stone head, ca. 900–200 B.C., Chavin de Huantar, Peru (Collection of the National Museum of Anthropology, Lima); see Figure 243.

258. Monument 13, Preclassic Period, ca. 1150 B.C.–A.D. 300, La Venta, Tabasco, Mexico (Collection of the La Venta Museum, Villahermosa).

259. Chinkultic disc, late Classic Period, ca. A.D. 600–800, Chinkultic, Chiapas, Mexico (Collection of the National Museum of Anthropology, Mexico City)

260. Detail of Stela 1 (rotated 90 degrees), late Preclassic Period, ca. A.D. 36, El Baul, Guatemala

261. Detail of Lintel 48, Classic Period, ca. A.D. 550–650, Yaxchilan, Chiapas, Mexico.

262. Pottery vessel, Preclassic Period, ca. 1150–550 B.C. Puebla, Mexico (Collection of the National Museum of Anthropology, Mexico City)

263. Incised image on a slate celt, Preclassic Period, ca. 1150 B.C.–A.D. 300, Simojovel, Chiapas, Mexico (Collection of the National Museum of Anthropology, Mexico City.

264. Incised image on a jade celt, Preclassic Period, ca. 1150 B.C.–A.D. 300, Arroyo Pesquero, Veracruz, Mexico (Collection of the Museum of Anthropology, University of Veracruz, Jalapa) see Figure 251.

265. Stela 11, late Preclassic Period, ca. A.D. 100–300, Kaminaljuyu, Guatemala (Collection of the Museum of Anthropology and Ethnology, Guatemala City).

PART 13

The Eye-Paw-Wing Complex

From dawn to dusk, the bird carries the sun on its daily flight across the sky.

Shanhai Jing
(Classics of Mountain
and Sea)
ca. 400–100 B.C.

266. Eye-paw-wing motives of China and America. a,b: late Shang Dynasty, ca. 1300–1100 B.C., China; c: ca. A.D. 1200–1700, Mississippi Valley, America; d: ca. A.D. 400–100, British Columbia; e–h: ca. A.D. 1200–1700, Mississippi Valley, America; i: 200 B.C.–A.D. 200; Izapa, Mexico; j–l: ca. A.D. 1200–1700, North America; m–o: ca. 1150–550 B.C., Mexico; p: ca. A.D. 1900, British Columbia; q: ca. 1150 B.C.–A.D. 300, Mexico.

267. a: ca. A.D. 900–1200, El Baul, Guatemala; b: ca. 1300–1100 B.C., China; c: ca. 1100–1000 B.C., China; d: ca. 900–200 B.C., Peru.

268. Eye-paw-wing motives on vessel, Chavin style, ca. 900–200 B.C., Peru (Collection of Dahlem-Berlin Museum, West Berlin)

269. Eye-paw-wing motive on vessel, Preclassic Period, ca. 1150–550 B.C., Tlatilco, Mexico (Collection of National Museum of Anthropology, Mexico City).

270. Eye-paw-wing motive, early Zhou Dynasty, ca. 1100–1000 B.C., China (Collection of the British Museum, London).

271, 272. Eye-paw-wing motives on vessels, Preclassic Period, ca. 1150–550 B.C., Tlatilco, Mexico (Collection of the National Museum of Anthropology, Mexico City).

273. Eye-paw-wing motive on a guang ceremonial vessel, late Shang Dynasty, ca. 1300–1100 B.C. (Collection of the Metropolitan Museum of Art, New York City).

274. Eye-paw-wing motive incised on bone, late Shang Dynasty, ca. 1300–1100 B.C., Anyang, China (Collection of the Academia Sinica, Taipei).

275. Eye-paw-wing motives on a lei ceremonial vessel, early Zhou Dynasty, ca. 1100–1000 B.C., China (Collection of the British Museum, London).

276, 277. Altar I (front and side views), Preclassic Period, ca. 1150 B.C.–A.D. 300, La Venta, Tabasco, Mexico (Collection of the La Venta Museum, Villahermosa).

277.

278–280. Eye-paw-wing motives, details of a *you* ceremonial vessel, late Shang Dynasty, ca. 1300–1100 B.C., China (Collection of the Freer Gallery of Art, Smithsonian Institution, Washington, D.C.).

After the sacrificial ceremony, the Emperor, in a kneeling-sitting position, spoke to his ministers and answered their questions concerning the Classics.

Fan Ye
Hou Han Shu
(History of the Later
Han Dynasty)
ca. A.D. 450

281. Guizuo (kneeling-sitting) anthropomorphic feline, Preclassic Period, ca. 1150 B.C.–A.D. 300, Puebla, Mexico (Collection of Dumbarton Oaks, Washington, D.C.).

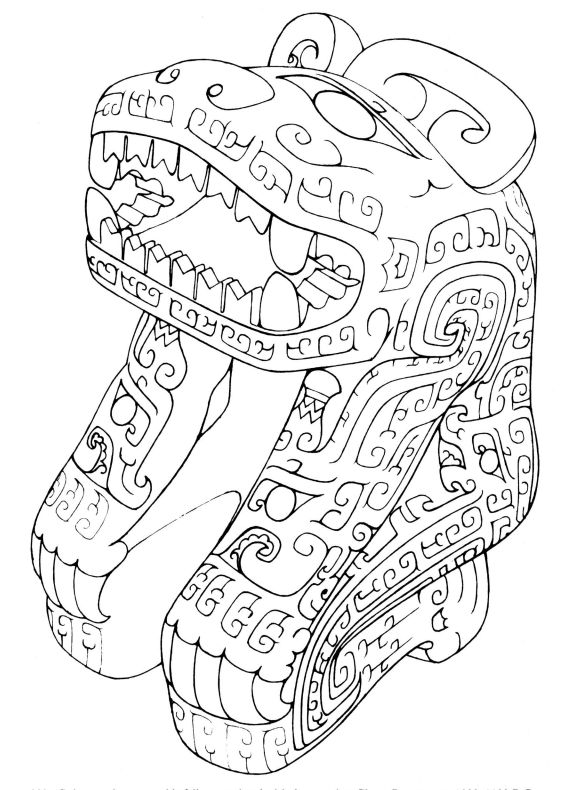

282. Guizuo anthropomorphic feline associated with dragons, late Shang Dynasty, ca. 1300–1100 B.C., Houjiazhuang, Anyang, Henan, China (Collection of the Academia Sinica, Taipei).

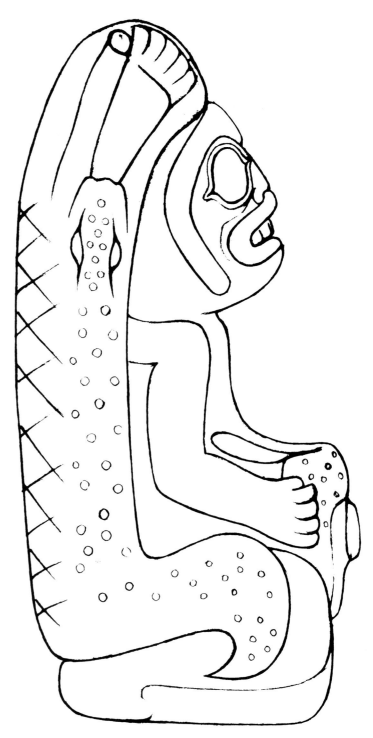

283. Guizuo figure associated with snake, ca. A.D. 100–400, Webster's Corners, Fraser River Valley, British Columbia (Collection of the Centennial Museum, Vancouver).

284. Guizuo figure associated with snakes, ca. A.D. 400–1000, North Saanich, Vancouver Island, British Columbia (Collection of John Hauberg, Seattle).

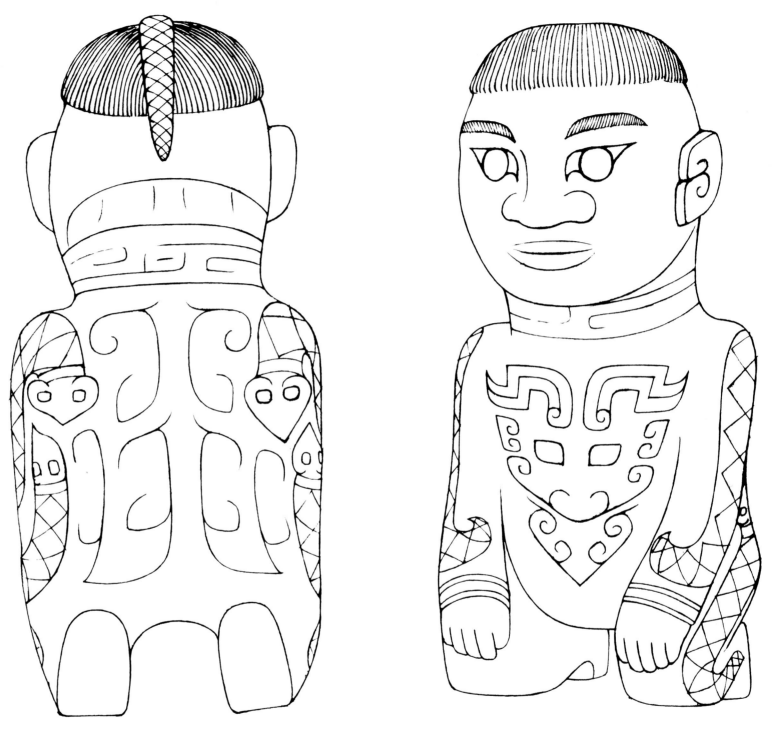

285. Jade guizuo figure associated with snakes (two views), late Shang Dynasty, ca. 1300–1100 B.C., Fuhao Tomb (No. 5), Anyang, Henan, China (Collection of the National Museum of History, Beijing).

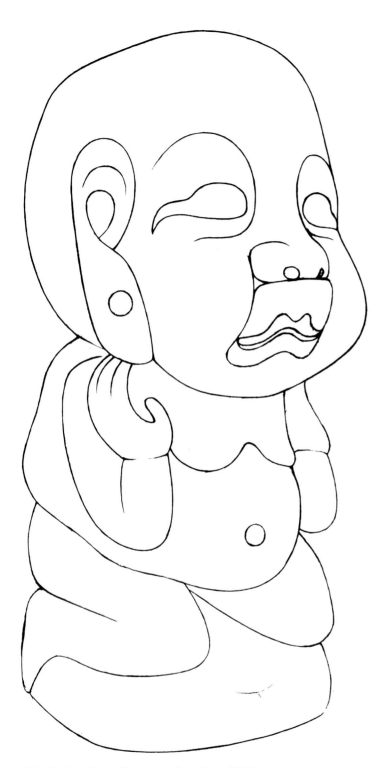

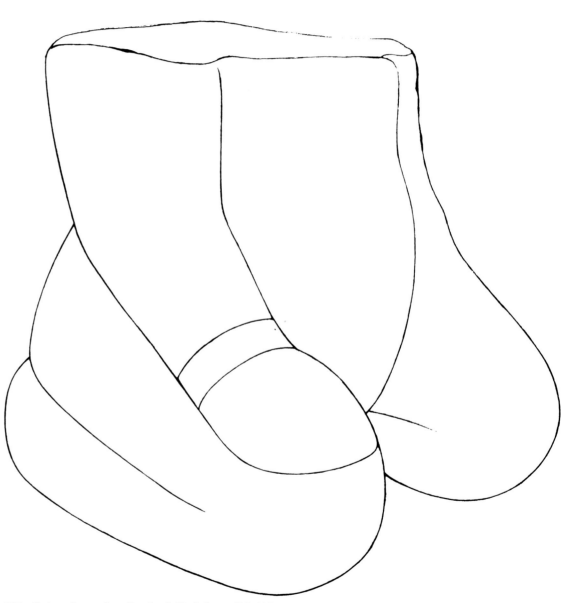

286. Guizuo figure, Preclassic Period, ca. 1150
B.C.–A.D. 300, El Quiche, Guatemala (Collection
of the Museum of the American Indian, Heye
Foundation, New York City).

287. Guizuo figure, late Preclassic Period, ca. 400–100
B.C., Tres Zapotes, Veracruz, Mexico (Collection
of the Regional Museum, Tres Zapotes).

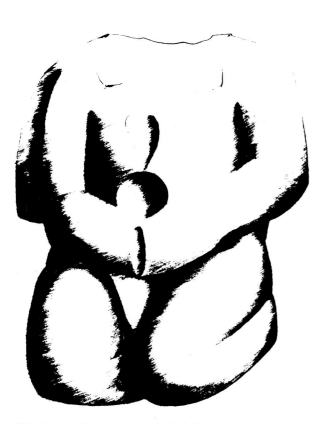

288. Guizuo figure, Preclassic Period, ca. 1150 B.C.–A.D. 300, La Venta, Tabasco, Mexico (Redrawn after Drucker, Heizer and Squier, 1959, Figure 63).

289. Jade guizuo figure, Preclassic Period, ca. 1150 B.C.–A.D. 300, La Lima, Ulua Valley, Honduras (Collection of the Middle American Research Institute, New Orleans).

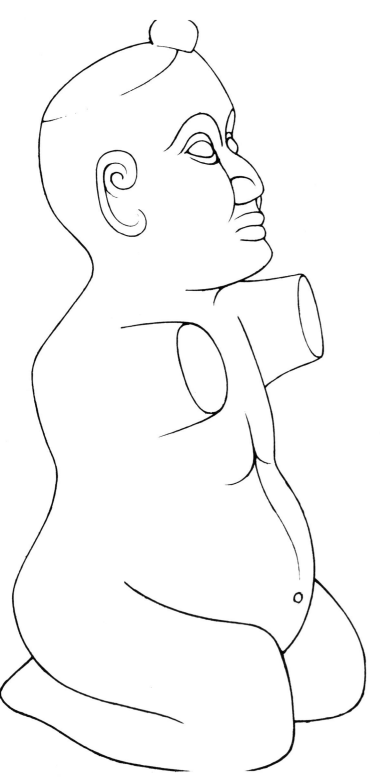

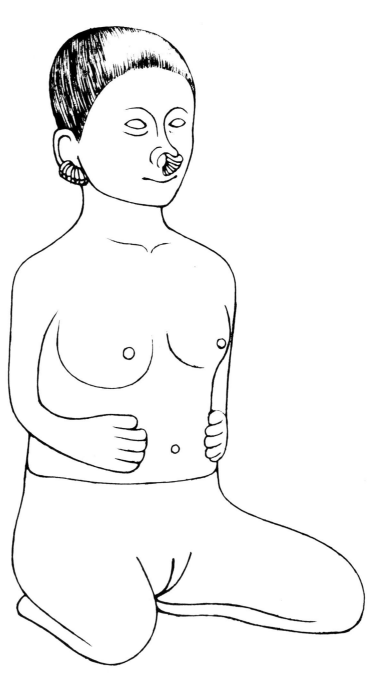

290. Guizuo figure, late Zhou Dynasty, ca. 400–200 B.C., China (Collection of the British Museum, London).

291. Guizuo figure, late Preclassic Period, ca. A.D. 100–300, Las Cebollas, Nayarit, Mexico (Collection of the National Museum of Anthropology, Mexico City, on loan to the American Museum of Natural History, New York City).

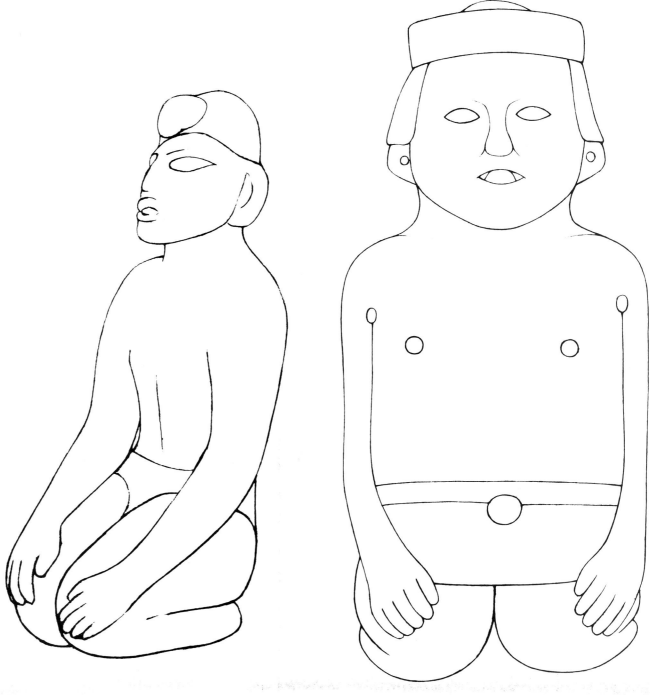

292. Guizuo figure, ca. A.D. 500, Turner Mound, Ohio (Collection of the Peabody Museum, Cambridge).

293. Guizuo figure, ca. A.D. 1200–1700, Tennessee (Collection of the American Museum of Natural History, New York City).

294. Guizuo figure, late Postclassic Period, ca. A.D. 1200–1500, Tenochtitlan, Mexico (Collection of the American Museum of Natural History, New York City).

295. Guizuo figure, Classic Period, ca. A.D. 400–800, Oaxaca, Mexico (Collection of the Dahlem-Berlin Museum, West Berlin).

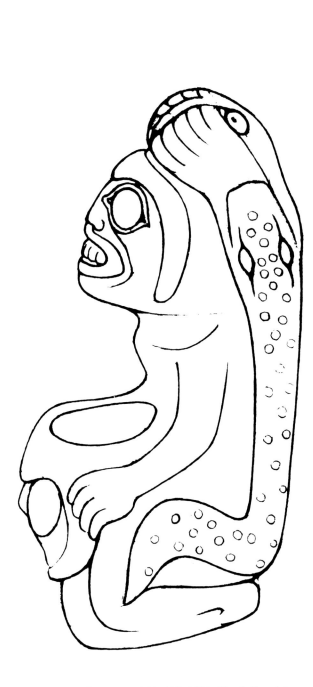

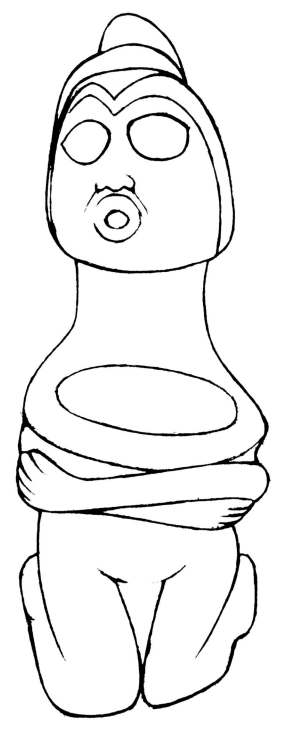

296. Guizuo figure, ca. A.D. 400–1000, North Saanich, Vancouver Island, British Columbia (Collection of John Hauberg, Seattle).

297. Guizuo figure, Marpole Phase, ca. 400 B.C.–A.D. 450), Marpole, Frazer Delta, British Columbia (Collection of C. E. Borden on loan to Museum of Anthropology, University of British Columbia).

298. Jade guizuo figure, late Classic period, ca. A.D. 700, Tomb beneath Temple I, Tikal, Peten, Guatemala (Collection of the Tikal Museum, Tikal).

299. Guizuo figure, late Zhou Period, ca. 500–300 B.C., China (Collection of the Nelson Gallery and Atkins Museum, Kansas City).

300. Jade guizuo figure, late Zhou Dynasty, ca. 500–300 B.C., China (Collection of the Fogg Art Museum, Cambridge).

301. Monument 5, Preclassic Period, ca. 1150 B.C.–A.D. 300, La Venta, Tabasco, Mexico (Collection of the La Venta Museum, Villahermosa).

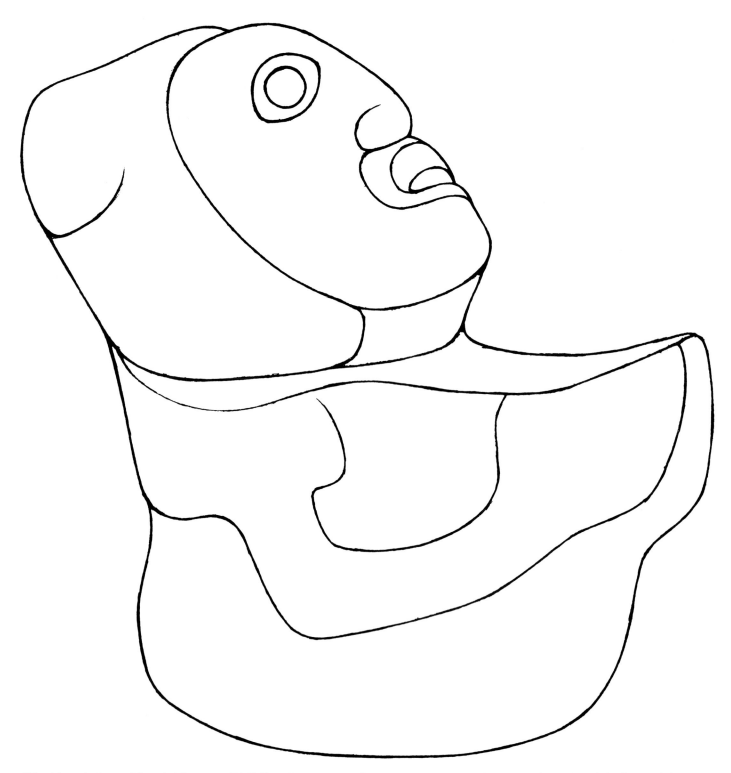

302. Marpole figure, Marpole Phase, ca. 400 B.C.–A.D. 450, Marpole, Fraser Delta, British Columbia (Collection of the Centennial Museum, Vancouver).

303, 304. Monument 70, Preclassic Period, ca. 1150 B.C.–A.D. 300, La Venta, Tabasco, Mexico (Collection of the Tabasco Museum, Villahermosa).

305. Jade guizuo figure, late Shang Dynasty, ca. 1400–1100 B.C., China (Collection of the Fogg Art Museum, Cambridge).

306. Jade guizuo figure, Preclassic Period, ca. 1150 B.C.–A.D. 300, La Lima, Ulua Valley, Honduras (Collection of the Middle American Research Institute, New Orleans).

307. Guizuo figure, Han Dynasty, 206 B.C.–A.D. 220, China (Collection of the Museum Cernuschi, Paris).

308. Guizuo figure, Preclassic Period, ca. 1150 B.C.–A.D. 300, El Quiche, Guatemala (Collection of the Museum of the American Indian, New York City), see Figure 286.

309. Jade guizuo figure, late Zhou Dynasty, ca. 500–300 B.C., China (Collection of the Fogg Art Museum, Cambridge).

310. Guizuo figure, late Zhou Dynasty, ca. 500–300 B.C., China (Collection of the Nelson Gallery and Atkins Museum, Kansas City).

311. Monument 5, Preclassic Period, ca. 1150 B.C.–A.D. 300, La Venta, Tabasco, Mexico (Collection of the La Venta Museum, Villahermosa).

312. Guizuo figure, late Preclassic Period, ca. A.D. 100–300, Abaj Takalik, Guatemala.

313. Guizuo figure, late Zhou Dynasty, ca. 400–200 B.C., China (Collection of the British Museum, London).

314. Guizuo figure, late Preclassic Period, ca. 400–100 B.C., Tres Zapotes, Veracruz, Mexico (Collection of the Regional Museum, Tres Zapotes).

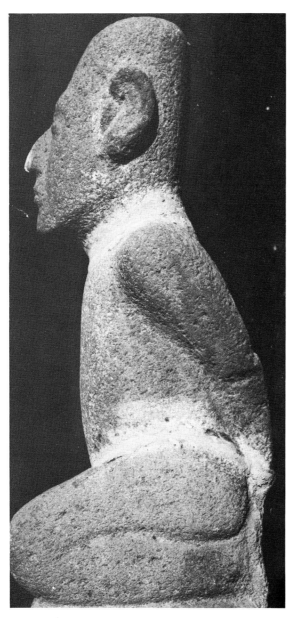

315. Guizuo captive (two views), late Preclassic Period, ca. 200 B.C.–A.D. 200, Highland Guatemala (Collection of the National Museum of Anthropology, Guatemala City).

316. Guizuo figure, ca. A.D. 1200–1700, Tennessee (Collection of the American Museum of Natural History, New York City).

317. Guizuo anthropomorphic figure, late Shang Dynasty, ca. 1300–1100 B.C., Houjiazhuang, Anyang, Henan, China (Collection of the Academia Sinica, Taipei).

318. Jade guizuo figure, late Zhou Dynasty, ca. 500–300 B.C., China (Collection of the Fogg Art Museum, Cambridge).

319. Jade guizuo figure, late Shang Dynasty, ca. 1300–1100 B.C., Anyang, China (private collection).

320, 321. Jade guizuo figure, late Shang Dynasty, ca. 1200 B.C., Fuhao Tomb (No. 5), Anyang, Henan, China (Collection of the National Museum of History, Beijing).

PART 15
The Totem Base

Yan Zi said [to Duke Jing of Qi]: I have heard that the people of Di compare themselves to the dragons and snakes. Now the beams of my lord's house are decorated with dragons and snakes; the columns are decorated with birds and animals. . . .

Yan Ying
Yan Zi Chun Qiu
(Master Yan's Spring
and Autumn Annals)
ca. 300 B.C.

322, 324. Pole-figure, Monument 52 (three views), Preclassic Period, ca. 1150 B.C.–A.D. 300, San Lorenzo, Veracruz, Mexico (Collection of the National Museum of Anthropology, Mexico City). Each of the stone sculptures in Figures 322–326 has a vertical trough in the back for fitting into pole or colume.

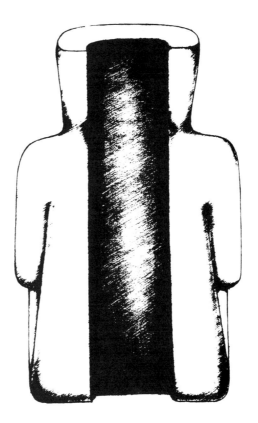

323. Pole-figure (two views, restored), late Shang Dynasty, ca. 1300–1100 B.C., Xiaodun, Anyang, Henan, China (Collection of the Academia Sinica, Taipei).

324. Pole-figure, Monument 52 (back view), see Figure 322.

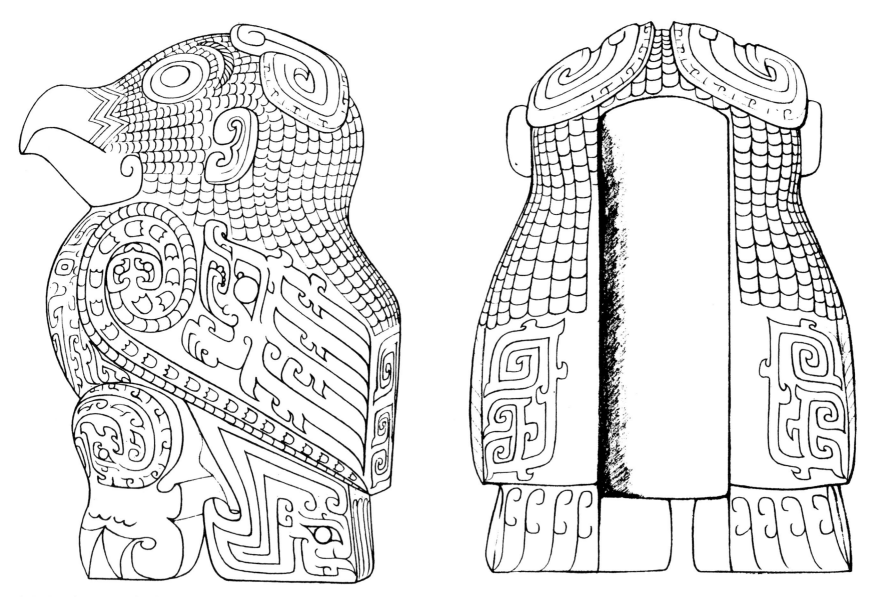

325. Pole-figure (two views), late Shang Dynasty, ca. 1300–1100 B.C., Houjiazhuang, Anyang, Henan, China (Collection of the Academia Sinica, Taipei).

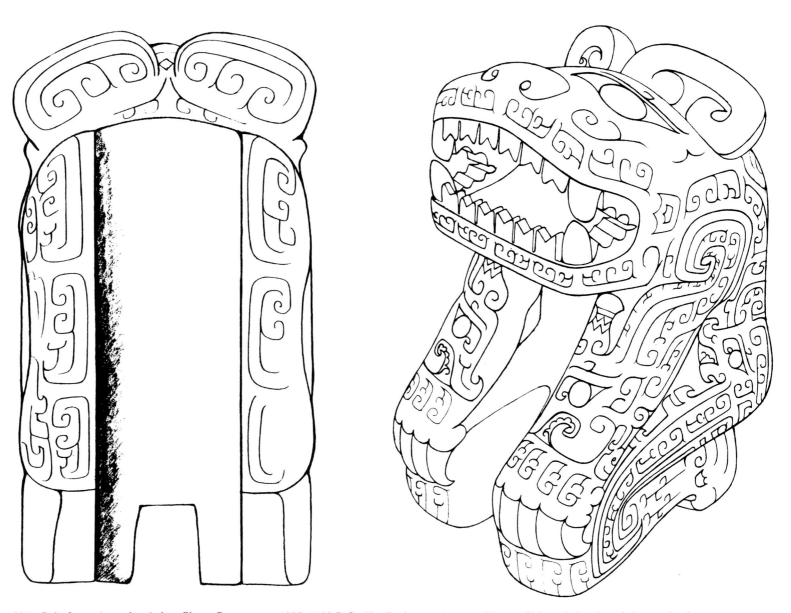

326. Pole-figure (two views), late Shang Dynasty, ca. 1300–1100 B.C., Houjiazhuang, Anyang, Henan, China (Collection of the Academia Sinica, Taipei).

There was a dragon cave on Mount Kui in
Wuchang. Whenever people saw a divine Kui
dragon fly in and out of the cave, the year was dry.
When people prayed to this dragon, however, it
rained.

Tao Qian
Shou Shen Hou Ji
(Sequel to the
Records of Spiritual
Manefestation)
ca. A.D. 400–500)

When rain is imminent, the dragons growl . . .
Their saliva produces a full array of fragrances,
their breath becomes clouds . . .

Wang Fu
of Han Dynasty
(206 B.C.–A.D. 220)
Quoted in
Er Ya Yi:
ca. A.D. 1175

327. Relief 1, portraying the sectional view of the life-giving deity's mouth, Preclassic Period, ca. 1150 B.C.–A.D. 300, Chalcatzingo, Morelos, Mexico.

328. Sun shield, late Classic Period, ca. A.D. 700, Temple of the Sun, Palenque, Chiapas, Mexico; see Figures 382–387.

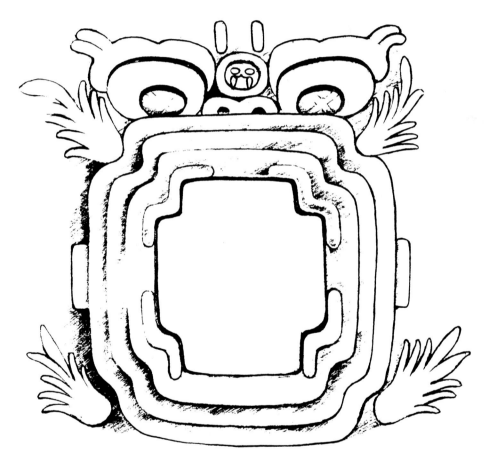

329. Mouth-cross, Preclassic Period, vicinity of Chalcatzingo, Morelos, Mexico (Collection of the Munson-Williams-Proctor Institute, Utica).

330. Mouth-cross, late Shang Dynasty, ca. 1300–1100 B.C., Anyang, Henan, China (Collection of the National Museum of History, Beijing); see Figures 141, 142, 353–359.

331. Mouth-cross clan name-glyph, late Shang Dynasty, ca. 1300–1100 B.C., Henan, China.

332. Mouth-cross clan name-glyph: Ya Zaorizhuan, portraying an animal under the sun and amidst plants (rubbing from a zun ceremonial vessel), late Shang Dynasty, ca. 1300–1100 B.C., China (Collection of the Freer Gallery of Art, Smithsonian Institution, Washington, D.C.).

333. Mouth-cross clan name-glyph: Ya Chou, portraying a spirit pouring elixir, late Shang Style, ca. 1300–1100 B.C., China.

The yellow dragon is the highest essence of all
spirits and the foremost of the four dragons.

Sun Rouzhi
Rui Ying Tu
(Pictorial Records
of Good Omens)
ca. A.D. 550

. . . For sacrifice to heaven, earth and four world
directions, six kinds of jade objects are made: blue
bi [disk] for the heaven, yellow zong [square tube]
for the earth, green gui for the East, red zhang for
the South, white hu for the West, and black huang
for the North.

Zhou Li
(Rites of Zhou)
ca. 206 B.C.–A.D. 220

East is associated with wood, its star being the
green dragon. West is associated with metal, its
star being the white tiger. South is associated with
fire, its star being the red bird. North is associated
with water, its star being the black warrior.

Wang Chong
Lun Heng
(On Equilibrium)
ca. A.D. 83

334. Fertility icon (three views) with animal heads incised on hip and shoulder joints, late Shang Dynasty, ca. 1300–1100 B.C., Anyang, Henan, China (Ex. Collection of J. D. Chen).

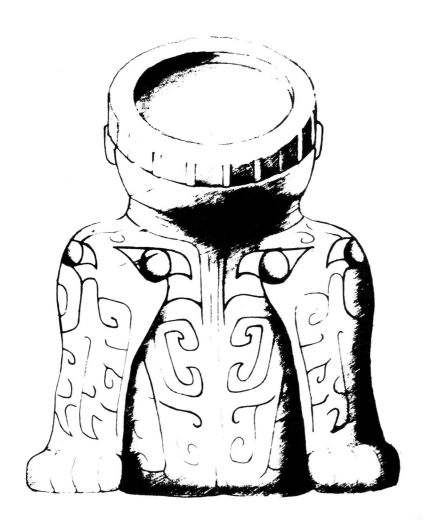

335. Kwakiutl ceremonial costumes (front and back views), early Twentieth Century, British Columbia (Collection of the Field Museum of Natural History, Chicago).

336. Kwakiutl ceremonial costumes (front and back views), early Twentieth Century, British Columbia (Collection of the Field Museum of Natural History, Chicago).

337. Anthropomorphic feline-dragon (two views), late Shang Dynasty, ca. 1300–1100 B.C., China (Collection of the Minneapolis Institute of Art, Minneapolis).

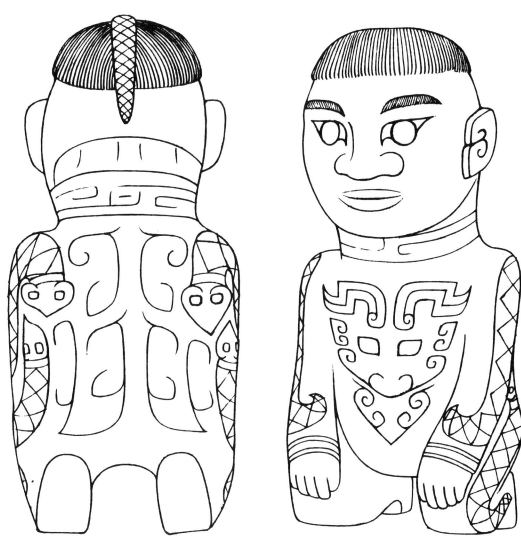

338. Jade ancestral icon (two views) with snakes incised on shoulder and hip, late Shang Dynasty, ca. 1200 B.C., Fuhao Tomb (No. 5) Anyang, Henan, China (Collection of the National Museum of History, Beijing).

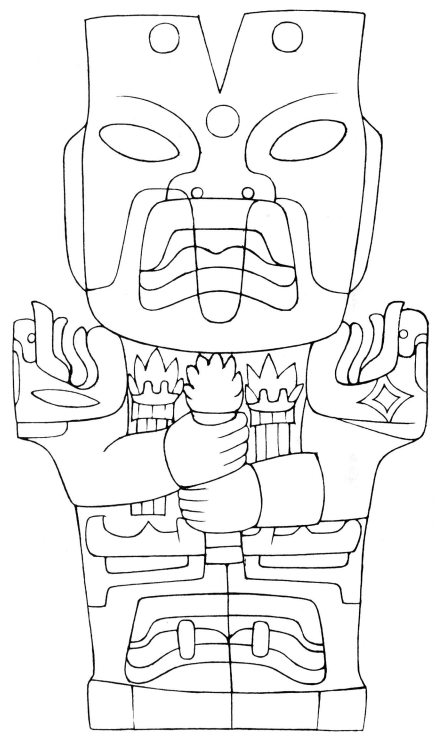

339. Serpentine icon with masks carved on shoulder and lower body, Preclassic Period, ca. 1150 B.C.–A.D. 300, Guerrero, Mexico (Collection of the Dallas Museum of Fine Arts, Dallas). Observe the four dragon profiles on the shoulder and the legs; see Figures 334, 343, and 346.

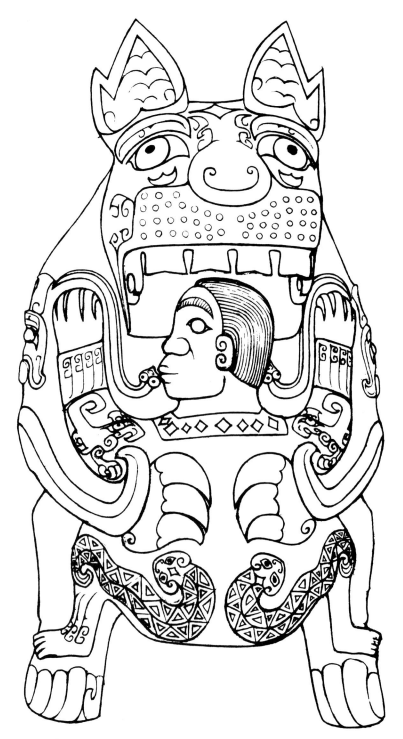

340, 341. Child held by a feline and ornated with bird-dragons on the shoulder, guei-dragons on the hip, late Shang Dynasty, ca. 1300–1100 B.C., Anhua, Hunan, China (Sumitomo Collection, Kyoto).

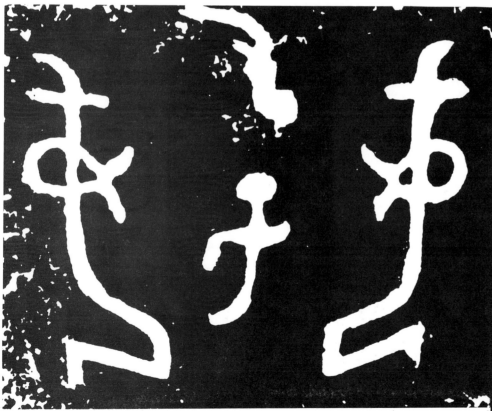

342. Fuhao clan-name glyphs, images of women dedicating or celebrating children, late Shang Dynasty, ca. 1200 B.C., Fuhao Tomb, Anyang, Henan, China (Collection of the Institute of Archaeology, Academy of Social Sciences, Beijing); see Figure 380, glyph on lower left corner.

343. Child held by a woman with dragon heads incised on the shoulder and knee joints, Preclassic Period, ca. 1150 B.C.–A.D. 300, Las Limas, Veracruz, Mexico (Collection of the Museum of Anthropology, University of Veracruz, Jalapa); see Figure 334.

 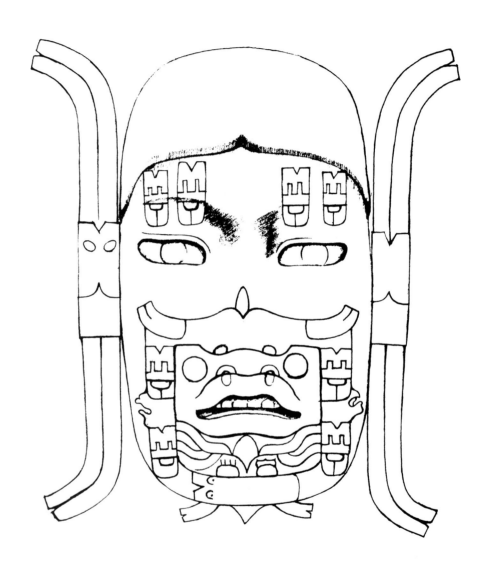

344, 345. Incised composite masks on the face of the Las Limas icon in Figure 343.

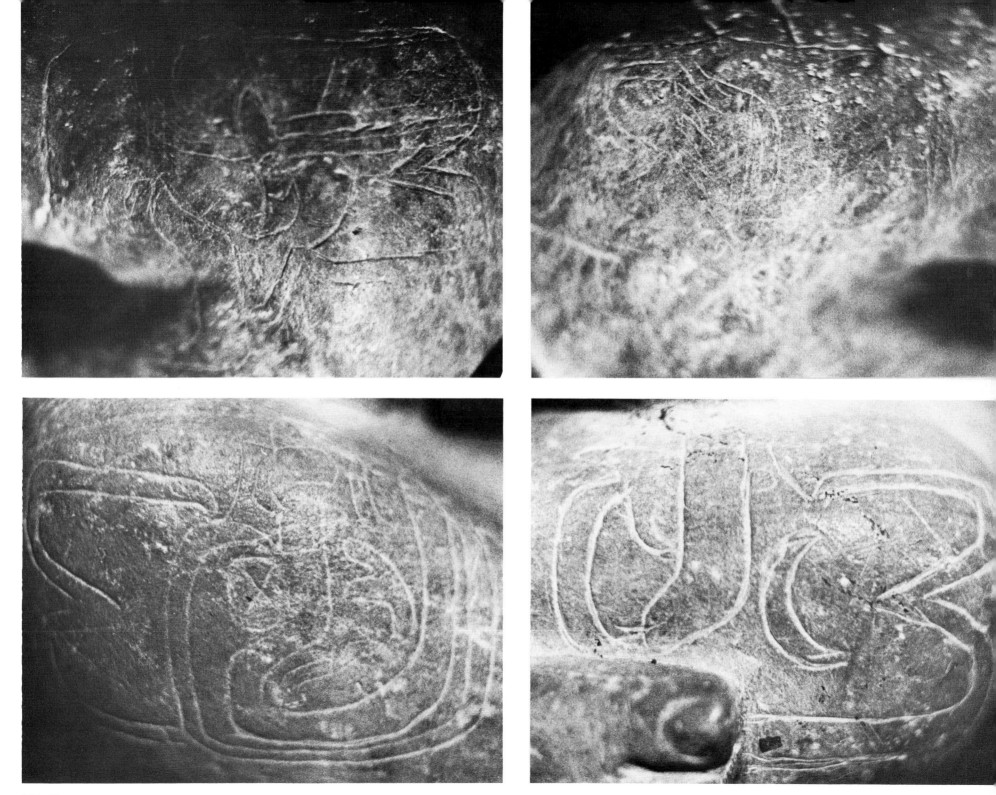

346. Upper row: incised dragon heads on the shoulder of the Las Limas icon (rotated 90 degree). Lower row: incised dragon heads on knee joints.

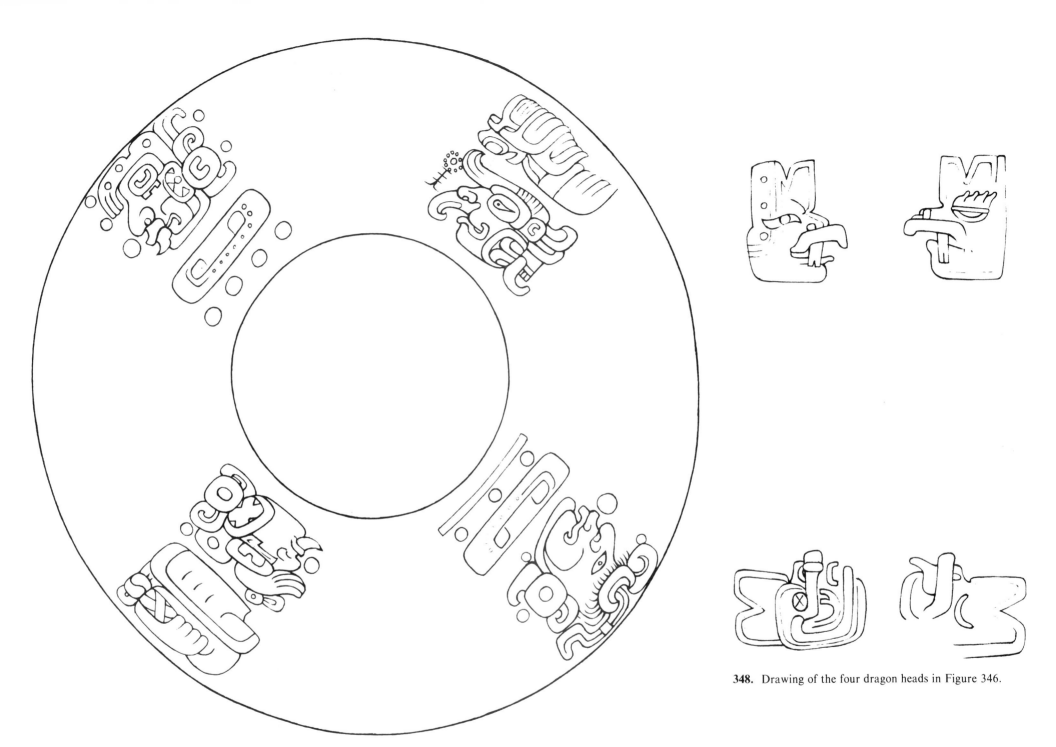

348. Drawing of the four dragon heads in Figure 346.

347, 349. Jade ceremonial flare incised with four iconographic profiles, ca. A.D. 200–400, Pomona, Belize (Collection of the British Museum, London).

349.

350. Jade bi (ceremonial disk) with four dragon masks,
Han Dynasty 206 B.C.–A.D. 220, China
(Collection of Minneapolis Institute of Art,
Minneapolis).

351. Jade zong-bi (ceremonial tube-disk), Shang
Dynasty, ca. 1766–1122 B.C., China (Collection
of the Minneapolis Institute of Art, Minneapolis).

352. Jade zong with four masks, late Shang early Zhou Dynasty, ca. 1200–1100 B.C., China (Collection of the Asian Art Museum, San Francisco).

353. Bronze iconographic mirror depicting the four cardinal animal-images, heaven and earth, Tang Dynasty, A.D. 618–906, China (Collection of the National Museum of History, Taipei).

354. Sun-eye cross, late Shang Dynasty, ca. 1400–1100 B.C., China; see Figures 330–333 and 383–387.

355. Riguang (sun-rays) bronze-mirror indicating eight cardinal points, Han Dynasty, B.C. 206–A.D. 220, China (Collection of the Fogg Art Museum, Cambridge).

356. Bronze mirror showing the twelve calendric branches represented by animal signs and the four cardinal images, Tang Dynasty, A.D. 618–906, China (Collection of the Victoria and Albert Museum, London).

357. Sun stone showing twenty calendric branches, eight cardinal points and four cosmic images, Postclassic Period, ca. A.D. 1479 (Collection of the National Museum of Anthropology, Mexico City).

358. Detail of the Sun Stone (Figure 357, lower portion) showing deities emerging from the mouths of the celestial dragons.

359. Detail of a painting on silk showing deities emerging from the mouths of the celestral dragons, note sun symbol on top, Tang Dynasty, A.D. 618–906, China (Collection of the Museum Guimet, Paris); see Figures 63–68, 74 and 75.

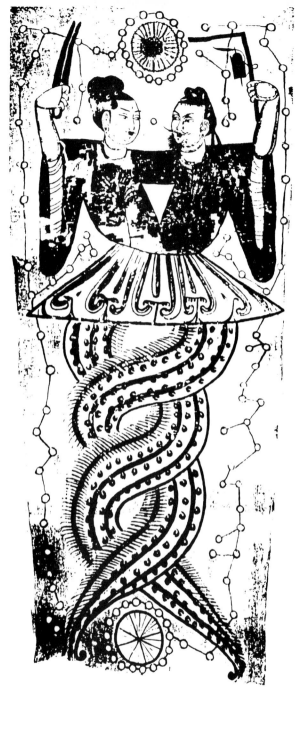

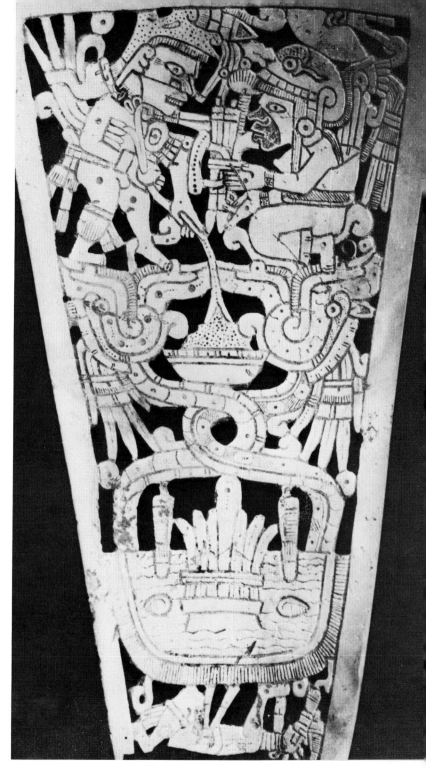

360. Intertwining anthropomorphic dragons (Fuxi and Nugua) and astrological images, Tang Style, ca. A.D. 900, China (Collection of the Archaeological Service, New Delhi); see also Figure 68.

361. Transterrestrial intertwining dragons (Mixcoatl and Tlazolteotl), Postclassic Period, ca. A.D. 1000–1250, Veracruz, Mexico (Collection of the Middle American Research Institute, New Orleans).

362. Dragon and tiger flanking a mask, Han Dynasty, B.C. 206–A.D. 220, China (Collection of the British Museum, London).

363. Anthropomorphic two-headed dragon, late Classic Period, ca. A.D. 750–800, Copan, Honduras; see Figure 384.

364, 365. Anthropomorphic two-headed dragon, early Zhou Dynasty, ca. 1100–800 B.C., China (Collection of the British Museum, London).

365.

366. Two-headed dragon with bifurcate glyph, lower
portion of Stela 3, late Preclassic Period, ca. A.D.
100–300, Abaj Takalik, Guatemala.

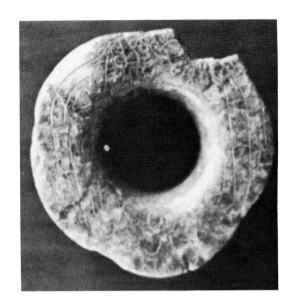

367. Jade earflares, Preclassic Period, ca. 1150 B.C.–A.D. 300, La Venta, Tabasco, Mexico (Collection of the National Museum of Anthropology, Mexico City).

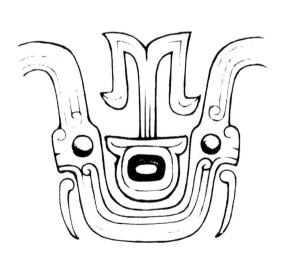

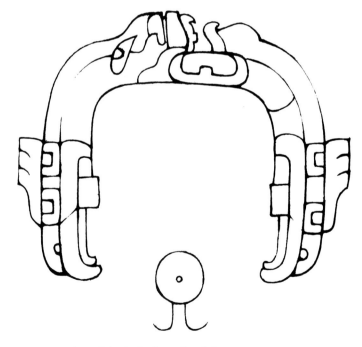

368. Two-headed dragon with bifurcate sun-eye motif, detail of a hu ceremonial vessel, middle Zhou Dynasty, ca. 900–600 B.C., China (Collection of the Art Institute of Chicago).

369. Drawing of the incised two-headed, anthropomorphic dragon on the earflare in Figure 367. Note bifurcated sun-eye glyph.

370, 371. Jade two-headed anthropomorphic dragon, Zhou Dynasty, 1122–256 B.C., China (Collection of the Freer Gallery of Art, Smithsonian Institution, Washington, D.C.).

371.

372. Two-headed dragon, upper portion of a stela, Nanbei Dynasty, ca. A.D. 450–550, China (Collection of the Boston Museum of Fine Arts, Boston). Note the standing deity at the lower center being protected by nine dragons.

377. Oracle glyphs, late Shang Dynasty, ca. 1400–1100 B.C., Henan, China. Row a–d: dragon pictographs; Row d: top five glyphs: double-headed dragon pictographs symbolizing rainbow. Row e, f: rain pictographs. Note the "inverted E" symbol which was also extensively used in Mesoamerica to signify rain. Row g–j: cleft-headed ancestral glyphs. Row k: ding ceremonial vessel symbolizing royal mandate. Row 1: light (kneeling-sitting figure with a flame-head). Row m, n: well-being, propitious (seated woman holding child). Row o: spirit (seated figure with a cross-head). Row p: brightness, enlightenment. Row q: sun (spinning fire-disc or sun-eye).

373. Spinning sun-dragon, early Zhou Dynasty, ca. 1000–800 B.C., China. See Figure 85, top: dragon as carrier of the sun across the sky. Almost identical myth existed in Mesoamerica.

375. Spinning sun-disk with four dragon profiles, ca. 900–200 B.C., Chavin de Huantar, Peru (Collection of the Museum of the American Indian, Heye Foundation, New York City); see Figure 347–352.

374. Spinning sun-eye two-headed dragon, early Zhou Dynasty, ca. 1000–800 B.C., China; see Figures 366–369.

376. Spinning sun-disk flanked by two dragons, detail of a fangyi, early Zhou Dynasty, ca. 1100–900 B.C., Meixian, Shaanxi, China (Collection of the National Museum of History, Beijing).

379. Stela 2, late Preclassic Period, ca. 200 B.C.–A.D. 200, Izapa, Chiapas, Mexico. See Figure 378, Row: o-q for comparable images.

380. Inscription on a bronze ceremonial vessel, early Zhou Dynasty, ca. 1100-1000 B.C., China. Observe the son-offering clan name-glyph at lower left corner and the bird initial glyph (preceding the date glyphs) at the upper right corner.

378. Oracle glyphs, late Shang Dynasty, ca. 1400–1100 B.C., Henan, China. Row a, b: town or city (buildings on earthen platform). Row c, d: high. Row e: city name-glyphs. Row f: capital. Row g: building. Row h–j: fantastic bird, synonymous to wind. Row k–l: bird. Row m, n: to obtain. Row o–q: sacrificial glyphs, each showing an inverted bird above an ancestral pole.

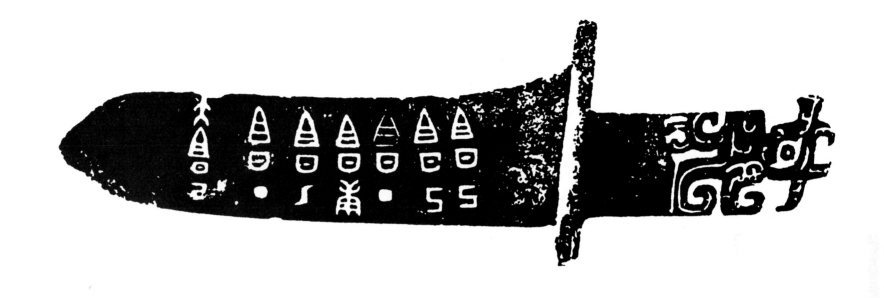

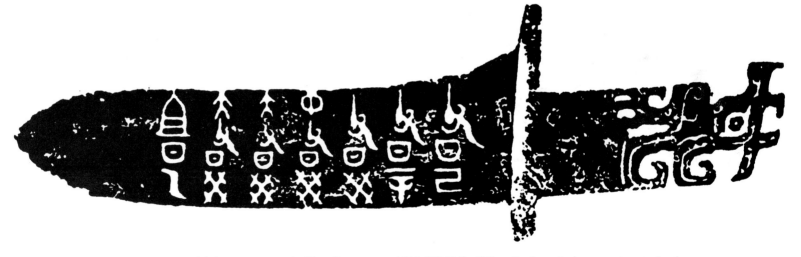

381. Inscriptions on bronze ceremonial dagger-axes, early Zhou Dynasty, ca. 1100–900 B.C., China. Each vertical row represents the day name-glyph of an ancester. As a group, the seven rows on each dagger-axe records the ancestral lineage of the ruling clan.

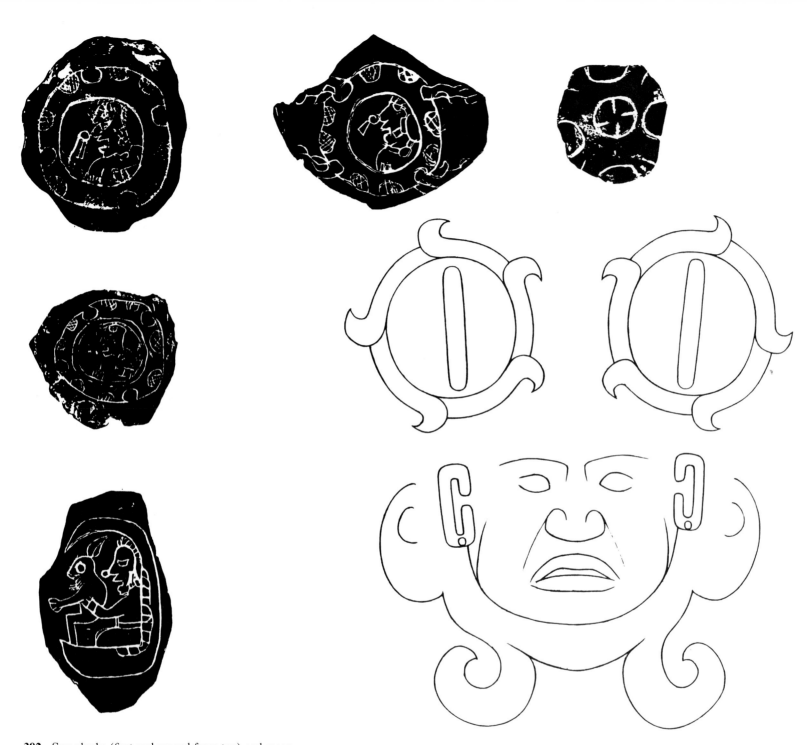

382. Sun glyphs (first and second from top) and moon glyph (bottom), late Classic Period, ca. A.D. 700–800, Uaxactun and Tikal, Peten, Guatemala (Collection of the National Museum of Anthropology, Guatemala City). The Chinese also traditionally represent the moon with a rabbit inside it; see Figure 68.

383. Sun glyphs. Top: late Classic Period, ca. A.D. 700–800, Tikal, Peten, Guatemala (Collection of the National Museum of Anthropology, Guatemala City). Bottom: incised images on a stone ball, Preclassic Period, ca. 1150 B.C.–A.D. 300, Pacific Coast, Mexico (Collection of the American Museum of Natural History, New York City). Observe the spinning sun-eye glyphs above the head; see Figures 373–376.

384. Top: two stylized dragon masks flanking the Kin sun-glyph, rubbing from a sello, Preclassic Period, ca. 1150 B.C.–A.D. 300, Tlatilco, Mexico. Bottom: two stylized dragon masks flanking the Kin sun-eye symbol, late Shang Dynasty, ca. 1400–1100 B.C., China (Collection of the Freer Gallery of Art, Smithsonian Institution, Washington, D.C.); see Figures 362–371.

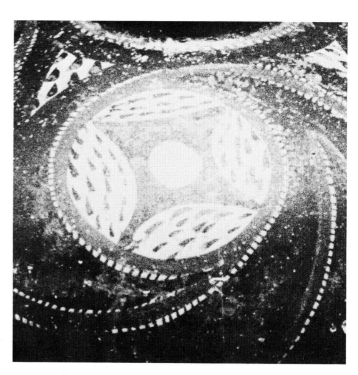

386. Kan-cross motif (in a stylized bird's eye), detail of a painted vessel, late Majiayao (Banshan) Period, ca. 2500–2000 B.C., Gansu, China (Collection of the Ostasiatiska Museum, Stockholm). Observe the water-drop motif surrounding the cross. In Mesoamerica this cross motif also symbolized rain and occurred often in the eyes of the rain deities. The Chinese counterpart of the Mesoamerican kan glyph is pronounced kwun (Cantonese) and kun (Mandarin), denoting: female, moon, cloudiness, earth and the Receptive.

385. Two stylized dragon masks flanking the sun-eye symbol, detail of a he ceremonial vessel, late Shang Dynasty, ca. 1400–1100 B.C., China (Collection of Freer Gallery of Art, Smithsonian Institution, Washington, D.C.). The Chinese counterpart of the Mesoamerican kin glyph is also pronounced kin (Cantonese) and chien (Mandarin), denoting: male, sun and the Creative in *I Jing,* ibid.

387. Banded cross and the spinning sun-motives on a ceremonial bell (Zhong, see photograph on the right), late Shang—early Zhou Dynasty, ca. 1200–900 B.C., China. The image involves 12 spinning suns and crosses with a stylized dragon mask at the center. On the forehead of the mask, a trifoliate element is exquisitely modeled; see Figures 216, 220–222.

CHAPTER V
The Forces, Mechanisms and Processes of Interhemispheric Cultural Diffusion

Years	Chinese Dynasties	North America	Periods	Mesoamerica — Gulf Coast — General Cultural Sequence*	Gulf Coast — San Lorenzo	Maya — General Cultural Sequence*	Maya — Guatemala Chiapa Pacific Coast	Central Mexico	Oaxaca	South America
1500 (AD)	Ming		Postclassic	Totonac				Aztec		Inca
	Yuan							Tenochtitlan		
	Jin					Mayapan			Mixtec	
	Liao			Huastec		Chicken Itza				
1000	Song	Mississippi Pueblos			Villa Alta			Toltec Tula	Monte Alban IV	
	Tang		Classic	El Tajin		Uxmal Palenque				Huari
	Sui									
500	Nanbei					Copan Tikal			Zapotec	Tiahuanaco
	Jin						Crucero			
	Sanguo							Teotihuacan		Nazca Moche
0 AD/BC	Han	Hopewell		Tres Zapotes		Kaminaljuyu				
	Qin	Adena	Preclassic		Remplas	Izapa Abaj Takalic				
500	E. Zhou			La Venta	Polagana			Cuicuilco	Monte Alban I	
							Conchas II			
				Olmec	Nacaste		Conchas I		Guadalupe	
1000	W. Zhou			San Lorenzo	San Lorenzo		Jocotal	Tlatilco	San Jose	Chavin
							Cuadros		Tierras Largas	
					Chicharras Bajio Ojochi		Ocos		Espiridian	
1500	Shang									
1900	Xia						Barra			

388. Abbreviated chronological chart of Chinese and American cultures.

*Sites with sculptural stelae and monumental architecture.

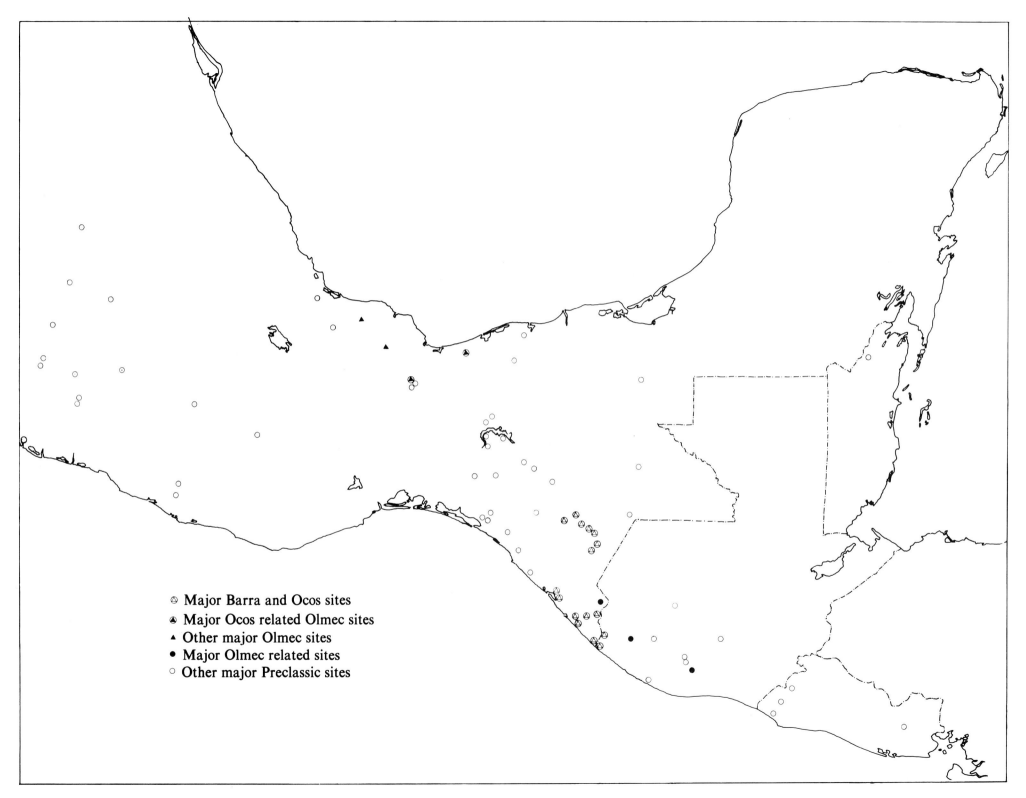

389. Principal Olmec and Olmec related sites in Mesoamerica.

Major Barra and Ocos sites
Major Ocos related Olmec sites
Other major Olmec sites
Major Olmec related sites
Other major Preclassic sites

Region / Stage	West China	North and Central China			East China		Years B.C.
	Upper Huanghe River	Middle Huanghe River	Laoha River	Middle Changjiang River	Lower Huanghe River	Lower Changjiang River	
Bronze Cultures	Siba	Shang	Xiajiadian	Shang	Shang	Shang	— 1000
	Qijia	Xia		Longshan	Longshan	Liangzhu	— 2000
Neolithic Cultures	Majiayao	Longshan	Hongshan	Qujialing			— 3000
				Daxi	Dawenkou	Majiabang	
		Yangshao					— 4000
					Qingliangang	Hemudu	
							— 5000
		Dadiwan Laoguantai	Peiligang	Cishan		Beixin	
							6000

390. Early cultural chronology of China.

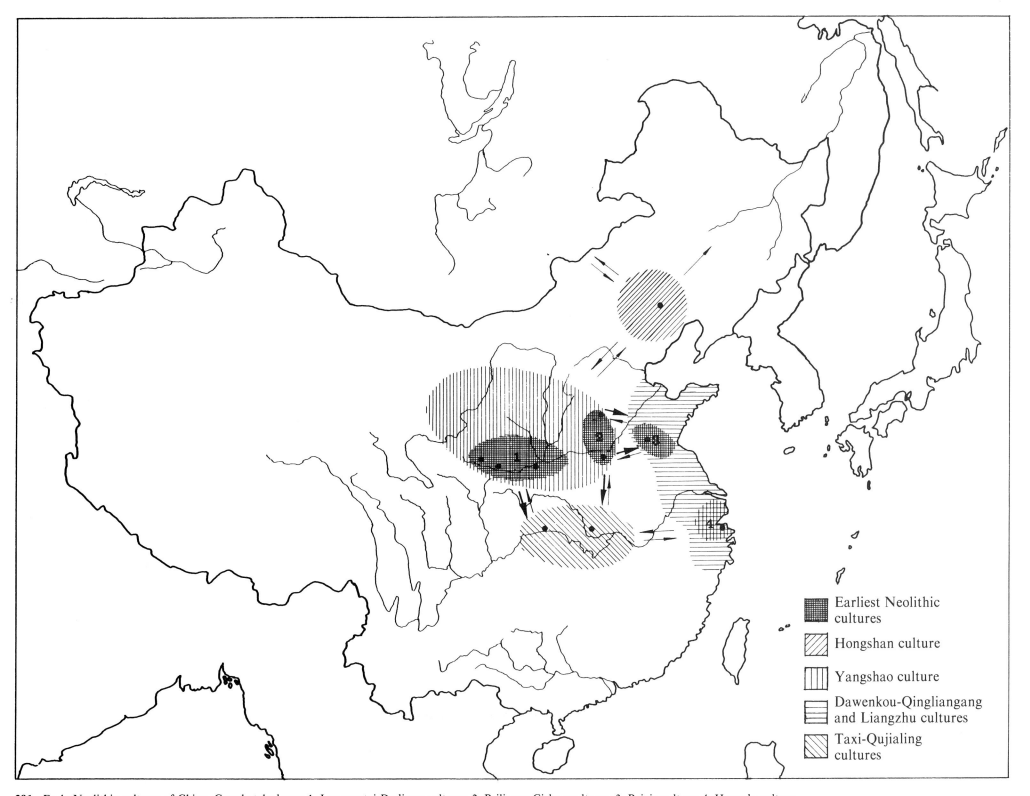

391. Early Neolithic cultures of China. Crosshatched area 1. Laoguantai-Dadiwan cultures; 2. Peiligang-Cishan cultures; 3. Beixin culture; 4. Hemudu culture.

Earliest Neolithic
cultures

Hongshan culture

Yangshao culture

Dawenkou-Qingliangang
and Liangzhu cultures

Taxi-Qujialing
cultures

392. Pre-Shang and early Shang cultures.

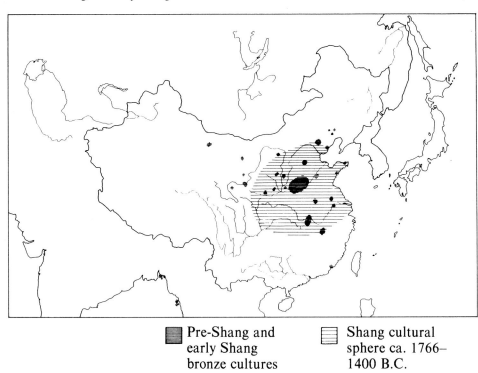

◾ Pre-Shang and early Shang bronze cultures

▤ Shang cultural sphere ca. 1766– 1400 B.C.

393. Late Shang Dynasty and the rise of Zhou culture.

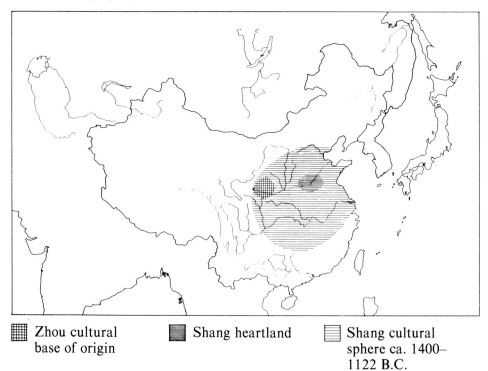

▦ Zhou cultural base of origin

▥ Shang heartland

▤ Shang cultural sphere ca. 1400– 1122 B.C.

394. Zhou Dynasty and the rise of Qin.

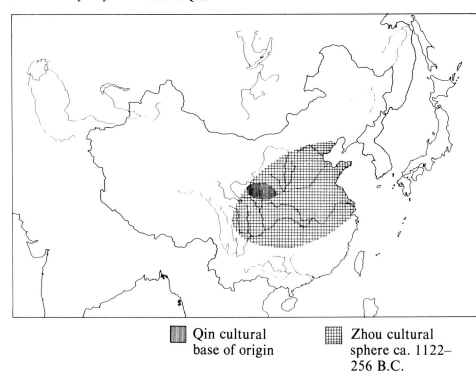

▥ Qin cultural base of origin

▦ Zhou cultural sphere ca. 1122– 256 B.C.

395. Qin, the first unified empire of China.

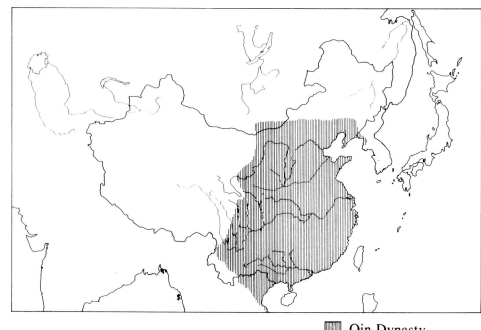

▥ Qin Dynasty 221–206 B.C.

396. Han Empire.

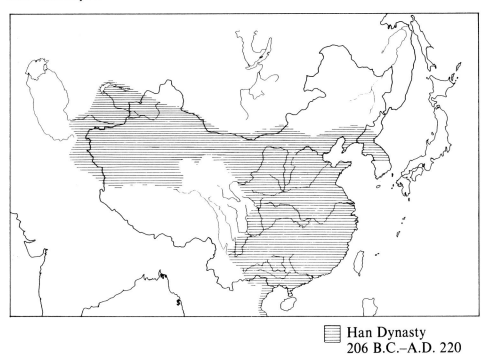

Han Dynasty
206 B.C.–A.D. 220

398. Western Jin Dynasty.

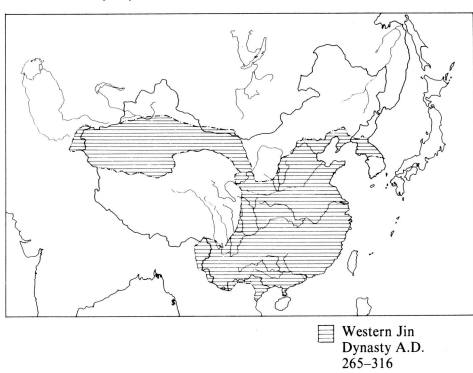

Western Jin
Dynasty A.D.
265–316

397. Sanguo: Wei, Shu and Wu Kingdoms.

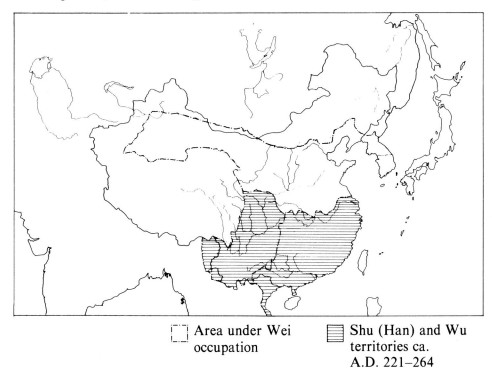

Area under Wei
occupation

Shu (Han) and Wu
territories ca.
A.D. 221–264

399. Eastern Jin Dynasty and the Qian Qin "barbarians".

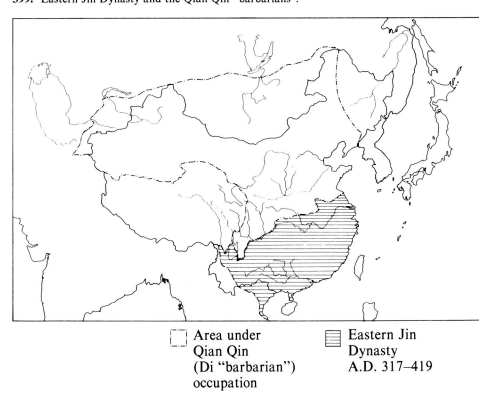

Area under
Qian Qin
(Di "barbarian")
occupation

Eastern Jin
Dynasty
A.D. 317–419

400. Liang Dynasty and the Eastern Wei, Western Wei "barbarians".

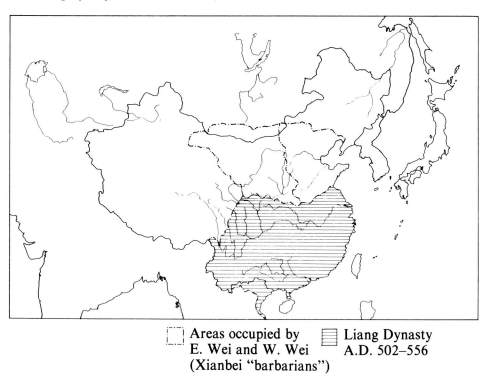

☐ Areas occupied by
E. Wei and W. Wei
(Xianbei "barbarians")

▤ Liang Dynasty
A.D. 502–556

401. Tang Empire.

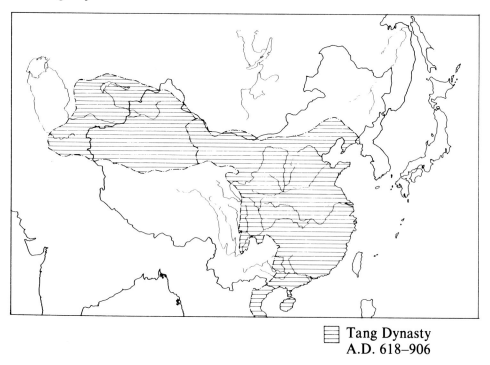

▤ Tang Dynasty
A.D. 618–906

402. Hou Tang, Hou Shu, Chu, Wu, Wuyue, Min and Nan Han.

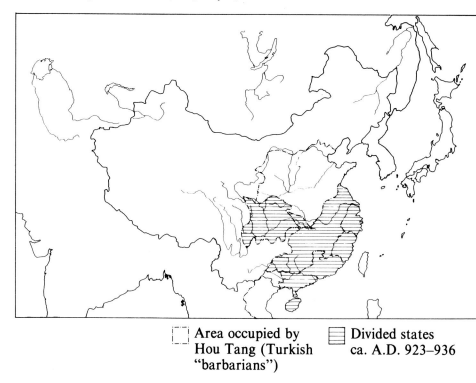

☐ Area occupied by
Hou Tang (Turkish
"barbarians")

▤ Divided states
ca. A.D. 923–936

403. Song Dynasty and the Jin "barbarians".

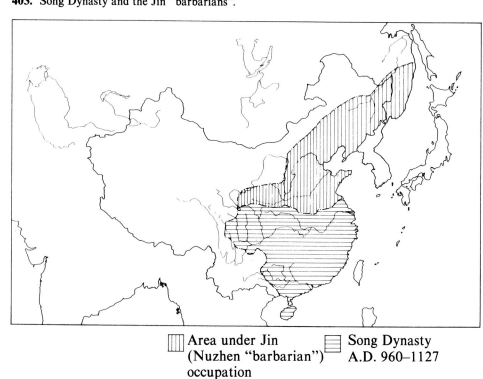

▥ Area under Jin
(Nuzhen "barbarian")
occupation

▤ Song Dynasty
A.D. 960–1127

404. Yuan (Mongols) Empire and allied hordes.

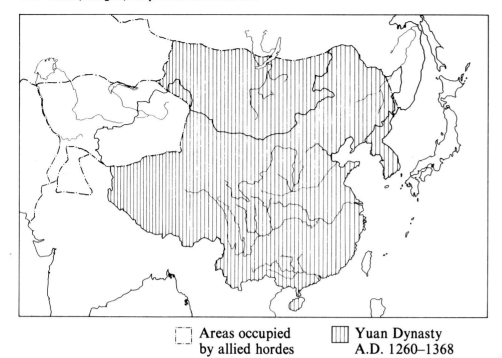

⌐—¬ Areas occupied ||||| Yuan Dynasty
   by allied hordes A.D. 1260–1368

406. Qing (Manchu) Empire.

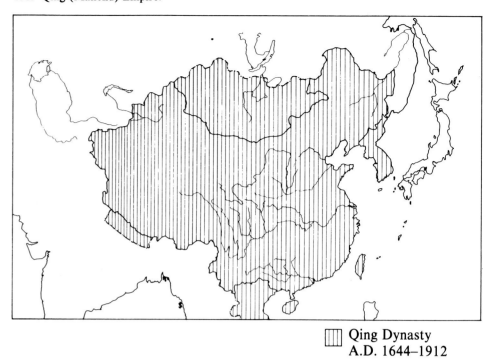

||||| Qing Dynasty
  A.D. 1644–1912

405. Ming Dynasty.

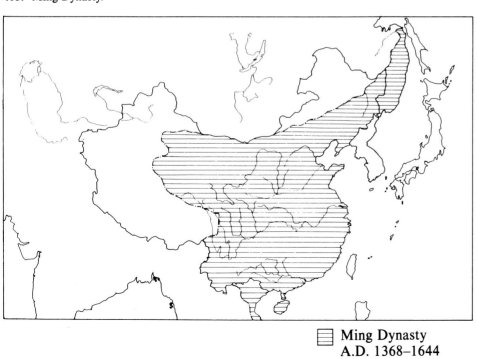

▤ Ming Dynasty
 A.D. 1368–1644

407. Contemporary China.

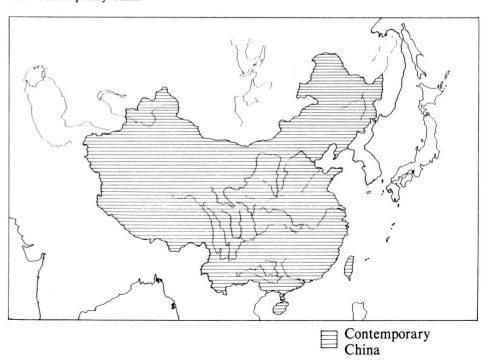

▤ Contemporary
 China

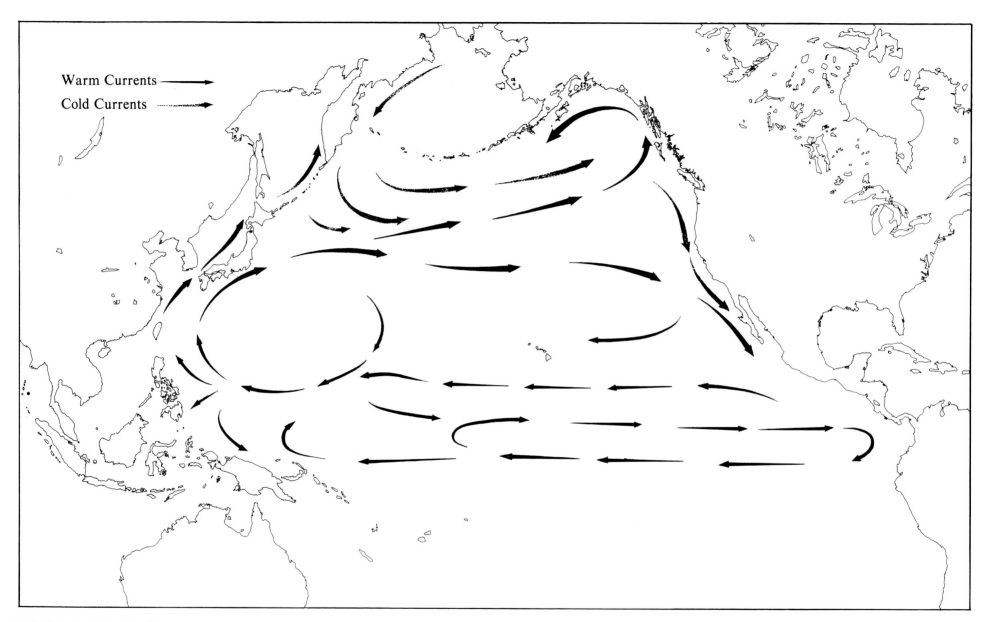

408. Principal North Pacific currents.

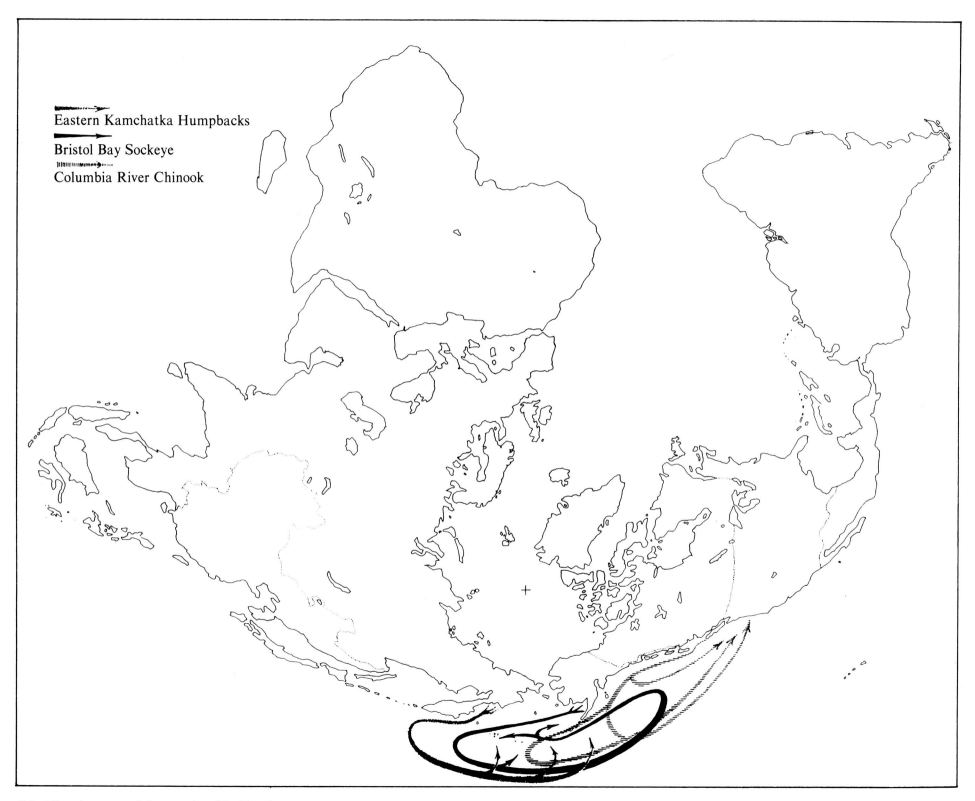

409. Migration routes of three species of Pacific salmon.

The end of the Pleistocene Ice Age was a milestone of man's vicissitudinous journey toward civilization. Favorable climatic changes precipitated the evolutionary process which was in progress since Homo errectus learned to use stone tools over one million years ago.

Warmer and wetter climate nurtured more abundant and extensive plant and animal resources. Population growth generated by these changes encouraged migration and innovative utilization of natural resources—cultivation of plants and domestication of animals. Settled agricultural villages appeared which ushered in a new era of human evolution. A self-sustaining chain of accelerated interactions was set in motion culminating in the birth, development and dissemination of cultures.

The more intensive, sedentary modes of food production gave rise to differentiated communities as well as specialized groups within a community. The resulting imbalance generated momentous forces which stimulated intercourse among peoples in the form of trade, territorial expansion and migration (of both peoples and ideas). It is through this interactive and cross-fertilizing process that cultures arose, first in the Old World and gradually spreading to the New World.

Why did "America's first civilization" abruptly emerge in one of the less endowed natural environments of the New World? How did this occur? What forces were at work? And via what process and through what mechanism?

The first question can be answered by my "hourglass" theory. It was not by accident that the first and highest manifestation of the New World cultures germinated and blossomed in Mesoamerica. These magnificent cultures owed their births, in no small degree, to the *strategic interactive location* of Mesoamerica. The American continents together can be visualized literally as an hourglass with Mesoamerica being the small passage in between. When the Americas were first populated by Asians, they inevitably funneled through Mesoamerica before dispersing in South America. Thus this area became the most strategic area in the New World, because it was there that peoples as well as ideas converged, interacted and cross-fertilized. In subsequent periods, the movement of peoples and goods (trade) in both directions through Mesoamerica was similarly unavoidable. Thus, Mesoamerica in general, and the Isthmus of Tehuantepec and the contiguous Pacific coastal plains in particular, were the logical location to become the birthplace of the "first civilization of America" (see Figures 7 and 389) because of the area's high frequency of interaction coefficient (FIC).[1]

The sequence of events which led to the sudden emergence and "take-off" of the Mesoamerican cultures may be described as follows:

1. Each succeeding wave or group of early Americans, in the process of migrating to South America, passed through Mesoamerica. In this process they brought to Mesoamerica not only new blood but also various semblances of Old World "cultural heritage".[2] The bio-cultural dynamics of this region gradually grew to such a charged state that the incidence of a suitable triggering mechanism would be sufficient to activate a "roaring take-off".
2. Such a triggering mechanism might well have been the intensification of conflicts between the Chinese and the surrounding nomadic peoples (invariably described by Classic Chinese historians as "barbarians") during the early second millennium B.C.

The alternating hegemony in east Asia of the Chinese with the surrounding nomadic peoples, activated a chain of events leading to the dislocation and subsequent emigration of people from east Asia. These emigrations resulted in sporadic and involuntary arrivals in the Americas. As immigrants in the Americas, these east Asians could well have provided the initial cultural stimuli and the succeeding cultural recharging (or reinforcement) necessary to generate such an emergence and development.

And what was the physical mechanism which implemented the arrival of these late immigrants (beginning ca. 2000 B.C.) in Mesoamerica? The location of Mesoamerica was again critical. It should be noted that there are two principal Pacific currents which could have carried Asian watercraft eastward across the Pacific: the Subartic Current and the North Pacific Current. The latter is the most favorable possibility (see Figure 408). In the event of Asian watercraft being swept into the North Pacific Current, their most probable land contact would have been the Pacific coast of either Mexico or Central America.[3]

Repeated mention of travel by watercraft is recorded in *I Jing* (Book of Changes). It is reported in the *Zhu Shu Ji Nian* (Bamboo Annals), that Emperor Mang (who ruled from ca. 2014 to 1996 B.C.) of the Xia Dynasty, in the year 2001 B.C., "went fishing in the Eastern Sea and caught big fishes." The *Shi Jing* (Book of Odes), in a passage describing the martial achievements of the Shang kings (ca. 1766–1120 B.C.) states: "The descendants of Wuding [who ruled from ca. 1766–1753 B.C.] . . . with their dragon banners fluttering, expanded the territories to the four seas."

Chen Yan of Beijing (Peking) University, in a recent article (titled, "Silk Roads of the Sea") documented that Chinese silk trade by sea routes had begun by 1121 B.C. during the Zhou Dynasty and by A.D. 166, the seaborne trading network had been extended to Rome, to the court of Emperor Marcus Aurelius.[4]

Trade, however, played only a minor role in the ancient Sino-American cultural contacts. The forces which activated the chain of diffusion of Asiatic cultures in general and Chinese culture in particular to the New World, were of a macro ecological and ethnological nature. The following brief review of the Chinese cultural context is offered in support of my premise.

The rise of the Chinese Neolithic cultures in the sixth millennium B.C. was generated by an interactive process of cultural evolution similar to that of Mesoamerica, as discussed earlier. The development of these cultures followed a pattern established in Paleolithic times by the Fen-wei chopping tool tradition and the Sankan small tool tradition (see Figure 15).

As is evident in Figures 32 and 391, nearly all early Paleolithic and Neolithic sites of significance in China were strategically located on the thoroughfare of human movement and interaction, particularly along the middle reaches of the Huanghe (Yellow River).

This region had always been China's main east-west artery (and practically the only viable route) linking the Pacific coastal plains with the western highlands and, still further west, with Central Asia. This artery subsequently became the eastern most section of "the Silk Road". Variously regarded by both traditional and contemporary scholars as "the cradle of Chinese civilization", "the Chinese cultural nucleus", or "the heartland of Chinese tradition", this area had been the focus of contention by many different peoples.

These constant struggles for hegemony (a term still applied by the Beijing government in describing the Sino-Russian conflicts) provided continual cultural exchange and cross-fertilization from which resulted the birth of the Chinese civilization in the early second millenium B.C. The continual combats for domination of the heartland also brought about massive movement and dislocation of peoples. As early as during the pre-dynasty period of ca. 2255–2205 B.C., various native tribes of the Huanghe (Yellow River) Valley were reported to have been driven to other regions by the precursor of the Xia Dynasty.

He banished the tribe of Gonggong to Youzhou [Hebei, north China], sent the tribe of Guandou to the Chong Mountains [Hunan, south China], drove the three tribes of Miao to Sanwei [southwest China], and annihilated the tribe of Gun in Yushan [Shandong, east China]. . . .[5]

Since then, virtually uninterrupted conflict between the people of the Yellow River valley and the surrounding "barbarians" have been recorded in various Chinese classic writings. The capital of the first historical dynasty of China (Xia, ca. 2205–1766 B.C.) was forced to relocate eight times[6], in an west-east pattern as a result of battles with the "barbarians". For similar reasons, the capital of the Shang Dynasty (ca. 1766–1122 B.C.) also was moved eight times.[7]

In 1122 B.C., a confederation of western "barbarians", under the Zhou leader Wu, marched eastward, fought a decisive battle in the fields of Mu on the banks of Huanghe and put an end to the Shang Dynasty (see Figures 392–394).

Despite close affiliations with the "barbarians", the Zhou people, having adopted the sedentary way of life in the middle reaches of the Yellow River valley, were immediately at war with the "have-not" peoples from all sides.

Our dukes' chariots are a thousand strong, equipped each with two spears and two bows and decorated with red tassels and green ribbons.

The footmen numbered thirty thousand, with sea shells and vermilion strings adorning their helmets.

A great roaring multitude, to drive out the intruding Rong Barbarians in the West and the Di Barbarians in the North; and to launch punitive expeditions against the Jingchu Barbarians in the South.[8]

In 771 B.C. the Zhou capital was overrun by the Quanrong ("Dog Barbarians"). The Zhou king was slaughtered and the seat of government was moved eastward to Luoyang. This was the beginning of a new era designated by historians as the Eastern Zhou Dynasty (770–256 B.C.) which existed almost in name only. Feudal lords of various ethnic Chinese divided the kingdom into independent contending states. To ward off the onslaught of the "barbarians" from the north and also to ward off each other, these states built extensive walls.

In 221 B.C. the western most state, Qin, succeeded in overpowering the other six states to the east, and established the first unified empire of China (see Figures 394 and 395). Under Qin Shihuangdi (First Emperor of Qin), the Great Wall of China was built, utilizing part of the existing walls of the defeated independent states. Some scholars believe the disruption of the southerly movement of the barbarians into China as a result of the Great Wall initiated a chain of counter-movements directly or indirectly causing the steppe barbarians of Alans, Goths, and others to bring down the Roman Empire.[9]

As we know, the Huns, defeated in their attempts to conquer China, eventually turned west and, driving the Goths before them caused the premature downfall of the Roman Empire.[10]

By extension, the transmission of this interactive chain of movement must have been felt also in northeast Asia and perhaps in the Americas. Heine-Geldern has pointed out the resemblance of pottery forms of Mesoamerica (Teotihuacan) to those of China at about this period.[11] To this I might add that the largest truncated pyramid (the First Emperor's tomb) in east Asia was built at this time. This pyramid measures approximately 230 feet in height and approximately 1500 feet each in width and length. Roughly three hundred years later the largest truncated pyramid in Mesoamerica of that time was also constructed in Teotihuacan, measuring 240 feet in height and 740 feet on each side.

Parallel to the formation of the first unified empire in China, a similar political transformation among the "barbarians" in the steppes north of China also took place. The first Xiongnu Empire (209–141 B.C.) was created encompassing a vast confederation of nomadic tribal groups of mainly Turanian ethnic affinity. The Qin Dynasty collapsed in less than two decades and was replaced by the Han (206 B.C.–A.D.

220). From this period onward the direction of "barbarian" invading thrust followed a "north to south" axis instead of the traditional "west to east" axis. Figures 396–407 illustrate the alternate dominance in China proper between the "barbarians" and the Chinese. Far differing from the commonly held view that China had been a self-contained, closed or stagnant nation, the sequence of maps provided here demonstrates the turbulent character of the Chinese historical development. Almost every other dynasty in China, after the Han period, was ruled by the "barbarians" who conquered China but adopted the Chinese way of life. The impact of these tempestuous racial-political convulsions must have been far-reaching. As a different (it was a civil war) but related case in point: the rise of the Beijing regime dislodged millions of Nationalists from the Chinese mainland to the island of Taiwan in the late 1940s. The influx from the mainland in turn, forced some of the native Taiwanese to seek refuge in America where they launched the so-called "independent movement".

Herein lies the propelling forces for trans- or circumpacific contacts, involuntary as they might have been.

So far I have attempted to trace the origin of the early Americans, their lithic industries, as well as the form and meaning of their material remains. I have outlined the processes, mechanisms and the motivating forces for interhemispheric cultural diffusion. There is no doubt in my mind that ancient American cultures are integral parts of the global cultural continuum, via genealogical heritage, as well as stimulative diffusion. There is equally no doubt in my mind that the people of the ancient Americas created their own magnificent cultural expression and personality. Cultures, however, like humans, are products of a protracted process of interactive evolution.

> No civilization has arisen from a single focus. If we must have a metaphor, we would do better to compare the progress of civilization to the propagation of waves on a rising tide. Its genesis is the interaction of cultures, and no isolated and homogeneous culture has ever risen much beyond its original level.[12]

The ancient Chinese and Americans comprehended the act of creation as interactive and dualistic in nature. They endowed their gods with like attributes. Do the products of their cultures support a monolithic, non-interactive, independent creation of ancient American cultures? I believe not.

The study of cultural genesis differs from the study of ethnological, lithic or ceramic origins. It involves not only descriptive analysis and scientific methodologies but also affective comprehension of inner meaning. Such study demands cognitive as well as intuitive awareness of the aesthetic gestalt: the empathetic ability to grasp the cultural whole which is greater than the sum of its parts.

In this regard, I find the discipline of Olmec archaeology most lacking. I present the following examples[13], not as a personal attack on the scholars involved, but rather as an earnest appeal for open-minded, inter-disciplinary and cross-cultural cooperation in the search for the true beginnings of the American cultures.

Monument H (Figure 410) is one of many blatant examples of visual illiteracy or, at best, visual insensitivity within the field of Olmec archaeology. This sculpture was first published in 1943, in the *National Geographic Magazine* and in the *Bulletin of the Bureau of American Ethnology,* as an owl. Thirty years later, in 1973, it was cataloged again as an owl (lechuza) in *Escultura monumental olmeca*[14]. At the present time (1983) it is still being exhibited, in an upside down position, as an owl!

As is clearly shown in Figures 411–413 (the photographs having been rotated 180 degrees), the sculpture is actually the head of the most common Olmec deity: God I—the anthropomorphic dragon.

It is difficult to comprehend, that in the forty years since Monument H was first published and subsequently placed in public exhibition, that not one single scholar noticed this work was placed upside down and misidentified as an owl.

Another problem extant in Olmec archaeology which deserves urgent address is the incidence of chronological ambiguity, temporal misplacement and stylistic misinterpretation. In my earlier publication (Shao, 1976, p. 101), I alluded to this problem.

As is evident in Figures 414–430, the commonly accepted 1150–900 B.C. Preclassic placement[15] of San Lorenzo Olmec monumental sculptures (and 900–600 B.C. for those at La Venta) is at best tentative, and at worst, like "Monument H", upside down.

Practically all major monumental Olmec sculpture was not produced at the sites at which they were excavated.[16] The importance of stylistic seriation is further underscored by the fact that at one time or another virtually all of these monuments were mutilated, buried, or reburied. "The overwhelming majority of San Lorenzo Tenochtitlan sculptures have no strategraphic associations whatsoever. . . ."[17] Thus, formal and iconographic correlation are doubly important in determining the interactive evolutionary sequence of Mesoamerican cultures.

As to the interaction of stimulus and response, the intermingling of the flow with the blocking of the flow: their coming cannot be prevented, their going cannot be stopped: underground things go on like shadows vanishing, back to life they come like echoes awakening. Comes the lightening release of nature's spring. . . .

Lu Ji, *Wenfu*
ca. A.D. 360

Notes

1. One of the measuring instruments of a statistic model for testing the validity of cultural diffusion, which I am constructing for another research project.
2. See Chapter III, Paragraph 1.
3. Betty Meggers, Clifford Evans and Emilio Estrada, 1965, ibid., p. 167.
4. Chen Yan, "Silk Roads of the Sea", *China Reconstructs,* December, 1982, pp. 47–50.
5. *Shu Jing* (Book of Historical Documents), ca. 1122 B.C.–A.D. 320.
6. *Zhu Shu Ji Nian* (Bamboo Annals), ca. 300 B.C.
7. Guo Moruo, *Historical Atlas of China,* Beijing: Atlas Press, 1979, Vol. 1, p. 12
8. *Shi Jing* (Book of Odes), ca. 900–500 B.C.
9. Joseph Needham, *Science and Civilization in China,* Cambridge: University Press, Vol. 1, 1954, pp. 183–184.
10. William McGovern, *The Early Empires of Central Asia,* Chapel Hill: North Carolina Press, 1939, p. 114.
11. Robert Heine-Geldern, "The Problem of Transpacific Influences in Mesoamerica", *Handbook of the Middle Americans,* Vol. 4, edited by Gordon Ekholm and Gordon Willey, 1966, p. 282.
12. Tatiana Proskouriakoff, "Olmec and Mayan Art: Problems of Their Stylistic Relations," *Dumbarton Oaks Conference on the Olmec,* Edited by Elizabeth Benson, Washington, D.C.: Dumbarton Oaks, 1968, p. 119.
13. In *Olmec Art: Form and Meaning* which is being prepared, many other such examples will be illustrated.
14. Beatriz de La Fuenta, *Escultura monumental olmeca,* Mexico: Instituto de Investigaciones Esteticas, Universidad Nacional Autonoma de Mexico, 1973, p. 300.
15. Michael Coe and Richard Diehl, 1980, ibid., p. 295.
16. Ibid., p. 297.
17. Ibid., p. 294. When a multitude of late monumental sculptures were buried at an early site, one or two of these sculptures were bound to be covered with earth possessing the original stratigraphic sequence of the *site.* The overwhelming majority of Olmec sculptures also have no stylistic and iconographic association with the ceramic sequences at major Olmec sites.

410. "Owl", Monument H, Preclassic Period, ca. 1150 B.C.–A.D. 300, Tres Zapotes, Veracruz, Mexico (Collection of the Regional Museum of the National Museum of Anthropology, Tres Zapotes). A case of visual illiteracy.

411–413. Olmec God I, (Figure 410 turned upside down).

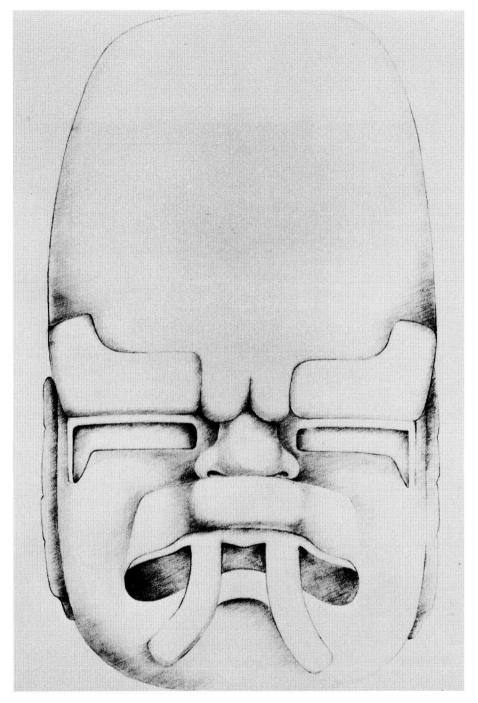

412.

413.

414. Bearded royal personage, detail of Stela 1, late Classic Period, ca. A.D. 869, Seibal, Peten, Guatemala.

415. Bearded royal personage, detail of Stela 3, Preclassic Period, ca. 1150 B.C.–A.D. 300, La Venta, Tabasco, Mexico (Collection of the La Venta Museum, Villahermosa).

416. Bearded royal personage, Stela C, late Classic Period, ca. A.D. 782, Copan, Honduras.

417. Bearded royal personage, Stela 2, Preclassic Period, ca. 1150 B.C.–A.D. 300, La Venta, Tabasco, Mexico (Collection of the La Venta Museum, Villahermosa).

418, 419. Bearded royal personage, Altar 7, Preclassic Period, ca. 1150 B.C.–A.D. 300, La Venta, Tabasco, Mexico (Collection of the La Venta Museum, Villahermosa).

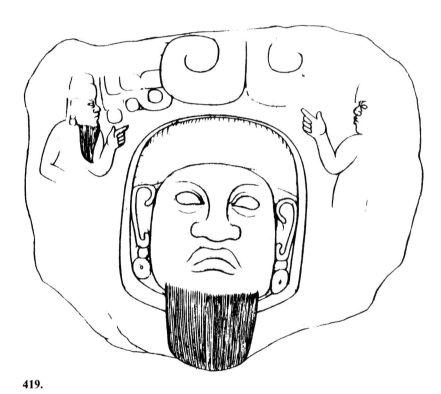

419.

420. Bearded royal personage, stone altar, Postclassic
Period, ca. A.D. 900–1500, Veracruz (Collection
of the Museum of Anthropology, University of
Veracruz, Jalapa).

421. Personage with bird-headdress, detail of a sculptured column, late Classic Period, ca. A.D. 750–900, El Tajín, Veracruz, Mexico.

422. Personage with bird-headdress, detail of Altar 7, Preclassic Period, ca. 1150 B.C.–A.D. 300, La Venta, Tabasco, Mexico (Collection of the La Venta Museum, Villahermosa).

423, 424. Altar 7, (side view), Preclassic Period, ca. 1150 B.C.—A.D. 300, La Venta, Tabasco, Mexico (Collection of the La Venta Museum, Villahermosa).

424.

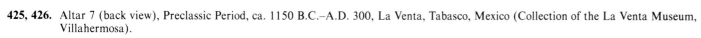

425, 426. Altar 7 (back view), Preclassic Period, ca. 1150 B.C.–A.D. 300, La Venta, Tabasco, Mexico (Collection of the La Venta Museum, Villahermosa).

427, 428. Olmec seated figure with stylized headdress, Monument 77, Preclassic Period, ca. 1150 B.C.–A.D. 300, La Venta, Tabasco, Mexico (Collection of the La Venta Museum, Villahermosa).

429. Aztec seated figure with stylized headdress, late Postclassic Period, ca. A.D. 1200–1500, Mexico, (Collection of the British Museum, London).

430. Olmec seated pole-figure with stylized headdress, Preclassic Period, ca. 1150 B.C.–A.D. 300, San Lorenzo, Veracruz, Mexico (Collection of the National Museum of Anthropology, Mexico City).

Bibliography

Aigner, J. S.

   1976 "Early Holocene Evidence for the Aleut Maritime Adaptation." *Arctic Anthropology,* Vol. 13, pp. 32–45.

   1978 "Important Archaeological Remains from North China." In *Early Remains in Early Paleolithic in South and East Asia,* pp. 193–232. (F. Ikawa Smith, ed.). The Hague: Mouton.

Aigner, J. S., Laughlin, W. S.

   1973 "The Dating of Lantian Man and the Significance for Analyzing Trends in Human Evolution." *American Journal of Physical Anthropology,* Vol. 39, pp. 97–110.

Alexander, H. L.

   1963 "The Levi Site: A Paleo-Indian Campsite in Central Texas." *American Antiquity,* Vol. 28, pp. 510–528.

An, Zhimin

   1947 "The Stone Knives of Anyang." *Yenching Journal of Chinese Studies,* Monograph Series No. 33.

   1954 "A List of Reference Books of Chinese Prehistory." *Yenching Journal of Chinese Studies,* Monograph Series No. 23.

   1959 "The Sites of Miaodigou and Sanliqiao." *Archaeological Excavations at the Yellow River Reservoirs Report,* No. 2. Beijing: Science Press.

   1965 "Trial Diggings on the Paleolithic Cave Deposits at Hsiaonanhai in Anyang, Honan Province." *Kaogu Xuebao,* No. 1.

   1973 "A Tentative Interpretation of the Western Han Silk Painting Recently Discovered at Changsha." *Kaogu Xuebao,* No. 1.

   1973 "The Chin Pan and Chin Ping Coins—A Study of the Gold Coins of the State of Chu and Han Dynasties and Some Related Problems." *Kaogu Xuebao,* No. 2.

   1978 "Mesolithic Remains at Hailarin Heilungkiang Province—With Notes on The Origin of the Microlithic Tradition." *Kaogu Xuebao,* No. 3.

   1979 "The Sites of Peiligang, Cishan and Yangshao—A Tentative Study of the Origin and Development of the Neolithic Culture on the Central Plains." *Kaogu Xuebao,* No. 4.

   1979–1980 "The Neolithic Archaeology of China—A Brief Survey of the Last Thirty Years." *Early China,* No. 5.

   1981 "Some Problems Concerning China's Early Copper and Bronze Artifacts." *Kaogu Xuebao,* No. 3.

   1982 *Essays on the Neolithic in China.* Beijing: Wenwu Press.

   1982 *History of Pottery and Porcelain in China.* Beijing: Wenwu Press.

   1982 "China's Neolithic Period." *China Reconstructs,* Vol. XXXI, No. 6.

   1982 "Paleoliths and Microliths from Shenja and Shaunghu, Northern Tibet." *Currently Anthropology,* Vol. 23, No. 5.

Anderson, D. D.

   1970 "Microblade Traditions in Northwestern Alaska." *Arctic Anthropology,* Vol. 6, pp. 2–16.

   1972 "An Archaeological Survey of Noatak Drainage, Alaska." *Arctic Anthropology,* Vol. 9, No. 1, pp. 66–117.

Andrews, E. Wyllys, V.

   1977 "The Southeastern Periphery of Mesoamerica: A View from Eastern El Salvador." In *Social Process in Maya Prehistory: Studies in Honor of Sir Eric Thompson,* pp. 113–134. (Norman Hammond, ed.). San Francisco: Academic Press.

Archaeological Team of Heilongjiang Province

1979 "Excavations of the Site of Xinkailiu in Mishan County." *Kaogu Xuebao,* No. 4, pp. 491–516.

Aveleyra Arroyo Deanda, L.

1965 "Una Nueva Cabeza Colosal Olmeca." *Boletin del Instituto Nacional de Antropologia e Historia,* num 20, pp. 12–14, Mexico.

Badner, Mino

1972 "A Possible Focus of Andean Artistic Influence in Mesoamerica." *Studies in Pre-Columbian Art and Archaeology,* No. 9. Washington, D.C.: Dumbarton Oaks.

Ball, Hal C.

1975 "Radiocarbon Dating of 'Pot Belly' Statuary in El Salvador." *Newsletter,* Vol. 4, No. 10, p. 4. Miami: Institute of Maya Studies of the Miami Museum of Science.

Balser, Carlos

1959 "Los 'Baby-Faces' Olmecas de Costa Rica." *Actas del XXXIII Congreso Internacional de Americanistas, San Jose, 20–27 Julio 1958,* tomo II, pp. 280–285. San Jose: Lehmann.

1961 "La Influencia Olmeca en Algunos Motivos de la Arquelogia de Costa Rica." *Imforme Semestral,* enero a junio 1961, pp. 63–78. San Jose: Instituto Geographico de Costa Rica, Ministerior de Obras Publicas.

1965 "El Jade Precolombino de America." *Boletin Imformativo, No. 15,* pp. 31–50. San Jose: Museo Nacional de Costa Rica.

1969 "A New Style of Olmec Jade with String Sawing from Costa Rica." *Verhand-lungen des XXXVIII. Internationalen Amerikanisten Kongresses, Stuttgart-Munchen, 12. bis 18. August 1968,* Band I, pp. 243–247. Munchen: Kommissionsverlag Klaus Renner.

1974 *El Jade de Costa Rica: Un Album Arqueolo'gico.* San Jose.

Beebe, B. F.

1980 "A Domestic Dog (Canis Familiaris) of Probable Pleistocene Age From Old Crow, Yukon Territory, Canada." *Canadian Journal of Archaeology 4.*

Benson, Elizabeth P.

1971 "An Olmec Figure at Dumbarton Oaks." *Studies in Pre-Columbian Art and Archaeology,* No. 8. Washington, D.C.: Dumbarton Oaks.

1976 "Motifs in Olmec Sculpture." *Actas del XXIII Congreso Internacionale de Historia del Arte: Espana entre el Mediterraneo yel Atlantico, Granada 1973,* Vol. I, pp. 65–80. Granada: Universidad de Granada, Departamento de Historia del Arte.

Benson, Elizabeth P., ed.

1968 *Dumbarton Oaks Conference on the Olmec.* October 28th and 29th, 1967. Washington D.C.: Dumbarton Oaks Research Library and Collection.

Berger, Rainer; Graham, John A.; and Heizer, Robert F.

1967 "A Reconsideration of the La Venta Site." In *Studies in Olmec Archaeology,* pp. 1–24, *Contributions of the University of California Archaeological Research Facility, No. 3.* Berkeley.

Bernal, Ignacio

1967 "La Presencia Olmeca en Oaxaca." Conferencia Mimeografiada, *Serie Culturas de Oaxaca,* num. 1. Mexico: Departmento de Difusion Cultural, Museo Nacional de Antropologia.

1968 "View of Olmec Culture." *Dumbarton Oaks Conference on the Olmecs,* pp. 135–142. Washington, D.C.: Dumbarton Oaks Research Library and Collection.

1968 "Olmecas y Olmecoides." Conferencia Mimeografiada, *Serie Los Olmecas*, Mexico: Departamento de Difusion Cultural, Museo Nacional de Antropologia.

1969 *The Olmec World.* (Trans. by Doris Heyden and Fernando Horcasitas.) Berkeley: University of California Press.

1971 "The Olmec Region-Oaxaca." *Contributions of the University of California Archaeological Research Facility, No. 11,* pp. 29–50, Berkeley.

Bernal, Ignacio, and Andy Seuffert

1979 "The Ballplayers of Dainzu." *Artes Americanae,* Vol. 2.

Black, R. F.

1974 "Late Quarternary Sea Level Changes, Umnak Island, Aleutians: Their Effects on Ancient Aleuts and Their Causes." *Quaternary Research,* Vol. 4, pp. 264–281.

Blom, Frans, and Lafarge Oliver

1926–1927 "Tribes and Temples: A Record of the Expedition to Middle America." Conducted by the Tulane University of Louisiana in 1925 2. Vols. *Middle American Research Series, Tulane University of Louisiana Publication I* New Orleans.

Boggs, Stanley H.

1950 " 'Olmec' Pictographs in the Las Victorias Group, Chalchuapa Archaeological Zone, El Salvador." *Notes on Middle American Archaeology and Ethnology,* Vol. IV, No. 99, pp. 85–92. Cambridge: Carnegie Institution of Washington.

Borhegyi, Stephan F. de

1961 "Miniature Mushroom Stones from Guatemala." *American Antiquity,* Vol. 26, No. 4, pp. 498–504.

Bove, Frederick J.

1978 "Laguna de Los Cerros: An Olmec Central Place." *Journal of New World Archaeology,* Vol. 2, No. 3, pp. 1–56.

Bruggemann, Jurgen, and Hers, Marie-Areti

1970 "Exploraciones Argueologicas en San Lorenzo Tenochtitlan." *Instituto Nacional de Antropologia e Historia, Boletin 39,* pp. 18–23.

Bryan, A. L.

1978 "An El Jobo Mastodon Kill at Taima—Taima, Venezuela." *Science,* Vol. 200, pp. 1275–1277.

Bryan, Alan Lyle, ed.

1978 *Early Man in America from a Circum-Pacific Perspective.* Edmonton: Archaeological Researches International.

Bushnell, Geoffrey H. S.

1964 "An Olmec Jade Formerly Belonging to Alfred Maudslay." *XXXV Congreso Internacional de Americanistas, Mexico, 1962 Actas y Memorias,* Vol. I, pp. 541–542. Mexico: Instituto Nacional de Antropologia.

Campbell, John M.

1962 "Prehistoric Cultural Relations Between the Artic and Temperate Zones of North American," (Campbell, John M. ed.). *Artic Institute of North America Technical Papers,* No. 11. New York: Johnson Reprint Corporation.

Carlson, John B.

1975 "Lodestone Compass: Chinese or Olmec Primary?" *Science,* Vol 189, pp. 753–760.

Carneiro, Robert L.

1970 "A Theory of the Origin of the State." *Science,* Vol. 169, No. 3947, pp. 733–738.

Carter, George F.

1963 "Plants Across the Pacific." *Memoirs, Society for American Archaeology,* Vol. 9, pp. 62–71.

1976 "Chinese Contacts with America: Fu-Sang Again." *Anthropological Journal of Canada.*

1977 "A Hypothesis Suggesting the Possibility of a Single Origin of Agriculture." In *Origins of Agriculture.* (Charles A. Reed, ed.). Chicago: Aldine Publishing Company.

Caso, Alfonso

1942 "Definicion y Estension del Camplejo 'Olmeca.' " *Sociedad Mexicana de Antropologia, Mayas y Olmecas,* Segunda Reunion de Mesa Redonda sobre Problemas Antropolocicos de Mexico y Centro America, pp. 43–46. Mexico.

1947 "Calendario y Escritura de las Antiguas Culturas de Monte Alban." *Obras Completas de Miguel O. de Mendizabal,* Vol 1. Mexico.

1964 "Posibilidades de un Imperio 'Olmeca.' " *Conferencia sustentada en El Colegio Nacional de Mexico, agosto 24, 1964.* Mexico.

1965 "Existo un Imperio Olmeca?" *Memoria del Colegio Nacional,* Tomo V, num. 3, pp. 1–52. Mexico.

1965 "Sculpture and Mural Painting of Oaxaca." In *Handbook of Middle American Indians,* Vol. 3, Part 2, pp. 849, 870. Austin: University of Texas Press.

1965 "Zapotec Writing and Calendar." In *Handbook of Middle American Indians,* Vol. 3, Part 2, pp. 931–947. Austin: University of Texas Press.

Caso, Alfonso; Bernal, Ignacio; and Acosta, Jorge R.

1967 "La Ceramica de Monte Alban." *Memorias del Instituto Nacional de Antropologia e Historia, XIII.* Mexico: Secretaria de Educacion Publica.

Ceravantes, Maria Antonieta

1967 "Una Estela Olmeca de Dos Caras." *Boletin del Instituto Nacional de Antropologia e Historia,* num. 28, pp. 32–35. Mexico.

1968 "Revision de una Escultura Olmeca de Arroyo Sonso, Veracruz." *Boletin del Instituto Nacional de Antropologia e Historia,* num. 33, pp. 46–50. Mexico.

1969 "Dos Elementos de uso Ritual en el Arte Olmeca." *Anales del Instituto Nacional de Antropologia e Historia, epoca 7al,* tomo I, 1967–1968, pp. 37–51. Mexico: Secretaria de Educacion Publica.

1974 "Una Nueva Escultura de San Lorenzo, Ver." *Anales del Instituto de Investigaciones Esteticas,* num. 43, pp. 57–62. Mexico: Universidad Nacional Autonoma de Mexico.

1976 "Le Estela de Alvarado." *Actas del XLI Congreso Internacional de Americanistas, Mexico, 2 al 7 de septiembre de 1974,* Vol. II, pp. 309–322. Mexico: Instituto Nacional de Antropologia e Historia.

Chang, Kwang-Chih

1977 *The Archaeology of Ancient China.* New Haven: Yale University Press.

1980 *Shang Civilization.* New Haven: Yale University Press.

1981 "In Search of China's Beginnings: New Light on an Old Civilization." *American Scientist,* Vol. 69, pp. 148–160.

Chapman, Anne M.

1957 "Port of Trade Enclaves in Aztec and Maya Civilizations." In *Trade and Market in Early Empires,* pp. 114–153. (K. Polanyl, C. M. Arsenberg, and H. W. Pearson, ed.). Glencoe: Free Press.

Chow, Benshun

1978 "The Distribution of the Woolly Rhinoceros and Woolly Mammoth," *Vertebrata PalAsiatica,* Vol. 6, No. 1, pp. 59.

Clewlow, C. William, Jr.

1970 "A Comparison of Two Unusual Olmec Monuments." *Contributions of the University of California Archaeological Research Facility, No. 8*, pp. 35–40. Berkeley.

1974 "A Stylistic and Chronological Study of Olmec Monumental Sculpture." *Contributions of the University of California Archaeological Research Facility, No. 19*. Berkeley.

Clewlow, C. William Jr.; Cowan, Richard A.; O'Connel, James F.; and Benemann, Charles

1967 "Colossal Heads of the Olmec Culture." *Contributions of the University of California, Archaeological Research Facility, No. 4*. Berkeley.

Cobean, Robert H.; Coe, Michael D.; Perry, Edward A., Turekian Kark K.; and Kharkar, Dinkar P.

1971 "Obsidian Trade at San Lorenzo Tenochtitlan, Mexico," *Science*, Vol. 174, pp. 666–671.

Coe, Michael D.

1957 "Cycle 7 Monuments in Middle America: A Reconsideration." *American Anthropologist*, Vol. LIX, No. 4, pp. 597–611.

1961 "La Victoria: An Early Site on the Pacific Coast of Guatemala." *Papers of the Peabody Museum, Harvard University*, Vol. 53. Cambridge.

1962 "An Olmec Design on an Early Peruvian Vessel." *American Antiquity*, Vol. 27, No. 4, pp. 579–580.

1962 "Preliminary Report on Archaeological Investigations in Coastal Guanacaste, Costa Rica." *Internationalen Amerikanisten Kongresses, Wien, 18–25 Juli 1960*, pp. 358–365. Verlag Ferdinand Berger, Horn-Wien.

1963 "Olmec and Chavin: Rejoinder to Lanning." *American Antiquity*, Vol. 29, pp. 101–104.

1965 *The Jaguar's Children: Pre-Classic Central Mexico*. New York: The Museum of Primitive Art.

1965 "Archaeological Synthesis of Southern Veracruz and Tabasco." In *Handbook of Middle American Indians*, Vol. 3, Part 2, pp. 679–715. Austin: University Texas Press.

1965 "The Olmec Style and Its Distributions." In *Handbook of Middle American Indians*, Vol. 3, pp. 739–775. (Robert Wacichope, ed.). Austin: University Texas Press.

1966 "An Early Stone Pectoral From Southeastern Mexico." *Studies in Pre-Columbian Art and Archaeology*, No. I. Washington, D.C.: Dumbarton Oaks.

1966 *The Maya*, London: Thames and Hudson.

1967 "An Olmec Serpentine Figurine at Dumbarton Oaks." *American Antiquity*, Vol. 32, No. I, pp. 111–113.

1967 "Solving a Monumental Mystery." *Discovery*, Vol. 3, No. I, pp. 21–26.

1968 *America's First Civilization*. New York: American Heritage and Smithsonian Institution.

1968 "San Lorenzo and the Olmec Civilization, In *Dumbarton Oaks Conference on the Olmec, October 28 and 29*, pp. 41–78. (Elizabeth P. Benson, ed.) Washington, D.C.: Dumbarton Oaks Research Library and Collection.

1970 "The Archaeological Sequence at San Lorenzo Tenochtitlan, Veracruz, Mexico." In *Magnetometer Survey of the La Venta Pyramid and Other Papers on Mexican Archaeology*, pp. 21–34. *Contributions of the University of California Archaeological Research Facility, No. 8*, Berkeley.

1972 "Olmec Jaguars and Olmec Kings." In *The Cult of the Feline: A Conference in Pre-Columbian Iconography, October 31 and November 1, 1970*, pp. 1–18. (Elizabeth P. Benson, ed.). Washington, D.C.: Dumbarton Oaks Research Library.

1973 "The Iconology of Olmec Art." In *The Iconography of Middle American Sculpture*, pp. 1–12. New York: The Metropolitan Museum of Art.

1977 "Olmec and Maya: A Study in Relationships." In *The Origins of Maya Civilization*, pp. 183–195. (Richard E. W. Adams, ed.). *School of American Research Advanced Seminar Series*. Albuquerque: University of New Mexico.

Coe, Michael D., and Diehl, Richard A.

1980 *In the Land of the Olmec*. 2 vols. Austin: University of Texas Press.

Coe, Michael D., and Flannery, Kent V.

1967 "Early Cultures and Human Ecology in South Coastal Guatemala." *Smithsonian Contributions to Anthropology 3.* Washington, D.C.: Smithsonian Institution.

Coe, William R.

1965 "Tikal, Guatemala, and Emergent Maya Civilization." *Science,* No. 3664, pp. 1401–1419.

Covarrubias, Miguel

1942 "Origen y Desarrollo del Estilo Artistico 'Olmec.' " In *Mayas y Olmecas: Segunda Reunion de Mesa Redonda Sobrey Problemas Antropologicos de Mexico y Centro America, Tuxtla Gutierrez, Chiapas,* pp. 46–49. Mexico: Sociedad Mexicana de Antropologia.

1944 "La Venta, Colossal Heads and Jaguar Gods." *The Review of Modern Art,* No. 6, pp. 24–33. Mexico.

1946 "El Arte 'Olmeca' o de LaVenta." *Cuadernos Americanos,* Vol. XXVIII, num. 4, pp. 153–179. Mexico.

1946 *Mexico South, the Isthmus of Tehuantepec.* New York: Alfred A. Knopf.

1954 *The Eagle, the Jaguar, and the Serpent.* New York: Alfred A. Knopf.

1957 *Indian Art of Mexico and Central America.* New York: Alfred A. Knopf.

1961 *Arte Indigena de Mexico y Centroamerica.* (Trans. by Sol Arguedas). Mexico: Universidad Nactional Autonoma de Mexico.

Crook, W. W., and Harris, R. K.

1958 "A Pleistocene Campsite near Lewisville, Texas." *American Antiquity,* Vol. 23, pp. 233–246.

Davis, E. L.

1978 "Association of People and a Rancholabrean Fauna at China Lake, California." In *Early Man in America from a Circum-Pacific Perspective,* pp. 183–217. (A. L. Bryan, ed.). *Occasional Papers No. 1* Edmonton: Department of Anthropology, University of Alberta.

De La Fuenta, Beatriz

1971 "En Torno a las Nuevas Cabezas Olmecas." *Anales del Instituto de Investigaciones Esteticas,* num. 40, pp. 5–11. Mexico: Universidad Nacional Autonoma de Mexico.

1972 "Escultura Monumental Olmeca." *Artes de Mexico,* num. 154, pp. 6–9, Mexico.

1973 *Catalogo de la Escultura Monumental Olmeca.* Mexico: Instituto de Investigaciones Esteticas, Universidad Nacional Autonoma de Mexico.

1975 *Las Cabezas Colosales Olmecas.* Mexico: Fondo de Cultura Economica.

1977 *Los Hombres de Piedra: Escultura Olmeca.* Mexico: Instituto de Investigaciones Esteticas, Universidad Nacional Autonoma de Mexico.

Demarest, A.; Switsur, R.; Berger, R.

1982 "The Dating and Cultural Associations of the 'Potbellied' Sculptural Style: New Evidence from Western El Salvador." *American Antiquity,* Vol. 47, No. 3, pp. 557–570.

Derevianko, A. P.

1978 "The Problem of Lower Paleolithic in the South of the Soviet Far East." *Early Paleolithic in South and East Asia,* pp. 303–315. (F. Ikawa-Smith, ed.). The Hague: Mouton.

1978 "On the Migrations of Ancient Man from Asia to America in the Pleistocene Epoch." *Early Man in America from a Circum-Pacific Perspective,* pp. 70–72. Edmonton: Archaeological Researches International.

Dikov, N. N.

1968 "The Discovery of the Paleolithic in Kamchatka and the Problem of the Initial Occupation of America." *Arctic Anthropologist,* Vol. 5, pp. 19–203.

1978 "Ancestors of Paleo-Indians and Proto-Eskimo Aleuts in the Paleolithic of Kamchatka." In *Early Man in America from a Circum-Pacific Perspective,* pp. 68–70. Edmonton: Archaeological Researches International.

Dillon, Brian D.

1975 "Notes on Trade in Ancient Mesoamerica." In *Three Papers on Mesoamerican Archaeology,* pp. 79–135. *Contributions of the University of California Archaeological Research Facility,* No. 24. Berkeley.

Dixon, Keith A.

1959 "Ceramics from Two Preclassic Periods at Chiapa de Corzo, Chiapas, Mexico." *New World Archaeological Foundation,* Papers 5.

1970 "Archaeology and Geology in the Calico Mountains: Results of the International Conference on the Calico Project." *Important,* 1:10 (Special Issue). Berkeley: California State University.

1977 "Early Man at Owl Cave: Geology and Archaeology of the Wasden Site, Eastern Snake River Plain, Idaho." *Paper Presented at the 42nd Annual Meeting of the Society for American Archaeology, New Orleans.*

Drucker, Philip

1943 "Ceramic Sequences at Tres Zapotes, Veracruz, Mexico." *Bureau of American Ethnology, Bulletin 140.* Washington, D.C.: Smithsonian Institution.

1947 "Some Implications of the Ceramic Complex at La Venta." *Smithsonian Miscellaneous Collection,* Vol. CVII, No. 8. Washington, D.C.: Smithsonian Institution.

1952 "La Venta, Tabasco: A Study of Olmec Ceramics and Art." *Bureau of American Ethnology, Bulletin 153.* Washington, D.C.: Smithsonian Institution.

1952 "Middle Tres Zapotes and the Preclassic Ceramic Sequence." *American Antiquity,* Vol. 17, No. 3, pp. 258–260.

1961 "The La Venta Olmec Support Area." *Kroeber Anthropological Society Papers,* No. 25, pp. 59–72, Berkeley.

Drucker, P.; Heizer, R. F.; and Squier, R. J.

1959 "Excavations at LaVenta, Tabasco, 1955." *Bureau of American Ethnology, Bulletin 170.* Washington, D.C.: Smithsonian Institution.

Duff, Wilson

1975 *Images Stone B.C.,* Toronto: Oxford University Press.

Easby, Elizabeth

1968 *Pre-Columbian Jades from Costa Rica.* New York: Andre Emmerich, Inc.

Easby, Elizabeth Kennedy, and John R. Scott

1970 *Before Cortes: Sculpture of Middle America.* New York: The Metropolitan Museum of Art.

Ekholm, Gordon F.

1950 "Is American Indian Culture Asiatic?" *Natural History,* Vol. 59, No. 8, pp. 344–351, 382.

1955 "The New Orientation Toward Problems of Asiatic-American Relationships." In *New Interpretations of Aboriginal American Culture History,* pp. 95–108, Anthropological Society of Washington.

1964 "The Possible Chinese Origin of Teotihucan Cylindrical Tripod Pottery and Certain Related Traits." *Congreso International de Americanistas, Actas y Memorias,* Vol. 35, No. 1, pp. 39–45.

Ekholm-Miller, Susanna

1973 "The Olmec Rock Carving at Xoc, Chiapas, Mexico." *Papers of the New World Archaeological Foundation, No. 32.* Provo: Brigham Young University.

Eliot, Smith G.

    1924 *Elephants and Ethnologists.* London: Kegan Paul, Trench, Trubner and Company.

    1927 *Culture: The Diffusion Controversy.* London: Norton.

    1933 *The Diffusion of Culture.* London: Watts and Company.

Ericson, J. E.

    1977 "Egalitarian Exchange Systems in California: A Preliminary View." In *Exchange Systems in Prehistory,* pp. 109–126. (T. K. Earle and J. E. Ericson, ed.). San Francisco: Academic Press.

Ericson, J. E.; Taylor, R. E.; and Berger R.

    1982 *Peopling of the New World.* Bellena Press Anthropological Papers No. 23. Los Altos: Bellena Press.

Estrada, Emilio, and Meggers, Betty J.

    1961 "A Complex of Traits of Probable Transpacific Origin on the Coast of Ecuador." *American Anthropologist,* Vol. 63, No. 5, pp. 913–939.

Ferrero, Luis

    1975 *Costa Rica Precolombina: Arqueologia, Etnologia, Tecnologia, Arte.* San Jose: Editorial Costa Rica.

Flannery, Kent V.

    1968 "The Olmec and the Valley of Oaxaca: A Model for Interregional Interaction Informative Times." In *Dumbarton Oaks Conference on the Olmec, October 28 and 29, 1967,* pp. 79–117. (Elizabeth P. Benson, ed.). Washington, D.C.: Dumbarton Oaks Research Library and Collection.

Fletcher, R. C., and Hofmann, A. W.

    1973 "Simple Models of Diffusion and Combined Diffusion—Infiltration Metasomatism." *Carnegie Institution of Washington Publications 634,* pp. 243–259. Washington, D.C.

Fitzhugh, William, ed.

    1975 *Prehistoric Maritime Adaptations of the Circumpolar Zone.* The Hague: Mouton.

Ford, James A.

    1969 "A Comparison of Formative Cultures in the Americas: Diffusion of the Psychic Unity of Man." *Smithsonian Contributions to Anthropology,* Vol. 2. Washington, D.C.

Forde, James A., and Webb, Clarence H.

    1956 "Poverty Point: A Late Archaic Site in Louisiana." *American Museum of Natural History, Anthropological Papers,* Vol. 46, No. 1.

Foshag, William F.

    1955 "Chalchihiutl—A Study in Jade." *American Mineralogist,* Vol. 40, No. 11–12, pp. 1062–1070.

    1957 "Mineralogical Studies on Guatemalan Jade." *Smithsonian Miscellaneous Collections,* Vol. 135, No. 5.

Fraser, Douglas

    1967 *Early Chinese Art and the Pacific Basin: A Photographic Exhibition.* New York: Columbia University.

    1972 "Early Chinese Artistic Influence In Melanesia?" In *Early Chinese Art and Its Possible Influence in the Pacific Basin,* Vol. 3, pp. 597–654. (Noel Barnard, ed.). New York: Intercultural Arts Press.

Funk, R. E.

    1972 "Early Man in the Northeast and the Late Glacial Environment." *Man in the Northeast,* Vol. 4, pp. 7–39.

Furst, Peter T.

    1972 "Symbolism and Psychopharmacology: The Toad as Earth Mother." *Religion en Mesoamerica, XII Mesa Redonda.* pp. 37–46. Mexico: Sociedad Mexicana de Anthropologia.

Gai, Pei

1977 "Preliminary Report on Upper Paleolithic Hutouliang Sites, Hopei, China." *Vertebrate PalAsiastica,* Vol. 15, No. 4, pp. 287–300.

1978 "From North China to North America." *China Reconstructs,* May, pp. 46–48.

Gay, C. T. E.

1966 "Rock Carvings at Chalcacingo." *Natural History,* Vol. 75, No. 7, pp. 57–61.

Gerasimov, M. M.

1964 "The Paleolithic Site on Malta: Excavations of 1956–57." In *Archaeology and Geomorphology of Northern Asia: Selected Works* (Arctic Institute of North America, Anthropology of the North: Translations from Russian Sources 5), pp. 3–32. (H. N. Michael, ed.) Toronto: University of Toronto Press.

Graham, John A.

1977 "Discoveries at Abaj Takalik, Guatemala." *Archaeology,* Vol. 30, No. 3, pp. 196–197.

Green, Dee F., and Gareth W. Lowe

1967 "Altamira and Padre Piedra: Early Pre-classic Sites in Chiapas, Mexico," *New World Archaeological Foundation, Papers 20.*

Green Robertson, Merle

1974 "The Quadripartite Bridge—A Badge of Rulership". In *Primera Mesa Redonda de Palenque,* Part I: A Conference on the Art, Iconography, and Dynastic History of Palenque; Palenque, Chiapas, Mexico, December 14–22, 1973, pp. 77–93. (Merle Greene Robertson, ed.), pp. 77–93. Pebble Beach: The Robert Louis Stevenson School.

Green Robertson, Merle; Rosenblum Scandizzo, Majorie S., and Scandizzo, John R.

1976 "Physical Deformities in the Ruling Lineage of Palenque, and the Dynastic Implications." In the *Art, Iconography and Dynastic History of Palenque,* Part III: Proceedings of the Segunda Mesa Redonda de Palenque, December 14–21, 1974—Palenque pp. 59–86. (Merle Greene Robertson ed.). Pebble Beach: The Robert Louis Stevenson School.

Grove, David C.

1968 "Chalcazingo, Morelos, Mexico: A Reappraisal of the Olmec Rock Carvings." *American Antiquity,* Vol. 33, pp. 486–491.

1968 "The Pre-Classic Olmec in Central Mexico: Site Distribution and Inferences." *Dumbarton Oaks Conference on the Olmecs,* pp. 178–185. Washington, D.C.: Dumbarton Oaks Research Library and Collection.

1969 "Olmec Cave Paintings: Discovery from Guerrero, Mexico." *Science,* Vol. 164, pp. 421–423.

1970 "The Olmec Paintings of Oxtotitlan Cave, Guerrero, Mexico." *Studies in Pre-Colombian Art and Archaeology, No. 6.* Washington, D.C.: Dumbarton Oaks Research Library and Collection.

1970 "Los Murales de la Cueva de Oxtotitlan, Acatlan, Guerrero." *Serie Investigaciones,* num. 23. Mexico: Institute Nacional de Antropologia e Historia.

1972 "Olmec Felines in Highland Central Mexico." In *The Cult of the Feline,* pp. 153–164. Washington, D.C.: Dumbarton Oaks Research Library and Collection.

1973 "Olmec Altars and Myths." *Archaeology,* Vol. 26, No. 2, pp. 128–135.

1973 Reivew of "Chalcacingo and Xochipala: The Beginnings of Olmec Art by Carlo T. E. Gay. *American Anthropologist,* Vol. 75, No. 4, pp. 1138–1140.

1976 "Olmec Origins and Transpacific Diffusion: Reply to Meggers." *American Anthropologist,* Vol. 78, No. 3, pp. 634–637.

Grove, David C., and Louise I. Paradis

1971 "An Olmec Stela from San Miguel Amuco, Guerrero." *American Antiquity,* Vol. 36, No. I, pp. 95–102.

Hammond, Norman

    1982 *Ancient Maya Civilization.* New Brunswick: Rutgers University Press.

    1982 The Exploration of the Maya World. *American Scientist,* Vol. 70, pp. 482–495.

    1982 Unearthing the Oldest Known Maya. *National Geographic,* July, pp. 126–140.

Harington, C. R.

    1972 "Evidence of Early Man in Old Crow Basin, Yukon Territory." *Arctic Circular,* Vol. 22, pp. 118–128.

    1978 "Quaternary Vertebrate Faunas of Canada and Alaska and their Suggested Chronological Sequence." *Syllogeus,* No. 15. Ottawa: National Museum of Natural Sciences.

Hatch, Marion Popenoe

    1971 "An Hypothesis on Olmec Astronomy, with Special Reference to the La Venta Site. *"Contributions of the University of California Archaeological Research Facility, No. 13,* pp. 1–64. Berkeley.

Haviland, William A.

    1977 "Dynastic Genealogies from Tikal, Guatemala: Implications for Descent and Political Organization." *American Antiquity,* Vol. 42, No. 1, pp. 61–67. Washington, DC: Society for American Archaeology.

Haynes, C. V. Jr.

    1964 "Fluted Projectile Points: Their Age and Dispersion." *Science,* Vol. 145, pp. 1408–1413.

    1967 "Carbon 14 Dates and Early Man in the New World." In *Pleistocene Extinctions: The Search for a Cause,* pp. 267–286. (P.S. Martin and H. E. Wright, Jr., eds.). New Haven: Yale University Press.

    1969 "The Earliest Americans." Science, Vol. 166, pp. 709–715.

    1973 "The Calico Site: Artifacts or Geofacts?" *Science,* Vol. 181, pp. 305–310.

    1973 "Artifacts of Early Man in the New World." *Science,* Vol. 182, pp. 1317–1372.

Heine-Geldern, Robert

    1954 "Die Asiatische Herkunft der Sudamerikanischen Metalltechnik." *Paideuma,* Vol. 5, No. 7–8, pp. 347–423.

    1956 "The Origin of Ancient Civilizations and Toynbee's Theories." *Diogenes,* Vol. 13, pp. 81–99.

    1959 "Chinese Influences in Mexico and Central America: The Tajin Style of Mexico and the Marble Vases from Honduras." *Congreso Internacional de Americanistas, Actas,* Vol. 33, No. 1, pp. 195–206.

    1959 "Chinese Influence in the Pottery of Mexico, Central America, and Colombia." *Congreso Internacional de Americanistas, Actas,* Vol. 33, No. 1, pp. 207–210.

    1959 "Representation of the Asiatic Tiger in the Art of the Chavin Culture: A Proof of Early Contacts Between China and Peru." *Congreso Internacional de Americanistas, Actas,* Vol. 33, No. 1, pp. 321–326.

    1964 "Traces of Indian and Southeast Asiatic Hindu-Buddhist Influences in Mesoamerica." *Congreso Internacional de Americanistas, Actas y Memorisa,* Vol. 35, No. 1, pp. 47–54.

    1966 "Problem of Transpacific Influences in Mesoamerica." In *Handbook of Middle American Indians,* Vol. 4, pp. 277–295. Austin: University of Texas Press.

    1972 "American Metallurgy and the Old World." In *Early Chinese Art and Its Possible Influence in the Pacific Basin.* Vol. 3, pp. 787–822. (Noel Barnard, ed.). New York: Intercultural Arts Press.

Heine-Geldern, Robert, and Ekholm, Gordon F.

    1951 "Significant Parallels in the Symbolic Arts of Southern Asia and Middle America." *International Congress of Americanists Proceedings,* Vol. 29, No. 1, pp. 299–309.

Heizer, Robert F.

1957 "Excavations at La Venta, 1955." *Bulletin of the Texas Archaeological Society,* Vol. XXVII, pp. 98–110, Austin, Texas.

1959 "Specific and Generic Characteristics of Olmec Culture." *Actas del XXXIII Congreso Internacional de Americanistas, San Jose, 1958,* Vol. II, pp. 178–182, San Jose.

1968 "New Observations on La Venta." *Dumbarton Oaks Conference on the Olmecs,* pp. 9–40. Washington, D.C.: Dumbarton Oaks Research Library and Collection.

1971 "Commentary on: the Olmec Region-Oaxaca." *Observations of the Emergence of Civilization in Mesoamerica. Contributions of the University of California Archaeological Research Facility,* No. 11, pp. 55–69. Berkeley.

Heizer, Robert F.; Drucker, P.; and Graham, J. A.

1968 "Investigations at La Venta." 1967. *Contributions of the University of California Archaeological Research Facility, No. 5,* pp. 1–34. Berkeley.

Heizer, Robert F., Graham, John A.; and Napton, Lewis K.

1968 "The 1968 Investigation at La Venta." *Contribution of the University of California, Archaeological Research Facility, Contributions No. 5,* pp. 127–154. Berkeley.

1960 "Olmec Lithic Sources." *Boletin del Centro de Investigaciones Anthropologicas de Mexico,* num 6, pp. 16–17, Mexico.

Hester, T. R., Heozer, R. F.; and Jack, R. N.

1971 "Technology and Geological Sources of Obsidian from Cerro de las Mesas, Veracruz, Mexico, with Observations on Olmec Trade." *Contributions of the University of California Archaeological Research Facility, No. 13,* pp. 133–142. Berkeley.

Henderson, John S.

1979 "Atopula, Guerrero, and Olmec Horizons in Mesoamerica." *Yale University Publications in Anthropology, No. 77.* New Haven: Yale University Press.

Holmes, W. H.

1907 "On a Nephrite Statuette from San Andres Tuxtla, Veracruz, Mexico." *American Anthropologist,* Vol. 9, pp. 691–701.

Hrdlicka, A.

1928 "The Origin and Antiquity of the American Indian." *Smithsonian Annual Report for 1923.* Washington, D.C.: Smithsonian Institution.

Hutterer, K.L.

1976 "An Evolutionary Approach to the Southeast Asian Cultural Sequence." *Current Anthropology,* Vol. 17, pp. 221–242.

Ikawa-Smith, Fumiko, ed.

1978 *Early Paleolithic in South and East Asia.* The Hague: Mouton.

1978 "The History of Early Paleolithic Research in Japan." In *Early Paleolithic in South and East Asia,* pp. 247–286. The Hague: Mouton.

1978 "Introduction: Early Paleolithic Tradition of East Asia." In *Early Paleolithic in South and East Asia,* pp. 1–16. The Hague: Mouton.

Inner Mongolian Team, Institute of Archaeology, Chinese Academy of Social Sciences

1982 "Hongshan Cultural Site at Xishuiquan, Chifeng." *Kaogu Xuebao,* No. 2, pp. 198.

Irving, W. N.

1978 "Pleistocene Archaeology in Eastern Beringia." In *Early Man in America from a circum-Pacific Perspective,* pp. 96–101, (A. L. Bryan, ed.). *Occasional Papers, No. 1.* Edmonton: Department of Anthropology, University of Alberta.

Irving, W. N., and C. R. Harington

1973 "Upper Pleistocene Radiocarbon-dated Artifacts from the Northern Yukon." *Science,* Vol. 179, pp. 335–340.

Izumi, Seiichi, and Terada, Kazuo, eds.

1972 *Andes 4: Excavations at Kotosh, Peru, 1963 and 1966.* Tokyo: University of Tokyo Press.

Jairazbohy, Rafique A.

1974 *Ancient Egyptians and Chinese in America.* London: George Prior Associated Publisher.

Jennings, Jesse D., ed.

1978 *Ancient Native Americans.* San Francisco: W. H. Freeman.

Jennings, Jesse D., and Norbeck, Edward

1964 *Prehistoric Man in the New World.* Chicago: The University of Chicago Press.

Jett, Stephen C.

1971 "Diffusion versus Independent Invention: The Bases of Controversy." In *Man Across the Sea: Problems of Pre-Columbian Contacts,* pp. 5–53. (Carroll L. Riley, et al., ed.). Austin: University of Texas Press.

Jia, Lanpo

1975 *The Cave Home of Peking Man.* Beijing: Foreign Languages Press.

1980 *Early Man in China.* Beijing: Foreign Languages Press.

Jia, Lanpo; Gai, Pei; and You, Yuzhen

1972 "Report on the Excavation of the Late Palaeolithic Site of Shihyu, Shohsien, Shansi." *Kaogu Xuebao,* Vol. 1, pp. 39–58.

Jia, Lanpo, and Wei, Qi

1976 "A Palaeolithic Site at Hsu-Chia-Yao in Yangkao County, Shansi Province." *Kaogu Xuebao,* No. 2, pp. 112–114.

Jia, Lanpo; Wei, Qi; and Li, Zhaorong

1979 "Report on the Excavation of Hsuchiayao Man Site in 1976." *Vertebrata PalAsiatica,* Vol. 17, No. 4, pp. 277–293.

Jimenez Moreno, W.

1942 "El Enigma de los Olmecas." *Cuadernos Americanos,* Ano 1, num. 5, pp. 113–135. Mexico.

1966 "Mesoamerica before the Toltecs." *Ancient Oaxaca,* pp. 1–82. John Paddock, ed. Stanford: Stanford University Press.

Joralemon, P. David

1971 "A Study of Olmec Iconography." *Studies in Pre-Columbian Art and Archaeology, No. 7.* Washington, D.C.: Dumbarton Oaks Research Library and Collection.

1974 "The Olmec Dragon." *A Study in Pre-Columbian Iconography.* New Haven: Yale University.

1976 "The Olmec Dragon: A Study in Pre-Columbian Iconography." *In Origins of Religious Art and Iconography in Preclassic Mesoamerica,* pp. 27–71. (H. B. Nicholson ed.). Los Angeles: Latin American Center, University of California.

Jorgensen, Joseph G.

1972 *Biology and Culture in Modern Perspective.* San Francisco: W. H. Freman and Company.

Kano, Chiaki

1979 "The Origins of the Chavin Culture." *Studies in Pre-Columbian Art & Archaeology.* Washington, D.C.: Dumbarton Oaks, Washington, D.C.

Kelley, David H.

1962 "Glyphic Evidence for a Dynastic Sequence at Quirigua, Guatemala." *American Antiquity,* Vol. 27, No. 3, pp. 323–335.

Kidder, Alfred V.

1947 "The Artifacts of Uaxactun, Guatemala." *Carnegie Institution of Washington, Publication 576*. Washington, D.C.: Carnegie Institution of Washington.

1965 "Preclassic Pottery Figurines of the Guatemalan Highlands." In *Handbook of Middle American Indians,* Vol 2, pp. 146–155. (Robert Wauchope, ed.). Austin: University of Texas Press.

Kidder, Alfred V.; Jennings, Jesse D.; and Shook, Edwin M.

1946 "Excavations at Kaminaljuyu, Guatemala." *Carnegie Institution of Washington, Publication 561*. Washington, D.C.: Carnegie Institution of Washington.

Klein, R. G.

1971 "The Pleistocene Prehistory of Siberia." *Quaternary Research* Vol. I, pp. 133–161.

Kobayashi, T.

1970 "Microblade Industries in the Japanese Archipelago." *Arctic Anthropology,* Vol. 7, pp. 38–58.

Krieger, A. D.

1964 "Early Man in the New World." In *Prehistoric Man in the New World,* pp. 28–81. (J. D. Jennings and E. Norbeck, eds.). Chicago: University of Chicago Press.

Krotser, George

1973 "El Aqua Ceremonial de Las Olmecas." *Instituto Nacional de Antropologia Boletin,* Volume 2, pp. 43–48.

Kubler, George

1962 *The Art and Architecture of Ancient America.* Baltimore: Penguin Books.

Lathrap, Donald W.

1966 "Relationships Between Mesoamerican and the Andean Areas in Archaeological Frontiers and External Connections." In *Handbook of Middle American Indians,* Vol. 4, pp. 265–276. (Gordon R. Ekholm and Gordon R. Willey, eds.). Austin: University of Texas Press.

1971 "The Tropical Forest and the Cultural Context of Chavin." In *Dumbarton Oaks Conference on Chavin, October 26th and 27th, 1968,* pp. 73–100. (Elizabeth P. Benson, ed.). Washington D.C.: Dumbarton Oaks Research Library and Collection.

Laughlin, W. S.

1975 "Aleuts: Ecosystem, Holocene History and Siberian Origin: Soviet and U.S. Scientists Join in a Study of the Origins of the First Americans." *Science,* Vol. 189, pp. 507–515.

Laughlin, W. S. and J. Aigner

1975 "Aleut Adaptation and Evolution." In *Prehistoric Maritime Adaptations of the Circumpolar Zone.* pp. 181–202. (W. Fitzhugh, ed.), The Hague: Mouton.

Laughlin, William S., and Harper, Albert B.

1979 *The First Americans: Origins, Affinities, and Adaptions.* New York, Stuttgart: Gustav Fischer.

Lee, Thomas A., Jr.

1969 "The Artifacts of Chiapa de Corzo, Chiapas, Mexico." *Papers of the New World Archaeological Foundation,* No. 26. Provo: Brigham Young University.

1974 "Mount 4 Excavations at San Isidro, Chiapas, Mexico." *Papers of the New World Archaeological Foundation,* No. 34. Provo: Brigham Young University.

Longyear, John M. III

1952 *Copan Ceramics: A Study of Southeastern Maya Pottery, Publication 597*. Washington, D.C.: Carnegie Institution of Washington.

Lorenzo, Jose Luis

1965 *Tlatilco: Los Artefactos, III*. Mexico: Instituto Nacional de Antropologia e Historia.

Lothrop, Samuel K.

1926 "Stone Sculptures from the Finca Arevalo, Guatemala." *Indian Notes,* Vol. III, No. 3, pp. 147–171. New York: Museum of the American Indian, Heye Foundation.

1955 "Jade and String Sawing in Northeastern Costa Rica." *American Antiquity,* Vol. XXI, No. 1, pp. 43–51.

Lowe, Gareth W., and Agrinier, Pierre

1960 "Mount I, Chiapa de Corzo, Chiapas, Mexico." *New World Archaeological Foundation, Papers 8.*

Luckert, Karl W.

1976 *Olmec Religion: A Key to Middle America and Beyond*. Norman: University of Oklahoma Press.

MacNeish, R. S.

1971 "Early Man in the Andes." *Scientific American,* Vol. 224, pp. 36–46.

1976 "Early Man in the New World." *American Scientist,* Vol. 63, pp. 316–327.

Marshak, Alexander

1975 "Olmec Mosaic Pendant." In *Archaeoastronomy in Pre-Columbian America,* pp. 341–377. (Anthony F. Aveni, ed.). Austin: University of Texas Press, Austin and London.

Martin, P. S.

1973 "The Discovery of America." *Science,* Vol. 179, pp. 969–974.

Matson Moctezuma, Eduardo

1966 "Un Juego de Pelota doble en San Isidro, Chiapas." *Boletin del Instituto Nacional de Antropologia e Historia, No. 25,* pp. 36–37. Mexico.

Maudslay, A. P.

1889–1902 *Biologia Centrali-Americana: Archaeology*. 1 Vol. Text, 4 Vols. Plates. London: R. H. Porter and Dulau and Company.

McBurney, C. B. M.

1975 "Early Man in the Soviet Union: The Implications of Some Recent Discoveries." *Proceedings of the British Academy of Sciences,* Vol. 61, pp. 171–221, London.

Medellin, Zenil A.

1960 "Monolitos Ineditos Olmecas." *La Palabra y el Hombre,* Vol. XVI, pp. 75–97, Xalapa.

1963 "The Olmec Culture." *The Olmec Tradition*. Texas: Museum of Fine Arts.

1971 "Monolitos Olmecas y Otros en el Museo de la Universidad Veracruzana." *Union Academique Internationale, Corpus Antiquitatum Americanenism,* Vol. V. Mexico: Instituto Nacional de Antropologia e Historia.

Meggers, Betty J.

1971 "Contacts from Asia." In *The Quest for America,* pp. 239–259. (Geoffrey Ashe, ed.). London: Pall Mall Press.

1975 "The Transpacific Origin of Mesoamerican Civilization: A Preliminary Review of the Evidence and its Theoretical Implications." *American Anthropologist,* Vol. 77, No. 1, pp. 1–27.

Meggers, Betty J.; Evans, Clifford; and Estrada, Emilio

 1965 *Early Formative Period of Coastal Ecuador: The Valdivia and Machalilla Phases. Smithsonian Contributions to Anthropology, 1.* Washington, D.C.

Melgar, Jose M.

 1869 "Notable Escultura Antgua." *Boletin de lo Sociedad Mexicana de Geografia e Estadistica,* Vol. 2, pp. 292–297.

Melgarejo Vivanco, Luis, Jose

 1975 *El Problema Olmeca.* Xalapa: Coatzacoalcos-Veracruz-Mexico.

Michael, Henry N.

 1964 *The Archaeology and Geomorphology of Northern Asia: Selected Works,* Arctic Institute of North America Anthropology of the North: Translation from Russian Sources/No. 5. Toronto: University of Toronto Press.

Milbrath, Susan

 1979 "A Study of Olmec Sculptural Chronology." *Studies in Pre-Columbian Art and Archaeology, No. 23.* Washington, D.C.: Dumbarton Oaks.

Miles, S. W.

 1965 "Sculpture of the Guatemala-Chiapas Highlands and Pacific Slopes, and Associated Hieroglyphs." *In Handbook of Middle American Indians,* Vol. 2, pp 237–275. (Robert Wauchope, ed.). Austin: University of Texas Press.

Miller, Arthur G.

 1977 "The Maya and the Sea: Trade and Cult at Tancah and Tulum, Quintana Roo, Mexico." In *The Sea in the Pre-Columbian World: A Conference at Dumbarton Oaks, October 26 and 27, 1974,* pp 96–140. (Elizabeth P. Benson, ed.). Washington: Dumbarton Oaks Research Library and Collections.

Mochanov, Y. A.

 1973 "Early Migrations to America in the Light of a Study of the Dyuktai Paleolithic Culture in Northeast Asia." *Paper presented for the 9th International Congress of Anthropological and Ethnological Sciences,* Chicago.

 1978 "Stratigraphy and Absolute Chronology of the Paleolithic of Northeast Asia." In *Early Man in America from a Circum-Pacific Perspective,* pp. 54–67. Edmonton: Archaeological Researches International.

 1978 "The Paleolithic of Northeast Asia and the Problem of the First Peopling of America." In *Early Man in America from a Circum-Pacific Perspective,* pp. 67–68. Edmonton: Archaeological Researches International.

Morlan, R. E.

 1978 "Early Man in Northern Yukon Territory: Perspectives as of 1977." In *Early Man in America from a Circum-Pacific Perspective,* pp. 78–95. (A. L. Bryan, ed.). *Occasional Papers No. I.* Edmonton: Department of Anthropology, University of Alberta.

 1979 "A Stratigraphic Framework for Pleistocene Artifacts from Old Crow River, Northern Yukon Territory." In *Pre-Llano Cultures of the Americas: Paradoxes and Possibilities,* pp. 128–145. (R. L. Humphrey and D. Stanford, eds.). Washington, D.C.: Anthropological Society of Washington.

 1980 "Taphonomy and Archaeology in the Upper Pleistocene of the Northern Yukon Territory: A Glimpse of the Peopling of the New World." *Archaeological Survey of Canada Mercury Series Paper,* Vol. 94, pp. 1–380.

Morley, Sylvanus Griswold

 1946 *The Ancient Maya.* Standford: Standford University Press.

Movius, H. L., Jr.

 1956 "New Paleolithic Site near Ting-ts'un on the Fen River, Shansi Province, North China." *Quaternaria,* Vol. 3, pp. 13–26.

Muller, Jon D.

1971 "Style and Culture Contact." In *Man Across the Sea: Problems of Pre-Columbian Contacts*. pp. 66–78. (Carroll L. Riley et al., ed.). Austin: University of Texas Press.

Muller-Beck, H.

1966 "Paleohunters in America: Origins and Diffusion." *Science,* Vol. 152, pp. 1191.

1967 "On Migrations of Hunters Across the Bering Land Bridge in the Upper Pleistocene." In *The Bering Land Bridge,* pp. 373–408. (D. M. Hopkins, ed.). Palo Alto: Stanford University Press.

Navarrete, Carlos

1959 "A Brief Reconnaissance in the Region of Tonala, Chiapas, Mexico." *Papers of the New World Archaeological Foundation,* No. 4.

1969 "Los Relives Olmecas de Pijijiapan." *Anales de Antropologia,* Vol. 6, pp. 183–195, Mexico.

1971 "Algunas Piezas Olmecas de Chiapas y Guatemala." *Anales de Antropologia,* Vol. VIII, pp 69–82. Mexico: Instituto de Investigaciones Historicas, Universidad Nacional Autonoma de Mexico.

1974 "The Olmec Rock Carvings at Pijijiapan, Chiapas, Mexico and Other Olmec Pieces from Chiapas and Guatemala." *Papers of the New World Achaeological Foundation,* No. 35. Provo: Brigham Young University.

Nelson, N. C.

1937 "Notes on Cultural Relations Between Asia and America." *American Antiquity,* Vol. 2, pp. 267–272.

Nicholson, H B.

1971 "Religion in Pre-Hispanic Central Mexico." In *Handbook of Middle American Indians,* Vol. 10, pp. 395–446. (Robert Wauchope, ed.). Austin: University of Texas Press.

1976 "Preclassic Mesoamerican Iconography from the Perspective of the Post-classic: Problems in Interpretational Analysis." In *Origins of Religious Art and Iconography in Preclassic Mesoamerica,* pp. 157–175. (H. B. Nicholson, ed.). Los Angeles: UCLA Latin American Center Publications.

1976 *Origins of Religious Art and Iconography in Preclassic Mesoamerica.* (Nicholson, H. B. ed.). Los Angeles: UCLA Latin American Center Publications.

Norman, Daniel, and Johnson, W. W. A.

1941 "Note on a Spectroscopic Study of Central American and Asiatic Jades." *Journal of the Optical Society of America,* Vol. 3, No. 1, pp. 85–86.

Norman, V. Garth

1973 "Izapa Sculpture, Part I: Album." *Papers of the New World Archaeological Foundation,* No. 30. Provo: Brigham Young University.

1976 "Izapa Sculpture Part 2: Text." *Papers of the New World Archaeological Foundation,* No. 30. Provo: Brigham Young University.

Okladnikov, A. P.

1974 *Ancient Cultures of Siberia.* (Translated by K. Kato and S. Kato). Tokyo: Kodansha.

1978 "Paleolithic of Mongolia." In *Early Paleolithic in South and East Asia.* pp. 317–325. (F. Ikawa-Smith, ed.). The Hague: Mouton.

Olsen, Stanley, J.

1974 "Early Domestic Dogs in North America and Their Origins." *Journal of Field Archaeology,* Vol. 1, No. 3–4, pp. 343–346.

Paddock, John, ed.

1966 "Oaxaca in Ancient Mesoamerica." In *Ancient Oaxaca: Discoveries in Mexican Archeology and History,* pp. 87–242. Stanford: Stanford University Press.

Parson, Lee A.

1967 "An Early Maya Stela on the Pacific Coast of Guatemala." *Estudios de Cultura Maya,* Vol. VI, pp. 171–198. Seminario de Cultura Maya, Universidad Nacional Autonoma de Mexico, Mexico.

1969 "Bilbao, Guatemala: An Archaeological Study of the Pacific Coast Cotzumalhuapa Region," Vol. 2. *Publications in Anthropology, 12.* Milwaukee: Milwaukee Public Museum.

1972 "Iconographic Notes on a New Izapan Stela from Abaj Takalik, Guatemala." *40th International Congress of Americanists,* Rome-Genova, Vol. 1.

1976 "Excavation of Monte Alto, Escuintla, Guatemala." *National Geographic Society Research Reports, 1968 Projects,* pp. 325–332, Washington, D.C.

1978 "The Peripheral Coastal Lowlands and the Middle Classic Period." In *Middle Classic Mesoamerica: A.D. 400–700,* pp. 25–34. (Esther Pasztory, ed.). New York: Columbia University Press.

Parsons, Lee A., and Jenson, Peter S.

1965 "Boulder Sculpture on the Pacific Coast of Guatemala." *Archaeology,* Vol. 18, No. 2, pp. 132–144.

Parsons, Lee A., and Price, Barbara J.

1971 "Mesoamerican Trade and Its Role in the Emergence of Civilization." In *Observations on the Emergence of Civilization in Mesoamerica,* pp. 169–195. (Robert F. Heizer, John A. Graham, and C. W. Clewlow, Jr., eds.). *Contributions of the University of California Archaeological Research Facility,* No. II. Berkeley: Department of Anthropology.

Phillips, Philip

1966 "The Role of Transpacific Contacts in the Development of the New World Pre-Columbian Civilizations." In *Handbook of Middle American Indian,* Vol. 4, pp. 296–315. Austin: University of Texas Press.

Pina Chan, R.

1955 "Chalcatzingo, Morelos, Mexico." *Direccion de Monumentos Prehispanicos, Informes,* num. 4. Mexico: Instituto Nacional de Antropologia e Historia.

1968 "El Problema de los Olmecas." Conferencia Mimeografiada, *Serie Los Olmecas,* num. 1. Mexico: Seccion de Difusion Cultural, Museo Nacional de Antropologia.

1968 "Los Olmecas en el Centro de Mexico." Conferencia mimeografiada. *Serie Los Olmecas,* num. 5. Mexico: Seccion de Difusion Cultural, Miseo Nacional de Antropologia.

1971 "Preclassic of Formative Pottery and Minor Arts of the Valley of Mexico." In *Handbook of Middle American Indians,* Vol. 10, pp. 157–178. Austin: University of Texas Press.

Pina Chan, R., and Covarrubias, L.

1964 *El Pueblo del Jaguar (Los Olmecas Arqueologicos).* Consejo para la planeacion e instalacion del Museo Nacional de Antropologia, Mexico.

1976 "Obsidian Exchange in Formative Mesoamerica." In *The Early Mesoamerican Village,* pp. 292–306. (Kent V. Flannery, ed.). New York: Academic Press.

Pohorilenko, Anatole

1975 "New Elements of Olmec Iconography: Ceremonial Markings." In *Balance y Perspectiva de La Antropologia de Mesoamerica y del Centro de Mexico, Arqueologia I, XIII Mesa Redonda,* pp. 265–281. Sociedad Mexicana de Antropologia.

1977 "On the Question of Olmec Deities." *Journal of New World Archaeology,* Vol. II, No. 1, pp. 1–16. Los Angeles.

Powers, William Roger

1973 "Paleolithic man in the Northeast Asia." *Arctic Anthropology, Vol. 10, No. 2, pp. 1–106.*

Prideaux, T.

1973 *Cro-Magnon Man.* Waltham: Little, Brown and Company.

Proskouriakoff, T.

1950 *A Study of Classic Maya Sculpture.* Carnegie Institute of Washington, Publication 593. Washington, D.C.

1968 "Olmec and Maya Art: Problem of their Stylistic Relation." *Dumbarton Oaks Conference on the Olmec,* pp. 119–134. Washington: Dumbarton Oaks Research Library and Collection.

1971 "Early Architecture and Sculpture in Mesoamerica." *Contributions of the University of California Archaeological Research Facility, No. 11,* pp. 141–156. Berkeley.

Quirarte, Jacinto

1973 "Izapan and Mayan Traits in Teotihuacan III Pottery." In *Studies in Ancient Mesoamerica,* pp. 11–29. (John Graham, ed.). *Contributions of the University of California Archaeological Research Facility, No. 18.*

1973 "Izapan-Style Art: A Study of Its Form and Meaning." *Studies in Pre-Columbian Art and Archaeology,* No. 10. Washington: Dumbarton Oaks.

1974 "Terrestrial/Celestial Polymorphs as Narrative Frames in the Art of Izapa and Palenque." In *Primera Mesa Redonda de Palenque,* Part I: A Conference on the Art, Iconography, and Dynastic History of Palenque; Palenque, Chiapas, Mexico. December 14–22, 1973, pp. 129–135. (Merle Greene Robertson, ed.). Pebble Beach: The Robert Louis Stevenson School.

1976 "Izapan Style Antecedents for the Maya Serpent in Celestial Dragon and Serpent Bar Contexts." *Actas del XXIII Congreso International de Historia del Arte: Espana entre el Mediterraneo y el Atlantico, Granada 1973,* Vol. 1, pp 227–237. Granada: Departmento de Historia del Arte, University de Granada.

1976 "The Relationship of Izapan-Style Art to Olmec and Maya Art: A Review." In *Origins of Religious Art and Iconography in Preclassic Mesoamerica,* pp. 73–86. (H. B. Nicholson, ed.). Los Angeles: UCLA Latin American Center Publications and Ethnic Arts Council of Los Angeles.

1977 "Early Art Styles of Mesoamerica and Early Classic Maya Art." In *The Origins of Maya Civilization,* pp. 249–283. (Richard E. W. Adams, ed.). *School of America Research Advanced Seminar Series.* Albuquerque: University of New Mexico Press.

1978 "Actual and Implied Visual Space in Maya Vase Painting: A Study of Double Images and Two-Headed Compound Creatures." In *Studies of Ancient Mesoamerica,* III, pp. 27–38. *Contributions of the University of California Archaeological Research Facility, No. 36.* Berkeley:

Rathje, William L.

1971 "The Origin and Development of Lowland Classic Maya Civilization." *American Antiquity,* Vol. 36, pp. 275–285.

Reichel-Dolmatoff, Gerardo

1972 *San Agustin; A Culture of Colombia.* New York: Praeger Publishers.

Riley, Carroll L.; Kelley, Charles J.; Pennington, Campbell; and Rands, Robert, eds.

1971 *Man Across the Sea, Problems of Pre-Columbian Contacts.* Austin: University of Texas Press.

Rouse, I.

1976 "Peopling of the Americas." *Quaternary Research,* Vol. 6, pp. 597–612.

Rowe, John Howland

1966 "Diffusionism and Archaeology." *American Antiquity,* Vol. 31, No. 3, pp. 334–337.

1967 "Form and Meaning in Chavin Art." In *Peruvian Archaeology: Selected Readings,* pp. 72–104. (John Howland Rowe, and Dorothy Menzel, eds.). Palo Alto: Peek Publications.

Sahagun, Fray Bernardino de

1969 *General History of the Things of New Spain.* (Trans. by Arthur J. O. Anderson and Charles E. Dibble.) 13 parts. *Monographs of the School of American Research, No. 14.* Santa Fe: The School of American Research and the University of Utah.

Sanders, William T.

1970 "Review of Dumbarton Oaks Conference on the Olmec." *American Anthropology,* Vol. 72, pp. 441–443.

Saville, M. H.

1929 "Votive Axes from Ancient Mexico," Parts 1 and 2. *Indian Notes,* Vol. VI, pp. 266–299, 335–342. New York: Museum of the American Indians, Heye Foundation.

Schele, Linda

1977 "Palenque: The House of Dying Sun." In *Native American Astronomy,* pp. 42–56. (Anthony F. Aveni, ed.). Austin: University of Texas Press.

Scholes, France V., and Dave Warren

1965 "The Olmec Region at Spanish Contact." In *Handbook of Middle American Indians,* Vol. 3, pp. 776–787. (Gordon R. Willey ed.). Austin: University of Texas Press.

Schondube, O.

1968 "Los Olmecas en el Occidente." Conferencia Mimeografiada. *Serie Los Olmecas,* num. 7. Mexico: Seccion de Difusion Cultural, Museo Nacional de Antropologia.

Schuiling, W., ed.

1972 *Pleistocene Man at Calico.* Bloomington: San Bernardiono County Museum Association.

Scott, John F.

1976 "Post-Olmec Mesoamerica as Revealed in its Art." *Actas del XLI Congreso Internacional de Americanistas, Mexico, 2 al 7 de septiembre de 1974,* Vol. II, pp. 380–386. Mexico: Instituto Nacional de Antropologia e Historia.

1977 "El Meson, Veracruz, and its Monolithic Reliefs." *Baessler-Archiv: Beitrage zur Volker-kunde,* N. F. Band XXV, Heft I, pp. 83–138. Berlin: Museum fur Volkerkunde and verlag von Dietrich Reimer.

1978 "The Danzantes of Monte Alban," 2 Vols. *Studies in Pre-Colombian Art and Archaeology, No. 19.* Washington: Dumbarton Oaks.

Serizawa, C.

1978 "The Early Paleolithic in Japan." In *Early Paleolithic in South and East Asia,* pp. 287–297. (F. Ikawa-Smith, ed.). The Hague: Mouton.

Sharer, Robert J.

1974 "The Prehistory of the Southeastern Maya Periphery." *Current Anthropology,* Vol. 15, No. 2, pp. 165–187.

Shao, Paul

1976 *Asiatic Influences in Pre-Columbian American Art.* Ames: Iowa State University Press.

1978 "Chinese Influences in Preclassic Mesoamerican Art." In *Diffusion and Migration: Their Roles in Cultural Development,* pp. 202–225. Calgary: University of Calgary Archaeological Association.

Sharer, Robert J. ed.

1978 *The Prehistory of Chalchuapa, El Salvador,* 3 Vols. Philadelphia: University of Pennsylvania Press.

Shook, Edwin M.

1971 "Inventory of Some Pre-Classic Traits in the Highlands and Pacific Guatemala and Adjacent Areas." In *Observations on the Emergence of Civilization in Mesoamerica,* pp. 70–77. (Robert F. Heiser, John A. Graham, and C. W. Clewlow, Jr., eds.). *Contributions of the University of California Archaeological Research Facility, No. 11.* Berkeley.

Shook, Edwin M., and Heizer, Robert F.

1976 "An Olmec Sculpture from the South (Pacific) Coast of Guatemala." *Journal of New World Archaeology,* Vol. I, No. 3, pp. 1–8.

Shook, Edwin M., and Kidder, Alfred V.

1952 *Mount E-III-3, Kaminaljuvu, Guatemala. Carnegie Institution of Washington, Publication 596.*

Smith, J. W.

1974 "The Northeast Asian-Northwest American Microblade Tradition (NANAMT)." *Journal of Field Archaeology,* Vol 1, pp. 347–364.

Smith, J. W., and Harrison, V.

1978 "An Early Unifacial Technology in Northern British Columbia." *Journal of Field Archaeology,* Vol. 5, pp. 116–120.

Smith, T.

1963 "The Main Themes of "Olmec" Art Tradition." *The Kroeber Anthropological Society Papers,* No. 28, pp. 121–213. Berkeley, California. Sociedad Mexicana de Antropologia, Ed.

Sohn, P.

1978 "The Early Paleolithic Industries of Sokchang-ni, Korea." In *Early Paleolithic in South and East Asia,* pp. 233–245. (F. Ikawa-Smith, ed.). The Hague: Mouton.

Sorenson, John L.

1955 "Some Mesoamerican Traditions of Immigration by Sea." *El Mexico Antiguo,* Vol. 8, pp. 425–439.

Spinden, Herbert J.

1913 "A Study of Maya Art: Its Subject Matter and Historical Development." *Memoirs of the Peabody Museum of American Archaeology and Ethnology, Harvard University,* Vol. VI. Cambridge.

Stirling, M. W.

1939 "Discovering the New World's Oldest Dated Work of Man." *National Geographic Magazine,* Vol. LXXVI, pp. 183–218.

1940 "An Initial Series from Tres Zapotes, Veracruz, Mexico." *Contributed Technical Papers, Mexican Archaeology Series,* Vol. I, No. 1. Washington, D.C.

1940 "Great Stone Faces of the Mexican Jungle." *National Geographic Magazine,* Vol. LXXVIII, pp. 309–334.

1941 "Expedition Unearths Buried Masterpieces of Carved Jade." *National Geographic Magazine,* Vol. LXXX, pp. 277–302.

1943 "Stone Monuments of Southern Mexico." *Bureau of American Ethnology, Bulletin 138.* Washington D.C.: Smithsonian Institution.

1947 "On the Trail of La Venta Man." *National Geographic Magazine,* Vol. XCI, pp. 137–172.

1955 "Stone Monuments of Rio Chiquito, Veracruz, Mexico." *Bureau of American Ethnology, Bulletin 157, Anthropological Papers, No. 43,* pp. 5–23. Washington, D.C.: Smithsonian Institution.

1957 "An Archaeological Reconnaissance in Southeastern Mexico." *Bureau of American Ethnology, Bulletin 164, Anthropological Papers, No. 53,* pp. 213–240. Washington, D.C.: Smithsonian Institution.

1961 "The Olmecs, Artists in Jade." In *Essays in Pre-Columbian Art and Archaeology,* pp. 43–59. Cambridge: Harvard University Press.

1965 "Monumental Sculpture of Southern Veracruz and Tabasco." In *Handbook of Middle American Indians,* Vol. 3, pp. 716–738. Austin: University of Texas Press.

1968 "Early History of Olmec Problem." *Dumbarton Oaks Conference on the Olmec,* pp. 1–8. Washington, D.C.: Dumbarton Oaks Research Library and Collection.

1968 "Aboriginal Jade used in the New World." *Congreso Internacional de Americanistas, Actas y Memorias,* Vol. 37, No. 4, pp, 19–28.

1968 "Three Sandstone Monuments from La Venta Island." *Contributions of the University of California Archaeological Research Facility, No. 5,* pp. 35–36. Berkeley.

Sun, Jianzhong; Wang, Yuhue; and Jiang, Peng

1981 "A Paleolithic Site at Zhoujia Youfang in Yushu County Jilin Province." *Vertebrata Palasiatica,* Vol. 19, No. 3, pp. 280–291.

Suzuki, M.

1974 "Chronology of Prehistoric Human Activity in Kanto, Japan, Part II: Time-Space Analysis of Obsidian Transportation." *Journal of the Faculty of Science,* Section 5, Vol. 4, pp. 395–469. Tokyo: University of Tokyo.

Tello, Julio C.

1956 "Arqueologia del Valle de Casma, Culturas: Chavin, Santa o Huaylas, Yunga y Sub-Chimu." *Publicacion Antropologica del Archivo Julio C. Tello de la Universidad Nacional Mayor de San Marcos,* Vol. 1, Lima.

1960 "Chavin, Cultura Matriz de la Civilzacion Andina, Primera Parte." *Publicacion Antropologica del Archivo Julio C. Tello de la Universidad Nacional Mayor de San Marcos,* Vol. 2, Lima.

Thompson, J. Eric S.

1948 An Archaeological Reconnaissance in the Cotzumalhuapa Region, Escuintla, Guatemala. *Carnegie Institution of Washington, Publication No. 574,* Washington, D.C.

1950 Maya Hieroglyphic Writing: An Introduction. *Carnegie Institution of Washington, Publication No. 589,* Washington, D.C.

1954 *The Rise and Fall of Maya Civilization.* Norman: University of Oklahoma Press.

1966 *The Rise and Fall of Maya Civilization.* Norman: University of Oklahoma Press.

1970 *Maya History and Religion.* Oklahoma: University of Oklahoma Press.

1973 "Maya Rulers of the Classic Period and the Divine Right of Kings." In *The Iconography of Middle American Sculpture,* pp. 52–71. New York: The Metropolitan Museum of Art.

Tian, Guangjin

1983 "Recent Archaeological Studies on the Xiongnu People in Nei Mongu". *Kaogu Xuebao,* No. 1.

Tolstoy, Paul

1963 "Cultural Parallels between Southeast Asia and Mesoamerica in the Manufacture of Bark Cloth." *Transactions, New York Academy of Sciences,* Ser. 2, Vol. 25, No. 6, pp. 646–662.

1972 "Diffusion: As Explanation and as Event." *In Early Chinese Art and Possible Influence in the Pacific Basin,* Vol. 3, pp. 823–841. (Noel Barnard ed.). New York: Intercultural Arts Press.

Tolstoy, Paul and Paradis, Louise I.

1970 "Early and Middle Preclassic Culture in the Basin of Mexico." *Science,* Vol. 167, pp. 344–351.

Tong, Zhuchen

1979 "On Microlithic Cultures in North and Northeast China." *Kaogu Xuebao,* No. 4, pp. 403–422.

Towle, Jerry

1973 "Jade: An Indicator of Trans-Pacific Contact?" *Yearbook of the Association of Pacific Coast Geographers,* Vol. 35, pp. 165–172.

Tozzer, Alfred M. (ed.)

1941 *Landa's Relacion de las Cosas de Yucatan: A Translation. Papers of the Peabody Museum of American Archaeology and Ethnology, Harvard University,* Vol. XVIII, Cambridge.

Tsou, Heng

1978 "Po, The Shang Capital at Zhengzhou." *Wenwu,* No. 2.

1979 "Research on the Hsia Culture." *Wenwu*, No. 3

1979 *The Archaeology of Shang and Chou*. Beijing: Wenwu Press.

1980 *Essays on Hsia, Shang and Chou Archaeology*. Beijing: Wenwu Press.

1981 "On the South Po and West Po." *Chungyuan Wenwu*, No. 3.

1981 "On the Zhengpo Theory." *Kaogu*, No. 3.

1982 "Theory and Methodology of Archaeology." *Kaogu Yu Wenwu*, No. 6.

1982 "Archaeological Investigation of the Henan, Hebei and Shansi Provinces." *Wenwu*, No. 6.

1982 "The Stamped Pottery Sites in South China and their Relationship to the Cultures of Hsia, Shang and Chou." *Wenwu Chikan*.

Wang, Chien

1978 "Archaeological Reconnaissances at Hsia-Chuan in Chinshui County, Shansi Province." *Kaogu Xuebao*, No. 3, pp. 259–288.

Wauchope, Robert

1962 *Lost Tribes and Sunken Continents*. Chicago: University of Chicago Press.

Webb, C. H.

1977 "The Poverty Point Culture." *Geoscience and Man*, Vol. 17.

Weiant, C. W.

1943 "An Introduction to the Ceramics of Tres Zapotes, Veracruz." *Bureau of American Ethnology, Bulletin 139*. Washington, D.C.: Smithsonian Institution.

Wenke, Robert J.

1980 *Patterns in Prehistory*. Oxford: Oxford University Press.

Westheim, P.

1957 *Ideas Fundamentales del Arte Prehispanico en Mexico*. Mexico: Fondo de Cultura Economica.

Willey, G. R.

1962 "The Early Great Styles and the Rise of the Pre-Columbian Civilizations." *American Anthropologist*, Vol. 64, No. 1, Part 1, pp. 1–14.

1966 *An Introduction to American Archaeology, I: North and Middle America*. Englewood Cliffs: Prentice Hall.

1971 *An Introduction to American Archaeology. II: South America*. Englewood Cliffs: Prentice Hall.

Willey, G. R., and Sabloff, J. A.

1974 *A History of American Archaeology*. San Francisco: W. H. Freeman.

Willey, Gordon R., and Sabloff, J. A., eds.

1979 *Pre-Columbian Archaeology*. San Francisco: W. H. Freeman and Company.

Yu, Ying-Shih

1967 *Trade and Expansion in Han China*. Berkeley: University of California Press.

Zhang, Xingfu and Zhang Zhunxeng, eds.

1981 *The Unearthed Bronzes of Shang-Zhou Dynasty in Henan Province: A Brief Introduction*. Beijing: Wenwu Press.

Zhang, Zhenhong

1981 "The Human and the Culture of the Paleolithic Period from Liaoning District." In *Verterata PalAsiatica*, Vol. 19, No. 2, pp. 184–192.